How to Work in
Stained Glass

How to Work in STAINED GLASS

ANITA & SEYMOUR ISENBERG

CHILTON BOOK COMPANY RADNOR
PENNSYLVANIA

*Unless otherwise noted, all projects shown are the
work of the authors*

Copyright © 1972 by Anita and Seymour Isenberg
First Edition
All rights reserved
Published in Radnor, Pa., by Chilton Book Company
and simultaneously in Ontario, Canada,
by Thomas Nelson & Sons, Ltd.
ISBN: 0-8019-5638-2
Library of Congress Catalog Card Number 70-184138
Designed by William E. Lickfield
Manufactured in the United States of America

Second Printing, October 1973
Third Printing, April 1974

To the members
of the
STAINED GLASS CLUB
who have learned
to see through a glass
not darkly

Acknowledgments

Any work of this nature involves a siphoning of certain considerations from various specialized reservoirs. Accordingly, we would like to thank the following:

National Lead Company for information on the physical characteristics of solder, as well as allowing us to reproduce cross sections of their lead caming.

The Fletcher-Terry Company for photographs and their chart of glass cutters.

The Esico Company for allowing reproduction of much of their soldering equipment and specifications.

The Talens Paint Company for painting techniques with Vercolor.

The Bond Adhesives Company, who provided material for the chapter on Glass Cements.

Frank Reusche for his guidance on some of the fired painting techniques.

Wayne Daniels, of *Creative Crafts* magazine, who photographed many of the processes.

And those members of the Stained Glass Club who prodded, poked and pried the authors to write a book of this sort as a general guide, and whose constant query, "Isn't it ready yet?" acted as inducement and spur from hazy outline to completed chapters.

Contents

Introduction

Surely one of the most beautiful sights in the world is a medieval stained glass window! Definitively executed, artistically wrought, centuried and imperious, potent and fragile—it splinters the light into a shower of colors and forms which hang before us in a movement without motion, continually replenished by the available day. A spectacle almost too commanding for sight alone, it gives one the feeling of wanting to bring other senses to bear in an effort to accumulate all possible impressions.

How was this art brought into being? Its origins are shrouded in mystery, as are the origins of glass itself. The earliest known representation of a stained glass window—the Wissembourg Disk with the head of Christ—goes back only as far as the late eleventh century. The art itself probably has its roots in the miniature paintings of Charlemagne's era; illuminated manuscripts and stained glass windows do have a certain resemblance. But it was during the eleven hundreds that stained glass as an art form came into prominence and by the year 1200 attained a prestige in the religious world that was to haunt the craft for centuries thereafter. For the medieval world attached a mystical significance to stained glass—they saw a substance that modifies, shapes, and colors the light passing through it as a parallel to the divine Word enhancing the body of man by passing through his spirit. This initial inflection became in time a characterization and finally a category which eventually left the art in the backwater of creative thought, as new forces and ideas came to seek media more adaptable to their expression.

THE MEDIEVAL WINDOW

Fig. 1. Many medieval windows depicted high personages of the church, like this bishop in the act of blessing someone.

THE TIFFANY ERA

It fell to Louis C. Tiffany, son of the famous jeweler, to give stained glass a recrudescence. His experiments with pigmentation led to the development of Tiffany Glass—a stained glass of color and luminescenses that no one before had imagined. A new interest was fired in this ages old craft, which began making its appearance in private dwellings. Tiffany was not alone in his researches; both Durand and John LaFarge, both of whom Tiffany knew as creative artists in their own right, were independently seeking the expansion of the basic modality, glass, into the world of art—and more specifically Art Nouveau. But Tiffany led the field among those who insisted that glass must be a strong enough contender among the other expressive media to stand on its own without relying on overlays of painting or other embellishments to sustain it.

Fig. 2. Early window with realistic figures. The dark tones and heavy leading help to produce the total effect.

He began adding various metallic oxides to the basic glass formula to get the effects he wanted. His goal was realized when in 1893 the new firm of Tiffany and Co. offered for sale objects of "favrile" glass. This word became his trademark. Taken from the Latin word *faber* meaning "smith"—that is, hand-crafted—he soon brought it into worldwide renown. The strength of color and variety of form finally achieved in favrile glass is still unequaled. But Tiffany used his glass not only in three dimensional objects, such as vases and lamps; he used it also in windows—along with rocks, seashells, pebbles and anything else that would give the effect he wanted. Graceful designs characterize his work, and because of the nature of the small-pieced undulating break lines, he used (possibly devised) a method of holding his glass together with copper foil as well as with lead. This more supple material could take the multiple tiers of his fenestrations without giving the bulky, staggered look that lead would of necessity present. It provided an equally natural adaptation to the three dimensional form, for each piece of glass, wrapped in its edging of copper foil, could be easily made to conform to a moulded surface and then soldered together to completion. Making such designs of small pieces of glass held together with copper foil and involving extreme technical skill has become known as the "Tiffany foil method," and we will discuss it, as well as the medieval leading technique, during the course of this book.

Fig. 3. Church windows were often designed as teaching aids, illustrating lessons from the Bible.

STAINED GLASS AND YOU

So we have, in this brief space, skipped over centuries of the history of the art of colored glass from its earliest appearance to its renaissance in the twenties. Its current position as a rapidly growing hobby for the crafts enthusiast, as well as its role in specific productions by artists of renown, have given it a permanent status among the creative media, made more tantalizing by the lack of information concerning the technique of working with it. Today we find more and more stained glass in homes and more and more people anxious to learn the craft. Such desire is evidenced by the great number of classes now teaching stained glass in colleges, universities and adult education courses throughout the country. Unfortunately, teachers of the art are still in short supply, and even where they are present it is difficult to find any text specific for the beginner and the somewhat more advanced worker in the medium. It is for such individuals that this book is intended.

A word of warning: Stained glass is not only an art but a discipline. To attempt any stained glass project and try short cuts or skimping on the steps involved can only lead to disaster. While the technique involved is exacting, it is not difficult, requiring only the willingness to learn. We have heard often the two common distress calls, "I'll never be able to cut glass," and "I'm just not artistic." Skill will come with practice; the other is a question of degree. If you can draw a square, put a diamond within it and a circle within that you have already produced a design that, transposed into stained glass, will amaze you with its beauty. Where you go from there is up to you.

It's that simple.

And that intriguing.

But that it is good for a man to feel the satisfaction of knowing his craft thoroughly there would be no need to go into this . . . But I, for my part, cannot understand the spirit of an artist who applies his art to a craft purpose and has not, at least, a strong wish to know all that pertains to it. —C. W. WHALL

PART I · Materials

CHAPTER 1

What is
Stained Glass?

The misconception prevalent among most people who have not taken the trouble to look into the subject at any length is that stained glass is window glass that has been in some way "stained" or colored over with some sort of dye. Nothing could be further from the truth, even though the name "stained glass" reinforces this error. The glass is actually impregnated with color in the factory where it is made while still in raw chemical form. In medieval times the "colors" or metallic oxides were added to the "batch" while it was molten, but most factories today mix the elements before any of them go into the furnace. The colors are thus not smeared into a sheet as an afterthought but are an integral part of the entire process.

Stained glass is composed of silica sand with approximately one per cent iron, soda ash, limestone and some borax. The percentage of iron in the sand is most important. Since sand can contain up to ten per cent iron, the content of this element has to be carefully checked, for too much of it will give a greenish cast to the glass, rather like the color of a Coca-Cola bottle. Such an overlay could, of course, be disastrous to the end color the factory is trying to produce. To get the actual color into the glass the factory uses various metallic oxides which are then mixed into the sand and other material at the very beginning of the operation. Each color has its own formula and is mixed by a special worker who, in many cases, becomes an expert in the particular mixture. Some of the chemicals used for coloring glass are as follows: for amber, sugar and sulphur; di-

THE STAINING PROCESS

1

chrome for green; copper oxides produce blues and the addition of cobalt gives still stronger blues. Red colors, which include rubies, oranges, yellows—in short, the entire royal family—come from selenium or in many instances gold salts, which explains the higher cost of this glass. Cadmium is another element whose oxides give the glass a yellow color. Other common elements used in oxide state are nickel and iron.

Coloring the glass is not quite as simple as merely mixing the pigments into the sand and limestone and heating it up. Humidity and temperature play a great part in the end result, as does the thickness of the furnace and the coefficient of expansion of the different oxides within the molten glass. It is because of this last factor especially that the finished stained glass sheet behaves so much more peculiarly than regular window glass when you go to cut it. The internal stresses and strains can be immense, especially in sheets with more than one color, such as "streakies." It should be borne in mind that glass is a homogeneous liquid—not a solid—and is susceptible to the laws of hydraulics just like other liquids. That means if you put pressure on one particular part of it with a glass cutter, you may set up a strain pattern through the sheet so that a fracture appears some distance away, the force being transmitted in a way similar to that of the hydraulic brake in a car. Naturally the larger the sheet you are using the greater the possibility of this happening. Regular window glass will almost always transmit the pressure equally in a radius surrounding the moving cutter and generally behaves itself much better than the stained glass with its rather nervous oxides. Some highly neurotic stained glass sheets simply fly apart at what may appear to be the merest touch of a cutter (Fig. 1-1). Fortunately they are in the minority, but even for those of us who have worked in the medium for years, there come times when we find our skill challenged by a sheet of glass that insists on going its own way no matter how accurate the cut.

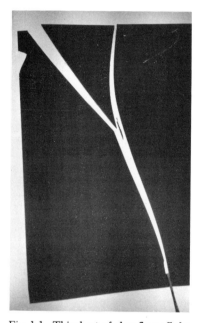

Fig. 1-1. This sheet of glass flew off the score line when slight pressure was applied from below using the glass cutter as a lever. The effect was of a sudden crumpling apart.

TYPES OF STAINED GLASS

Stained glass in general is broken down into two main categories: antique and cathedral. Within these ranges are found other characterizations involving the transparency and texture of the finished sheet. It must be remembered that the basic mixing of pigments follows pretty much the same process in all stained glass manufacture; from then on, the process varies depending on what the end result is going to be.

Antique Glass

This glass is not so named because of its own specific antiquity but because it is hand-blown, as was the glass in medieval times. Once the glass has become molten in the furnace, a glass blower picks up a certain amount of it on the end of his pontil and blows it into a long cylinder (Fig. 1-2). Sometimes the cylinder is blown into a mold. Such a mold can be made of apple wood and may have designs carved into it to give the finished glass a pattern. However, most of the "seeds," "bubbles" and other "movement" within the glass itself that are so characteristic of antique hand-blown glass are due to the art of the glass blower. "Trapped sunlight" is the way one admirer of antique glass expressed his pleasure at these small air pockets, which give the effect of miniature reflectors when the light flashes among them.

Once the antique glass cylinder has been blown, the ends are cut off and it is sliced down the center with a hot knife. It is then placed on its side in an oven, cut side uppermost, and allowed to fall flat with the heat, thus making it into a sheet of glass. Such a blown cylinder may be done free hand—that is without a mold, and will be extremely uneven in thickness; even the ones blown in a mold may vary in thickness from ¼ inch to almost ¾ inch in the same sheet!

Hand blown glass is made mostly in factories in France, Germany and England and its purchase entails the additional expense of any imported item. However the character and beauty of antique glass more than makes up the difference, aside from the fact that such glass contains shades and hues of every possible quality.

Antique glass is usually sold in sheets of about six square feet with rounded edges. This size is easily packed for export with minimum breakage.

Fig. 1-2. A cylinder of stained glass with top and bottom "bottle bottoms" cut off. This cylinder is cut in half when hot, placed in an oven and flattened into a sheet of stained glass.

Cathedral Glass

This is a domestic glass. It is "double rolled" by machine, the rollers of which may be embossed with a texture to be impressed on the glass sheet. The glass is of a constant thickness—usually ⅛″—and in general is easier to work with than antique glass, though this is by no means always the case. Since cathedral glass is made in the United States, it is quite a bit cheaper to buy than the imported antique but, while it is both beautiful and striking in its own right, it does not have the extensive range of tones furnished by the imported material. Nor does it have the definitive "character" of antique glass; the quality of individuality is not nearly as pronounced. All the same, the worker in glass will find much beauty in the product to amaze and delight him.

Opalescent Glass

A large proportion of cathedral glass is the so-called "opalescent glass," which, as its name implies, is a material almost opaque to light. Rather than allowing the light rays to pass directly through it, it spreads them within its surface confines to point up its own colors and designs. Opalescent glass is never of one color except when it is pure white or pure black (even when it is pure white it is usually of some white-on-white design). Much of it has quite dramatic mixtures of colors spread throughout the sheet in whorls and darting lines, which are given movement and life when light illuminates it from behind (Fig. 1-3). Opalescent glass, alone among stained glass, can also be seen by reflected light. Due to its dense makeup it does not lose its hues and tones with the disappearance of backlighting as do most stained glass windows when the sun goes down. This quality makes it a natural choice for articles where it is desired to keep a color tone at all times, such as lamps and room dividers which are not provided with backlighting. In lamps it is a particularly happy choice, for the opalescent glass hides the bulb that otherwise would be plainly seen as a "hot spot."

Because of the quite direct flow of color line across such a sheet of glass beginners can be misled into thinking the glass has a "grain" somewhat like wood. The question then arises whether to cut with or across the "grain." In fact, glass has no grain whatsoever and the appearance is misleading; whatever grain there is comes from the color alone and does not relate to underlying layers of glass. Opalescent glass is somewhat more difficult to cut than any other type of stained glass; it is harder, and requires a special cutter and generally more pressure than antique or other cathedral glass. We will go into this at length in the chapter on glass cutting.

Flashed Glass

This is a form of antique glass (generally) which is made with one color layer on top of another. Various combinations are available, for example, blue flashed on yellow, red on white, red on yellow, blue on orange, etc. You can easily tell a piece of flashed glass by scratching at a corner with a glass cutter or just chipping a small bit away. The underlying color will show through. Any color flashed on white or

Fig. 1-3. A sheet of opalescent glass held up to the light. You can readily see the whorls of color and "grain."

clear glass is particularly easy to tell simply by holding an edge of the glass up to the light. You can readily make out the clear underlying portion with the thin layer of color on top of it (Fig. 1-4).

Flashed glass is a particularly beautiful type of stained glass and has two main purposes. The first is to combine two colors so as to get a melding of both that will add yet another hue to the color range; the second is for etching purposes. By using the proper materials (see Chapter 17 on Etching and Painting) it is possible to dispense with portions of the flashed upper layer according to a predetermined design and thus allow the bottom layer to show through. The procedure can be as complex or as simple as you care to make it—from simply etching out the eye of an animal on a small figurine to the stained glass windows of Chagall.

Streakies

Here are very dramatic examples of stained glass art. Streakies pretty much follow their name. They are sheets of colors streaked across the surface. They are similar in this to opalescent glass, but being transparent they have a delicacy and impressiveness that can be breathtaking when the light streams through. Some of the best streakies—and most of them are English—could be put in a frame as they are. In fact, unless you are cutting fairly large pieces of such glass you can mar more than you create by using them since you may entirely lose the color flow. Many of the English Streakies, in addition to combining wide ranges and flow of colors, also add a rippling of the glass itself—a textural component that makes the colors simply dance across the sheet, though providing a most uncertain cutting surface. We have in our studio several German Streakies that we have never been able to bring ourselves to cut simply because there seems to be no way to possibly improve on the beauty of the glass as it already exists.

Streakies are particularly effective when used in windows as sunsets, cloud-filled skies, ocean waves, landscapes, rainbows—or even the Manhattan skyline. They also serve well as mountains or simply abstract colorations in less specific works. They may be employed in free-form objects and for animals—butterfly wings made from them are especially alluring.

Granite Backed Glass

This is a designed sheet with a very rough back to disperse the light more effectively. A common

Fig. 1-4. Detail from the "Pirate" window (see color section). The pocket, buttons, sleeve stripes were all etched from flashed glasses.

Fig. 1-5. Crackle glass showing the lines running through the surface.

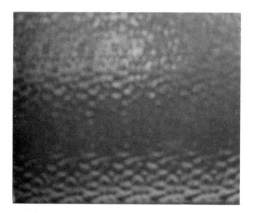

Fig. 1-6. A sheet of flemish glass showing highlights of the characteristic "pock-marked" effect as the light comes through.

Fig. 1-7. Stained glass shutters may be made of rectangular pieces of opalescent glass fitted into wooden frames.

question is, which is the "right" side of such a piece of glass? The "right side" of any glass is the side you think is best for your purpose; there are no hard and fast rules. Don't try cutting on the granite side, however. Just one look at it may make your glass cutter's wheel fall off. If you cut on the smooth side you should find granite backed glass no more difficult to work with than any of the other cathedral glasses. It does scare some beginners, however.

Hammered Glass

Here is yet another type of cathedral glass with a textural quality looking as though it had been tapped by a small and persistent hammer. The indentations are all quite uniform and when the light hits them they act like multifarious facets. Again there is a rough and a smooth side to this glass; again the choice is yours as to which side to put forward.

Crackle Glass

This is an antique glass which has been dipped quickly in water immediately after being formed. The shock of this contact forms definite fracture lines throughout the sheet. The glass is removed from the water before these lines can splinter the piece. As the glass then slowly cools, these fracture lines become embedded in the subsurface in a pattern that is most artistic and delightful (Fig. 1-5).

Crackle glass comes in almost all colors although ranges within a specific color are not available. This is a type of "figured" glass with the figurations—that is the crackling—running throughout the sheet. Strangely enough there is usually no problem cutting this glass but it is wise to be careful as you are dealing with a rather fragile type. (Fig. 1-6).

Flemish Glass

This is a decorative glass with deep channels running helter-skelter throughout the sheet. These channels are actually indentations caused by the rollers of the machine, and while the color may change, the indentations all look pretty much alike. There is a certain lack of individuality about flemish glass which is not noticed as much perhaps with either hammered or granite backed glass, perhaps because the indentations in flemish glass are so large and so readily apparent.

This is not a good glass to use in great quantity as it will tend to cheapen any other type of glass you may be using. Used by itself it tends to give a monotonous and unimaginative effect. With flemish glass more than with any other type discussed so far, a little bit goes a long way.

Slab Glass

While this is a form of stained glass, it is strictly speaking another type of endeavor altogether. Slab glass or "dalles" are thick chunks of glass approximately eight inches by twelve inches and one inch thick. They require special materials for their use—mainly epoxy or cement—and they may be used in complete blocks or broken up into glass chunks with a slab glass wedge. Light filtering through these chunks gives the effect of precious stones.

We will devote an entire chapter to the use of this glass alone.

By its very nature stained glass, to give its full effect, must be backlighted. Far from being a limiting factor, however, such lighting can be worked into a general decor so as to seem logical and imaginative. During the day stained glass windows are naturally infused with outside light. Such windows change their hues and tones in infinite variety—and indeed their entire appearance—as the light outside waxes toward noon and wanes into evening. From the brilliant, jewel-like quality of hot sunlight to the meditative light of early afternoon and the solemn perspectives of gathering twilight, they alter their personality in a manner indulged in by no other expressive medium. And once night comes and the lights are on inside, the windows, turned as it were inside out by incandescence, glow toward the street. That's a lot of activity for one art form (Figs. 1-7 and 1-8).

Of course you don't have to incorporate an entire window to get your effect. Many hobbyists fabricate small free-form objects to hang in a window. Small panels may also be so exhibited as may stylized animals, flowers, insignias or what have you (Figs. 1-9 and 1-10). These may be suspended from the wooden molding or hung by small plastic suction hooks to the glass of the window itself. It is recommended that you use a clear "fish line" to attach the glass; metal wire is awkward and noticeable.

Stained glass mobiles give an intriguing effect to a space. It is not necessary for such an object to be constructed entirely of glass pieces; stained glass hangings interspersed with many other materials, from pieces of forged metal to lengths of bamboo, provide an interesting comment. The arrangement is what gives charm and wit to the involved material, though no amount of arrangement can enliven essentially dull components.

STAINED GLASS EFFECTS

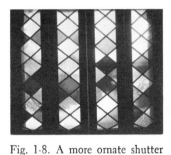 

Fig. 1-8. A more ornate shutter which employs lead lines in a diamond pattern.

Fig. 1-9. Door panel in the home of Mr. and Mrs. William Lee, New York.

Fig. 1-10. Free form duck in our studio window. Ducks in the background are real.

Fig. 1-11. Stained glass room divider. The frame is metal and is hinged together. Courtesy: Hope Pepe.

Fig. 1-12. Clock face of stained glass. The piece is illuminated during the night and reflects the daylight at other times. It really works, too. Courtesy: Elliott Weiner.

Those who wish to provide themselves with panels of stained glass but don't want to take up window space may find a lightbox the answer. Such a procedure is not really radical. Oils and watercolors hanging on walls usually have a light over them so they may be seen to best advantage. The lights illuminating a lightbox are far less obtrusive and certainly as effective. Lightboxes need not be expensive. You can get one made for about the cost of a good frame. The wood and design of a lightbox might well be varied to set off the work on display within. Nor does it have to be especially thick so that it stands uncomfortably away from the wall. There should just be room inside for the fluorescent lights to be set into recesses made for them; the backing covered by silver foil or a similar reflecting material; and the stained glass itself, which is placed with one-quarter inch molding to hold it. The back panel should be screwed, not nailed, into place to provide for the replacement of bulbs. While the final product is somewhat heavier than a picture of commensurate size, it will hang on the wall with little difficulty, as long as it is well supported. As for an off-on switch, either a simple line switch may be used or a small switch set right into the lightbox itself.

The most ornate type of lightbox is of course the stained glass lampshade. As we have previously stated, the glass employed in these creations is generally of an opalescent or granite-backed cathedral variety—both for diffusion of the light and in order to hide the bulb. Shades come in all shapes and sizes though basically they are of four types: the straight panel—usually with a skirt of some sort; the bent panel, which generally has a crown; the small, pieced lamp which may be so fabricated over its entire surface or only in its lower portion, having bent panels for the top; and the lantern, which is basically a straight panel lamp with a very small inside dimension. These will all be discussed further in the chapter on lampshades (Chapter 13).

Room dividers and fireplace screens—a type of modified room divider—have been produced by workers in the stained glass art, as well as clock faces, three dimensional panels, double glazed hangings to get the effect of glass on glass, self-supporting abstracts and figurines—in one case a full orchestra; tryptichs and entire ceilings. The interaction of light and color produces a vivacity that in turn enhances the imaginative powers of those working with the material, so that almost anything becomes a possibility. And the possibilities are endless (Figs. 1-11 and 1-12).

CHAPTER 2

Lead Came– The Ubiquitous Skeleton

Lead came is the chief support of works of stained glass. Like the bony skeleton, it is rigid where essential, yielding where necessary, compliant always. Such cames are available for our purposes in six-foot lengths of varied dimensions and designs.

The word "came" is an Old English word meaning "string" or "length." It is also occasionally spelled "calme." The lead cames we work with in stained glass are made by an extrusion process. That is to say, they are pushed through a steel die with a great amount of force. This die then channels and shapes them (Fig. 2-1). Contrary to general belief, came lead is pure lead with almost no additions. Certain cames may be tougher than others. Round came, for instance, is generally harder to cut and somewhat more difficult to work with than flat came. Probably this is due to the fact that it contains more lead within it to make up for the difference in shape.

While other materials have come into use, such as zinc bars, copper foil, brass rods, etc., lead is still the basic material that shapes stained glass creations.

Lead came serves a dual purpose. Basically, it holds the different pieces of colored glass together to conform to a pre-existing pattern or design. It also forms of itself a geometric or abstract design or, indeed, a pictorial design, which in an overall view, can add to or detract from the creative endeavor. A knowledge of the idiosyncrasies of lead is essential to anyone desiring to work in the stained glass art, for lead is neither secondary to nor less beautiful in the finished product than the glass itself.

Fig. 2-1. The extrusion process. This particular picture shows an extrusion press producing lead pipe. The only difference between this and came is the die and the fact that came is put in boxes in straight pieces instead of being coiled. Courtesy: National Lead Co.

PURPOSE OF LEAD CAME

9

HOW CAME IS
MEASURED

Lead came is always measured across the top surface, not across the channeled side—nor is the depth of the channel necessarily a factor in measuring lead. Since the channel may be pinched or enlarged, such a measurement would be inconstant. The top surface, however, does not change to any degree, and it's here that we measure whether the lead is $\frac{1}{16}$, $\frac{1}{8}$, $\frac{3}{16}$, $\frac{1}{2}$ inch, etc. Hobbyists generally stay in the range of $\frac{1}{16}$ to $\frac{1}{4}$ inch lead came, but if a fairly extensive project of wide dimensions is under consideration, you might want to go into the large leads, from the standpoint of both strength and design (Fig. 2-2).

Fig. 2-2. A length of lead came showing the "heart" and the top, or measuring, surface.

Whether came is round or flat applies also to a description of the top surface. Most leads come either way.

H OR U CAMES

H cames have two channels, one on either side with a wall or "heart" in the middle, and are shaped like an H on its side. This lead heart is usually $\frac{1}{16}$ of an inch. H leads are "inside" leads, accommodating themselves to pieces of glass in each channel. They are used within a panel or window. U cames or "high heart" cames are "outside" leads used for finishing off a single surface that will show, as in hanging panels or the skirts of lamps. They have only one channel which is considerably deeper than an H channel and their use gives a completed look to a panel or window, the edges of which will not be covered by molding.

Don't use H leads on the outside of a work such as a lamp, hoping to slice away the remaining open channel. This only ends up making the whole piece look very sloppy.

WIDENING AND NARROWING
THE CHANNELS

The channel width of lead came measures about $\frac{1}{4}$ inch. This accommodates the majority of different colored glasses. There are occasions, however, when in using hand-blown antique glass the lead channel may prove either too wide or more often than not, too narrow for the glass in question. English streaky glass, with its variable thicknesses throughout the sheet, is especially difficult to get into the ordinary lead channel.

To narrow the channel, it need only be pinched against the glass by running the broad blade of a lead or putty knife against it. To open the channel, a special instrument called a lathkin is used, and we will be considering this procedure and this instrument in a later chapter. There are occasions where a particularly thick piece of glass is to be accommodated, and here a portion of the lead channel must be opened to a width that may be totally out of line with the rest of the strand. This is permissible, providing enough of the lead grasps the edge of the glass so that you do not see a gap between the two.

Nothing seems simpler than this process, yet like most other procedures in this craft, it can be made extensively difficult through poor technique. Basically, the glass is simply slipped within the lead channeling once the channeling has been opened sufficiently to receive it. However, since the lead is generally flat against the table, and the glass being slid into it is also flat against the table, the trick is to get the glass into place without bending the lead all out of shape so that it looks like a dissolute pretzel. We have seen numerous students tapping glass into channels with varying degrees of frustration, only to find on examination that the glass was hooked onto the bottom channel wall. All their tapping had done was to mash that bottom channel wall so that the whole piece of lead had to be replaced. Glass will usually go into the channels quite easily if you slide the blade of your leading knife under the glass, raising it a slight amount from the table. This will give it enough height to miss catching on the lower flange of the came (Fig. 2-3). The glass will then click securely into place, and it will take very little tapping to lock it within the lead.

A word about tapping: This must always be done with caution rather than exuberance, and is an activity which should only be performed as a finishing procedure. Do not use a hammer to tap glass into the lead came, as you will surely shatter your pieces. The back of your leading knife, if it is weighted, is force enough, and if you have taken the pains to see that your glass fits correctly, you need very little tapping to make it seat properly. If your glass does not fit correctly, all the tapping in the world will only make a misfit into a disaster.

All lead came below ½″ size, and sometimes even that, must be stretched. Came should only be stretched prior to use. This process not only straightens the came of all kinks and twists, but makes it much easier to work with, as it firms up and tones the lead. The process of stretching is best done by placing one end of the came in a lead stretcher or vise and pulling, gently at first, with pliers at the other end (Fig. 2-4). You will actually feel the lead give and elongate. A quicker tug will probably snap the lead and send you flying across the room. It is a good idea to keep one foot behind you during the

FITTING THE GLASS TO THE CAME

Fig. 2-3. Place the blade of the lead knife under a piece of glass you want to seat in a channel. This will raise the edge of the glass just enough to clear the lower flange of the lead.

Fig. 2-4. Stretching a piece of came. The lead stretcher holds one end, you the other.

STRETCHING THE CAME—
A BASIC PROCESS

stretching process, no matter how carefully you pull —lead came has a sense of humor. Another method of stretching the lead is to simply step on one end and pull upwards on the other. This procedure works only for the thinner leads from $\frac{1}{16}''$ through $\frac{3}{16}''$. Unstretched lead is never wise to work with, as it will not follow the cavortings of the design, but will tend to stand away from the glass.

DESIGNING WITH LEAD

Many individuals, artists in other mediums, come to stained glass still thinking in terms of their previous craft, be it oils, water colors, or sculpture, and attempt to adapt that knowledge to stained glass. They soon find that the stained glass medium has rules of its own, especially in terms of design. One must always keep in mind not only what can and what cannot be cut in glass but what the leading procedure will do to these cuts. Points, especially, tend to disappear, swallowed up by the lead. If you have a number of points coming together at any one place, you will end up with a mass of lead and solder which may be far from what you had in mind. Let the lead work with you in the design. If you need a long, thin line, don't try to cut it out of glass; use a wide piece of lead instead. If you want the eye to follow along a certain direction, let the lead lines carry the flow to that area. Remember, lead came is an integral part of the design; it is not there simply to "glue" the glass pieces together. Lead lines that wander erratically over the surface of a work to no ostensible purpose detract from what otherwise might be a very pleasing prospect. The type of lead you use depends on the effect you want to produce and the amount of strength you need. Don't fall into the trap of designing with small pieces of glass, and then swallow them up with large pieces of lead.

In this regard, you might well consider mixing various sizes of lead within the same panel, as a painter would mix different brush strokes depending on what he wanted to emphasize and what he wanted to tone down. It is not essential or artistic to stick to one type of lead throughout a window or a panel. All of this must be noted in the original design or blueprint, and only when this is completed to the worker's satisfaction should the actual glass cutting and leading begin (Figs. 2-5, 2-6, 2-7, 2-8).

Fig. 2-5. A bold pattern showing sweeping lead lines radiating from an off-center focus. Leads used here were mostly ¼″ and ⅜″.

Fig. 2-6. A more delicate pattern of lead lines giving a spidery effect, the curves to complement the roundels scattered through these panels. Lead sizes ¼″–¾₁₆″.

STORAGE

Lead came resembles nothing so much as long strands of spaghetti combined with the sinuousness of snakes. If you throw them together in a bin any old way, you will have a fine old time untangling them. The best way to store six-foot lengths of came is in a wooden or cardboard box with one end knocked out so that the came can be extracted horizontally. You can divide the box into compartments and have different size came in each, or just pile one box on top of another. Arrange for this space underneath your work table. Remember, do not stretch the came until you are actually ready to use it. If you do not have enough came to make a box worthwhile, drape your six-foot lengths over padded hooks or wire hangers. *Do not* roll your came, as this process only makes it more difficult to stretch and work with.

Lead has a tendency to form an oxidative coating on its surface, a process which will be increased by dampness. This coating is fairly tough and is impervious to solder and flux. If your lead has a dull finish, it has probably become oxidized, and this coating must be removed if you expect to do any soldering. It is best removed with a stiff wire brush, similar to a suede brush, which can be purchased in any hardware store. It is not necessary to remove this coating until the soldering process is ready to begin, at which time simply scrub each joint with the wire brush, and you will see the shiny, newly minted surface of the lead reappear quite rapidly. Some workers make it a habit to scrub each joint, even if the lead still looks fairly new. They claim that a much neater soldering job is achieved in this fashion.

Lead came should never be cut with scissors or tin snips, as the blades will crush the end or twist it. Lead should only be cut with a leading knife, or a knife which has been adapted for this procedure. One of the more dangerous methods of cutting lead came is using a razor blade. While this implement is something almost everyone has on hand about the house, there is a distinct possibility a corner of it may chip off against an unexpectedly stiff portion of lead and get you in the eye. Even more likely, the thin blade may twist and suddenly break against the lead, mitering your fingers. To cut straight lengths of came, a utility knife with a rugged blade may be used. It hasn't the shape or activity of a good lead knife, and the novice will probably become dissatisfied with it fairly rapidly, but at least it does work. A heavy-duty linoleum knife may function as a lead knife if an edge is put on the back surface. It then resembles a professional leading knife and is at least a step in the right direction toward functional work in stained glass.

For the serious hobbyist, the only way to cut lead is with a professional leading knife. The method of

Fig. 2-7. One aspect of a garden scene. It shows a stark, emphatic use of line with fairly wide leads—¼" to ½".

CUTTING PROCEDURES AND MITERING

Fig. 2-8. Another aspect. An extremely ornate and nimble flow of lead line in the bouquet of flowers. This was a very difficult leading but worth it in terms of the end result. Even without the colors of the glass (see color section) the lead lines are striking.

cutting is always the same. The cut is made across the top surface of the came, not across the channeled side. The blade is placed gently on top of the came and a slight pressure is exerted with a side-to-side rocking motion. This sends the blade through the lead with an agility that cannot be duplicated by any other technique. Remember, excessive pressure is not needed and is not wanted, as it will only crush the more delicate cames. The side-to-side rocking motion is as important as the knife, as it is this, not excessive pressure, that does the slicing. It is recommended that the beginner learn to cut came correctly from the start. It will make for a much more whole-hearted enjoyment of the craft.

The mitering of came, or the cutting of angles so that one lead fits neatly against another, can only be accomplished easily with a leading knife. Lead cames should be mitered to fit as snugly as possible against each other. This makes for more smoothly soldered joints and a much neater final result.

CORNERING

Fig. 2-9. Demonstrates lock-in corner technique. The upper lead fits into the slot cut into the came on the right. The process is reversed below.

The corners of a window or panel involve the butting of one lead came against another at right angles. For purposes of strength and neatness, it is advisable to interlock these cames without showing an enormous bulge of solder. This is accomplished by splicing one into the other in a lock-and-key effect. While this is not a procedure universally adhered to by workers in the craft, it does provide good, tight corners which will hold to the dimension originally planned for them (Fig. 2-9).

LEAD POISONING

Lead poisoning is one of the first topics inquired into by beginners in stained glass. It is interesting to note that many professional workers in the craft know little about this subject. The fact of the matter is that it is possible, in extreme cases where poor hygiene is a way of life, to get lead absorbed into the body. Anyone handling lead for long periods of time will find on his fingers a deposit of the lead oxides. Providing he exercises good hygiene, washing the hands with soap, water and a brush when leaving the studio, these deposits will come right off and there will be absolutely no problem. However, if he's in a rush and decides to eat a sandwich with hands still dirty, or if he has a habit of licking his fingers, a certain amount of lead will be absorbed.

We have seen individuals working with lead while reading instructions who, while turning pages, would wet their fingers unconsciously with their tongue. Fortunately we were able to stop this particular procedure. Keep in mind the fact that lead is potentially a material which can weigh you down. The worker who is neat and clean in his work habits need have no fear of lead poisoning. As far as the danger of lead fumes liberated during the soldering process (another question generally asked), such fumes are negligible.

Remember that lead particles and lead oxides stick in the pores of the skin. They are not absorbed into the body unless ingested. Naturally, if you have any cuts on your fingers, they should be well bandaged before working with lead cames. Personally, we, ourselves, know of no one either beginner or professional working in the stained glass art who has ever suffered any difficulty with lead no matter how slight. We do feel, however, that one cannot err on the side of caution, and while we certainly do not advise anyone to wear gloves, we feel that certainly the skin of the hands should be thoroughly cleansed before leaving the workshop.

Needless to say, all lead should be kept out of the reach of children, especially babies, who show an unfortunate propensity to chew things that are left lying about.

A. *The H Cames*

The H cames, as previously noted, are inside leads —that is, lead used within a panel or lamp to accommodate a piece of glass to either side. While there are almost infinite styles and variations, we will discuss six of the major H leads in common use. Keep in mind that lead cames may be made for special purposes if one wishes to invest in having dies made. Dies are expensive. Of course, there are milling machines which are sold for making your own style came lead—indeed, there are also cames that are sold specifically for milling. We don't know anyone who has a milling machine, but if your acquisitions run this way, this is the material you would use. You could then turn out an almost endless supply of unusual leads, but if you are like the rest of us, you will settle for some of the tried and proven ones described below (Fig. 2-10).

1. *⅛″ Came—No Room for Error.* One-eighth inch H came is a very thin lead indeed. It is the smallest H came. In rounded form, it appears even thinner than it does in flat, since the ledging is so much less. There really is no room for error in using this lead. Your glass cutting must be precise because there is very little overhang to cover mistakes. In fact, this lead is not advised for beginner use unless glass edges are sanded, and even then, if the sanding

TYPES OF CAME

Fig. 2-10. Some H leads. From left to right: Thin ⅛″; heavy ⅛″ ³⁄₁₆ round; ¼ round, ¼ flat; ⅜ round; ½″ flat and ¾ and 1″ flat cames.

is not done correctly, the sanded edge will show beyond the limit of the came. One-eighth inch lead is used mainly for very small pieces of glass or for large pieces, where the lead line is so secondary to the overall design that just a hint of it is all that is required. It furnishes, as you may imagine, very little strength, and a design using a long unbroken length of this came must be carefully thought out in advance. It is extensively used in hanging objects, such as mobiles or small animals, where it is quite at home, since it goes around only small pieces of glass.

2. $\frac{3}{16}''$ *Came—A Beginner's Lead.* Here is the novice's friend—wider than the $\frac{1}{8}''$ but not as bulky to inexperienced fingers as the $\frac{1}{4}''$. As is true of all these leads, $\frac{3}{16}''$ comes in both round and flat shapes with the flat being somewhat easier to manipulate. Glass cutting need not be as specifically precise as with $\frac{1}{8}''$ came, though, of course, it is a good habit to always cut your glass as precisely as possible. Because of the small overhang in this lead, it will not accept thick pieces of antique glass, and if such glass is indicated in the design, avoid using the $\frac{3}{16}''$ lead in those areas. With this one exception, you will find this a basic lead for intermediate panels, mobiles, and windows, since it furnishes a feeling of delicacy without fragility and adapts well to inner and outer curves.

3. $\frac{1}{4}''$ *Came—Lamp Makers' Pride.* It isn't true that this lead is used exclusively for lamps, but it is the most popular lead for such creations, especially in rounded form. In its flat shape it is used more in windows and panels. The $\frac{1}{4}''$ rounded lead gives enough room for lamp panels to angle within it, without showing the edge of the glass. Yet it does not appear too bulky or make the lamp too heavy. This lead also contributes enough strength to hold the lamp firm. The rounded edge serves to intensify the three-dimensional effect of such an object and gives a finished appearance to the surface. In windows or panels, $\frac{1}{4}''$ flat lead gives a more definite line to the work than either $\frac{1}{8}''$ or $\frac{3}{16}''$, and, of course, adds more rigidity, too.

4. $\frac{3}{8}''$ *Came—For Professional Windows.* With this size we leave the hobbyist leads and go into leads used mainly by professional studios. $\frac{3}{8}''$ came is a stiff, heavy lead, which firmly clutches the glass on either side and gives a definitive linear quality to the window. It will not conform well to sharp curves, nor should it be used at such a portion of the design. In its rounded form it may be employed in the larger type lampshades, but it will provide more of a bulky effect here than the $\frac{1}{4}''$. With the $\frac{3}{8}''$ we

get into heavier and therefore more expensive leads, as lead is sold primarily by weight.

5. *½", ¾" and 1" Lead Cames—Strength and Flexibility.* These are all professional leads and are used by the hobbyist infrequently, if at all. They provide more strength than flexibility. They are rugged leads, are difficult to work with and are generally used in very, very large windows. They provide a design of definitive linear flow and basically can only be used with large pieces of glass. Although these leads are much more rugged than the hobbyist leads, they are worked with in exactly the same fashion. They need not be stretched quite so much. Occasionally you will find a piece of one of these wide leads used in a smaller work of thinner and more delicate line to form an emphasis or stark exclamation in the overall design. Such use is a procedure that calls for the utmost discretion on the part of the designer, since it can overbalance the entire work if used incorrectly.

B. *The U or End Cames*

Used on borders or surfaces of glass where no other piece of glass abuts, these are basically finishing cames. They give a completed appearance to the work, instead of leaving an empty H channel dangling. They are a very popular lead with hobbyists and are very seldom used by professional studios. Basically, this is because professional studios deal mainly with windows of very large dimension and design.

1. *¹⁄₁₆" Styles—Back-to-back Leads.* Here is a very mobile and accommodating came. There are two widths—¼" and ⅛" measured across the channel.

The ⅛" U width is very popular with hobbyists since it gives a more delicate effect to the finished piece and grips the glass tightly. The wider ¼" U is used where the glass employed is antique and of varying thicknesses some of which may not fit into the thinner ¹⁄₁₆" U. Remember the ¹⁄₁₆" measurement applies to the "arm" of the U which is pictured as lying on its side. It is not a measurement of the channel width. There is no comparable H came to this particular U—the smallest H came being ⅛".

It is the particularly narrow channel that gives this ¹⁄₁₆" U lead the functional capacity that endears it to fabricators of free form items. It can take angles up to 60° and yet cling to the glass. Its flat side is perfectly suited to the application of a sister lead against it. Two such leads soldered together where they meet along their length, give the "back-to-back" effect, even though each is individually involved in

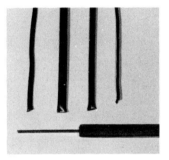

Fig. 2-11. Some flat cames. From left to right: ³⁄₁₆ U, ⅜ H, ⅜ U and ¹⁄₁₆ U. Below is an example of reinforced came with the center rod partly removed from the lead to show its position within the came.

wrapping around a different piece of glass. In using this lead, each piece of glass after being cut is wrapped with the came. The ends are soldered together and the wrapped pieces are then placed back on the pattern and solder flowed along the surfaces where they meet. This is a very rapid technique for putting together free form objects such as hanging mobiles, small animals, shade pulls, pendants, etc. It is one of the more popular techniques among beginners in this craft, and we will go into it further in a later chapter (see Chapter 15).

2. $\frac{3}{16}$"—*Finish for Small Panels*. This is the first of the truly "high heart" cames. It is used along flat surfaces as a finishing lead where the panel is to be hung in a window and where no molding is involved. $\frac{3}{16}$" lead will take curves providing they are not too abrupt. If the curve is not a gentle one, this lead will tend to kink. Either it must be smoothed very gently as you go, or small triangles must be cut out of it to take the bend, and the lead soldered at these areas after being pulled together. It is rather like taking a dart in the material for a dress. There is no rounded version of this particular lead. It is a popular lead for lamp shades, where it is used mainly as the bottom of the skirt. It is also used where three dimensional objects must be soldered together at angles, where use of an H lead would involve too much bending of the channels. $\frac{3}{16}$" U lead is amenable to a number of shapes and designs if it is worked carefully and with patience. It can prove as balky as a mule if it is simply tugged or pushed into awkward areas. Because of its flat surface, it will fit against a sister lead with very little trouble, providing the glass cutting is reasonably done. A very straight and neat soldered joint can be accomplished by use of such a lead.

A secondary use of this lead is as a "belt" to close the seams of lamps. When $\frac{3}{16}$" U is flattened out completely, it has just the proper shape and width to form a smooth bridge over the seam between body and skirt. We will discuss this further in the chapter on fabricating lamps.

3. $\frac{1}{4}$" *Round—A Lamp Lead*. This lead specializes in curves of three-dimensional objects, the most common of which are the skirts of straight panel lamps or the bottom curved portion of lamps with bent panels. It may also be used to wrap roundelles— spun glass circles—within a flat panel, providing you press the lead firmly enough against the roundelle's surface to make sure it grips. $\frac{1}{4}$" round does its job superbly where it is called for, though it is not called for too often. It has a use as well in stained glass

jewelry and stained glass belt buckles where peculiar curves must be followed in three-dimensional form. It is a fairly heavy lead and comes only in rounded form. It complements ³⁄₁₆″ H and ¼″ H leads and may be used with either of them. Since ¼″ H round is used extensively in lamps, the ¼″ U round may be a logical choice for the skirt if the curve is too abrupt for ³⁄₁₆″ U.

4. *³⁄₈″—For Large Panels and Windows.* ³⁄₈″ U lead is the largest size U lead generally used. It complements ¼″ H leads. Remember that we are dealing here with a very deep channel running the entire width of the came, a space almost ³⁄₈ of an inch deep. The tendency for beginners to forget this is regrettable, because they find out too late that having designed a little too close to the border, their shapes are swallowed up by this rather hungry lead. Another problem arises when beginners cut their inside H leads a little too long so that when the bordering U lead is put on, it covers over these inside H's. This leads to bumps in the panel if the leads are not pulled out and re-cut. However, if used correctly, and its use does take some practice, the ³⁄₈″ heavy duty U lead will give a finished effect which is worth the time and trouble it takes to learn how to use it. This lead will not take curves well and should not be used as a wrap around lead. It gives too bulky an appearance.

C. *Specialized Cames*

These cames all have some peculiarly distinctive feature marking them for a specific use. They are not general purpose leads. They are more expensive than the leads so far described.

1. *Reinforced Cames.* These leads have a hollow heart, through the center of which is run a flat steel rod. This gives these cames a very stiff support quality, though they may still conform to the most gentle bends of the design. While these H leads may be used to run from side to side in a large panel for strength and may be worked in the design to this effect, they are mainly used as border leads. They cannot be cut through with the ordinary lead knife though they are cut with a hacksaw quite easily and smoothly. It is possible to diminish the number of reinforcing bars if enough of this type lead is used. When designing for this lead, it is necessary to allow for its greater heart. The wider size pattern scissors are used (see Chapter 7). Naturally this lead is used only on fairly large windows and even there, with discretion.

2. *Colonial and High Heart Cames.* These rather

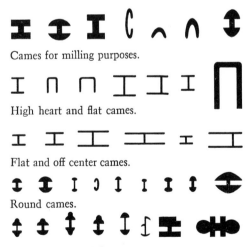

Cames for milling purposes.

High heart and flat cames.

Flat and off center cames.

Round cames.

Colonial and High heart cames.

Fig. 2-12. Some lead cames in cross section.

ornate leads are applicable to very special types of windows. We find them generally in the "leaded window"—that is, one which contains clear glass cut into shapes of recurring pattern, such as diamonds, squares, rectangles, etc., rather than in windows of colored glass in pictorial or free form pattern. Use of these cames is an adventure in discretion, since they can be rather overpowering.

3. *Off-Center Cames.* Here are H leads where the heart is placed away from the center, infringing on one channel. Thus we have one channel shallow and one channel deep. This lead can be used where two pieces of glass abut, one of which is thin, the other extremely thick. The thick piece can be given a wider flap of lead to fit into whereas the thin piece will be satisfied with a narrower channel. In this manner, for example, you can get away with using $\frac{3}{8}''$ lead rather than going into a heavier $\frac{1}{2}''$ or $\frac{3}{4}''$ or even $1''$ lead which is liable to overbalance the window with its wider lead line.

4. *Extra Wide Cames.* All these widths may be purchased with a channel that is almost double the width of the usual sized channels. This is to allow the placing of either very thick pieces of antique glass or the process of "double glazing," that is, one piece of glass placed on top of another of a similar or different color, the two then imbedded into this wide channel of lead. Interesting and novel effects can be obtained in this fashion, and two and even three tiers of glass can be placed together, depending upon the effect you want to achieve.

H CAME AS OUTSIDE LEAD

There are times when it is necessary to use H came as an outside lead. Professional studios invariably do just this. Since they are involved in making large windows, the edges of which will be covered with molding, whatever lead they use around these edges will not show. The use of an H lead in this type of work leaves an empty channel, which gives a certain margin for error should the dimensions of the window prove too tight. In this case, the extra channel may be shaved off to make the window fit. Hobbyists may follow this idea in making a panel that is going to fit into a wooden frame, such as a door panel. However, where the outside border is going to show, a U lead must be used or the work will look unfinished.

BUYING LEAD

Lead is sold in six-foot lengths and varies in price according to the width of the strip. The wider the strip, the more it will weigh and therefore the more it will cost. Lead came costs anywhere from 70 to 80 cents a six-foot length for the thinner leads, and 80 cents to $1.00 per length from there on up to the ½″ leads. Beyond that, it is not unreasonable to expect to pay between $1.00 to $2.00 per length. Where reinforced or other specialized came is concerned, the price may be even higher. The beginner will stick pretty much with the thinner and lower priced leads and should be able to supply his needs quite adequately at a nominal cost. Any major supplier of materials can be considered a source of information for purchase of any of the lead reviewed in this chapter.

SUMMARY

While we have attempted to give a description of both the lead cames themselves and some idea of how they are used, we could not cover each type of came that is made. There are unquestionably sizes betwixt and between those we mentioned as well as sizes larger and wider. If you learn to work with the leads mentioned, you will be able to work with any style. Remember that, like smiles, there is a lead for every purpose.

CHAPTER 3

The
Soldering Process

WHAT IS SOLDERING?

Soldering is a process for joining metals. In order to do this, we use a mixture of metals—an alloy—as a bonding agent. Heated to a certain temperature, such an alloy splints the metals. While not all metals fall into the category of those that can be soldered, most of the ones used in the stained glass art are solderable. These include lead, tin, sheet metal, bronze, copper and the so-called "white metal."

The soldering process occurs when the metal pieces to be soldered are heated above the melting point of the solder itself. This process can occur very quickly, and in our case the more quickly it occurs, the better the soldering process will be. Since lead has a fairly low melting point, we must take care not to heat it so it melts from under our hand. This is a common mistake made by beginners. Soldering occurs when, the proper temperature being reached, a bonding takes place between the solder and the metals being joined. The solder flows over the surfaces of the opposing metals by capillary action to produce neat, smooth joints. A proper solder should flow very easily over the heated surfaces. It should not be necessary to keep going over a joint to even it out. If you have to fuss with it, something is wrong with the solder, the flux, the metals to be joined, or the soldering equipment.

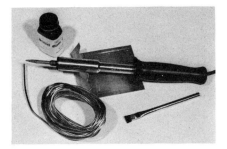

Fig. 3-1. Flux, flux brush, solder (60/40 solid core ⅛″), soldering iron and stand.

Welding is another process for joining metals. It is not used in stained glass work. Braising is closely associated with welding because of the high temperatures required to do the job. Both braising and welding involve joining metals of higher melting points than lead. The only way lead strips can be joined

22

together in a metal-to-metal bond is by soldering. It is this process that we now intend to explore.

We would like to emphasize that when we use the term "solder" or "soldering" we are not speaking of so-called "liquid solder" or "cold solder." Both of these are really glues. Plastic bonds formed by the liquid solders break down and disintegrate at temperatures which are well below the melting point of the tin-lead combination that forms the metal-to-metal bond of which we speak. In fact, such cold solders should not be used where a strong metal-to-metal joining is required.

The most extensively used solders are those which are composed of lead and tin in specific percentages. In naming any alloy, the more expensive metal is always given first place. Thus, a 60/40 solder is one containing 60% tin and 40% lead. 60/40 solder is the only solder which is extensively used in stained glass work.

Lead has a melting temperature of 621°F. Tin has a melting temperature of 450°F. Combined, however, in solder form, they melt at 361°F. To get a completely molten state of combinations of the two, is to run a gamut of temperatures between

CHARACTERISTICS OF SOLDER

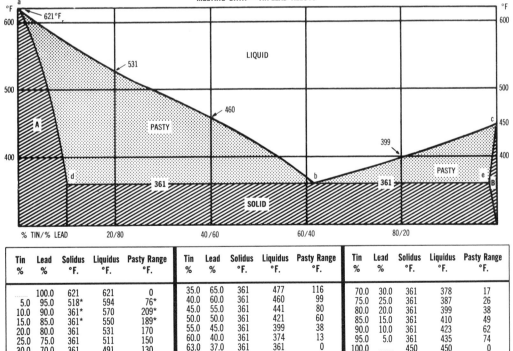

MELTING DATA — TIN-LEAD ALLOYS

Tin %	Lead %	Solidus °F.	Liquidus °F.	Pasty Range °F.	Tin %	Lead %	Solidus °F.	Liquidus °F.	Pasty Range °F.	Tin %	Lead %	Solidus °F.	Liquidus °F.	Pasty Range °F.
	100.0	621	621	0	35.0	65.0	361	477	116	70.0	30.0	361	378	17
5.0	95.0	518*	594	76*	40.0	60.0	361	460	99	75.0	25.0	361	387	26
10.0	90.0	361*	570	209*	45.0	55.0	361	441	80	80.0	20.0	361	399	38
15.0	85.0	361*	550	189*	50.0	50.0	361	421	60	85.0	15.0	361	410	49
20.0	80.0	361	531	170	55.0	45.0	361	399	38	90.0	10.0	361	423	62
25.0	75.0	361	511	150	60.0	40.0	361	374	13	95.0	5.0	361	435	74
30.0	70.0	361	491	130	63.0	37.0	361	361	0	100.0		450	450	0
					65.0	35.0	361	367	6					

*These are preferred values for engineering purposes but are not equilibrium values. At equilibrium the eutectic limits are 19.5—98% tin. (June 1944)

Fig. 3-2. Courtesy: National Lead Co.

the very solid to the partly solid, partly liquid, to the entirely liquid state.

Let us examine that a little more closely. A solder of, let us say 20/80 composition, which would be 20% tin–80% lead, would have to be heated up to 531°F. to be completely liquid—a very high temperature for use in stained glass, indeed almost as high as the melting temperature of lead. This particular percentage of 20/80 goes to a liquid very slowly and very sluggishly and has a temperature range of 361–531 degrees before it is entirely liquid. We can see, therefore, that this percentage of solder is more of a paste; and indeed, it is used mostly for plumbing even though it is really too sluggish even for that. Certainly it is too unwieldy a combination for the pin-point soldering of lead joints, which requires a fast melt and a fast freeze with as little heat as possible. On the other hand, a 60/40 solder need be heated only to approximately 370° before it goes into a completely liquid state. It goes solid again at 361°, leaving a working zone of temperature of only 9 degrees. This is exactly right for stained glass work (Fig. 3-2).

There is a combination of tin and lead which goes immediately to a liquid from a solid with no working zone at all. It is practically instantaneous. This is a combination of 63% tin and 37% lead. The instant shift from solid to liquid is called the eutectic point of the solder.

SUMMATION

The more tin you add to lead, the lower the melting point of the lead–tin combination and the smaller the workable zone of the solder, that is, the zone where it goes from completely solid to completely liquid. A solder of 63/37 would have no workable zone at all, since it would go solid–liquid, liquid–solid instantaneously. The closest solder to that point which still has a workable zone, that is, a 9 degree zone in which one can solder, is 60/40. The addition of tin beyond this point will raise the working zone gradually between 361° to 450°, the melting point of tin.

"SHAPES" OF SOLDER

There are two shapes in which solder is generally sold, bar solder and wire solder. Wire solder comes in different dimensions. We have found that the best physical shape in which to use solder with stained glass is ⅛" solid core wire solder. This width allows the maximum amount of solder to flow onto the iron and thence to the joint to give the best possible and neatest appearing joint. To use solder of a diameter less than ⅛" is simply to use up a greater amount of material and time to achieve a poor result. As for bar solder, it is totally inadequate for stained glass work and we mention it only to decry its use.

There are solders on the market which contain a core of material, usually a resinous flux. These should be avoided, as the resin will hinder, not help, your work. We have found it eventually gums soldering tips and makes it very difficult to get the finished stained glass product clean, as the resin also gums the glass. In fact, it keeps oozing out of the soldered joints long after the piece has been finished—a cloudy activity that you can well do without. Use solid core solder *only* in percentages of 60/40 and avoid being under this particular cloud.

CORE SOLDER

While it is the soldered joints that hold the entire stained glass work together, they should deemphasize their importance by modestly staying in the background. Nothing is more ungainly than bulges of solder arthritically sitting in great humped masses over the joints of a panel or lamp. Leads that have been pitted and burned in an attempt to solder them will also add to the generally crippled effect.

PROCEDURE FOR A GOOD SOLDER JOINT

Fig. 3-3. The authors demonstrating a soldering technique. Note the smoothness of the joints. Courtesy: *The Suburbanite.*

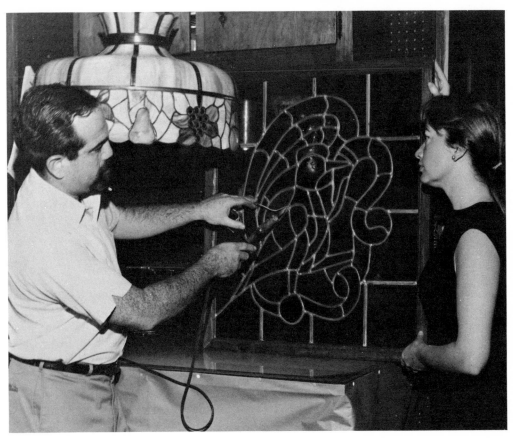

The best procedure for ending up with a good, substantial solder joint which will still appear neat and clean involves the following steps:

1. Clean all joint surfaces before doing anything else.
2. Make sure that your lead cames are properly fitted together, that is, that they abut one another as closely as possible with as little space between as possible.
3. Make sure you are using the correct soldering flux for the work you are doing.
4. Keep your iron at the proper temperature and use the proper solder.
5. Make sure each joint is clean after you have soldered it.

Let us discuss the above point by point:

1. *Cleaning the Joint's Surfaces*

A clean surface is half the battle. If there are any particles of dirt or grease, or any oxides covering the lead, they will interfere with the soldering process. Do not use a cleaning solution on lead came in an attempt to clean the surfaces. We advise a mechanical cleansing with a copper wire or very fine steel wire brush (Fig. 3-4). This will not scratch the glass but will allow enough abrasive quality to strip the oxide coat and any other interfering material from the lead. In cases where the lead is so old and oxidized that even a wire brush will not remove the coating, it may be done by scraping the surface with the blade of your lead knife until the shiny underportion appears. Only this surface is solderable. It goes without saying that the soldering tip should also be clean or it will not only refuse to pick up solder but its application against an otherwise clean joint will dirty it, so that it becomes unsolderable. The use of strong inorganic acids such as hydrochloric or sulphuric as cleansing agents is not recommended. These acids release fumes which are highly toxic, and the acids themselves are extremely dangerous.

2. *Fit Your Lead Cames Together Properly*

The lead cames should be approximated so that the solder can easily be drawn into the space between them and cover the ends with one easy flow. This means that the cames should be mitered or so cut as to correspond closely one with the other. No wide gap should be present between the ends (Fig. 3-5). They should be sliced with a sharp instrument, preferably a leading knife, which provides a clean and true end-to-end meeting. Attempting to bridge over

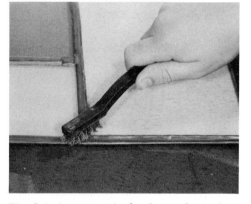

Fig. 3-4. A copper wire brush may be used to clean the joints to allow the solder to flow evenly.

Fig. 3-5. The lead came should butt together as shown allowing for a smooth soldered joint.

a wide gap between the leads will not only lead to a messy and hunchbacked solder joint, but will waste a good bit of solder, and time and temper as well. It is better to do a leading job correctly step by step than try to make up in Step III for what obviously should have taken place in Step I.

3. *Use a Proper Flux*

We will have a word to say about fluxes themselves shortly. Be sure that the flux you are using is the correct one for the work under consideration. In stained glass we use a very specific flux, the main ingredient of which is oleic acid. This can be mixed with other material to give it a quality which will make the solder flow smoothly and evenly. However, no amount of flux will do any good if the joint surface is not clean. The flux may be applied to the parts to be soldered by brushing or dipping these parts. If it is a flat panel, obviously you must brush it on. We very rarely dip joints into flux in stained glass work. In brushing flux on to a joint, it is important to use an "acid" brush. This is a stiff bristle brush which is itself impervious to the flux. Its stiffness is essential to work the flux into the lead surface and through any remaining oxide coat that may be present. The better you work the flux into the surface of the lead came, the more easily the solder will flow. It is not necessary to flood the area with flux. A small amount properly applied will work better than an ocean of it drowning the joint. Don't be afraid to scrub the flux into the joint. Simply wiping it on gently is not enough.

4. *Keep Your Iron at the Proper Temperature*

The soldering iron is the most familiar and the best method of heat application. We will be discussing it shortly in detail. It is important to select an iron large enough to have sufficient heat capacity to perform its function at a reasonable rate of speed. But don't let it get too hot. An iron that is too hot will refuse to pick up solder and will end up burning the joint surfaces away. This cratering effect of the lead cames is unsightly and makes for the extra work of patching the missing surfaces with solder. Watch your iron. Don't let it get so hot that it takes over the job on its own. On the other hand, if your iron is not hot enough, you will end up "dragging" the solder, with an end result showing waves of frozen metal in peaks and valleys over the joint. No amount of re-smoothing with an iron insufficiently heated will rectify this.

No matter how much soldering you may have

Fig. 3-6. Note how the leads are mitered to fit snugly one against the other.

done in wiring circuits or plumbing or work around the house in general, you will find that soldering lead is a different situation altogether. It is best to practice on scrap lead for fifteen or twenty minutes until you get the feel of the material. You will be amazed how rapidly the lead will melt away from your overheated soldering iron. Better to have this happen on scrap rather than on lead which you are attempting to use in a piece of finished work.

Of course, if you are not using the proper solder, you will be hindered all along the line, even if your iron *is* adequate.

5. *Clean the Joints After They Are Soldered*

Flux residues tend to make the glass tacky and smudgy. There are organic solvents which may be used as cleaning agents, such as carbon tetrachloride, but we mention this specific agent only to condemn it. While an excellent solvent, its use is accompanied by so much danger that it should be ruled out completely, no matter how well your studio is ventilated. Unfortunately, simple soap and water will not clean away the flux residues and oxide coatings from the glass nor will any of the routine glass cleansers like Windex. The best material we have found is our own cleaning and polishing powder, which can be used either wet or dry over the entire surface. This powder probably works best when used dry, although it does tend to fly around the room. So close the doors when you are working with it. Used wet, it forms a paste, and while more elbow grease must be applied to get it to work properly, it doesn't take to the air quite so readily. Cleaning and polishing powder should be sprinkled over the entire finished work on one surface and then the surface scrubbed with a heavy floor brush over glass and lead alike. This powder not only picks up and breaks down all flux residues and dirt that have collected on the glass and lead, but it also dries the putty with which many finished stained glass panels are impregnated.

THE FLUXES

A flux is a material which, placed on metals to be soldered, cleans the surfaces and enables the solder to take hold. Without it, the soldering process is frustrated. The solder will simply roll off. Many ideas have been advanced to explain the action of fluxes. Basically, their purpose is to remove and to keep any oxides from forming on the metal surface during its heating and soldering. Fluxes also prevent any oxidation of the molten solder. A flux must be readily displaced by the solder so as not to interfere with the wetting and bonding of the solder to the underlying metal. In order to perform the above require-ments, it is important that the flux remain stable over the soldering range. Good soldering technique calls for the selection of the mildest flux that will do the job. While fluxes fall into three main classes, corrosive, intermediate and non-corrosive, non-corro-sive fluxes are too weak and corrosive fluxes generally too strong for stained glass work.

A non-corrosive flux, such as is used in resin "core" solder, has the disadvantage previously mentioned of oozing from the lead joints. A corrosive flux, for in-stance, one containing an inorganic acid, eventually attacks the lead, leading to pitting of the surfaces.

Most fluxes used in stained glass work are in liquid form, since they are easier to work with that way. A flux may be used in the form of a paste with no diminution of its value. For ease of operation, how-ever, a liquid is preferred. It is easier to scrub a liquid into the lead with the soldering brush and much easier to get it out of the jar. One basic dis-advantage of the liquid flux is the readiness with which the jar goes over, fluxing the table top and losing material. In order to frustrate this particular tendency, one should consider keeping only a small amount of flux in the bottle while working, so that when the soldering iron cord tangles in it, or the piece one is working on bumps against it and it over-turns, one does not lose the entire amount of flux on hand.

The poor tool blames its workman. In this cate-gory of reproach, few items employed by the stained glass artisan are apt to get hotter under the collar than the soldering iron. Its revenge for unjust re-sponsibility is to impeach the quality of the work, fragment the artistic impulse and waste money, time and temper. Here are a few soldering iron types which should *not* be used in stained glass work and which will let you know it in terms of your end result:

The Featherweight

This item costs somewhere between $1 and $3 and is available on the bargain counter of your hardware store. The tip is not replaceable. Wattage varies be-tween 25 and 50 watts. Such an iron is strained beyond its capacity when it comes to melting solder over a wide unit area, such as a lead joint. The pin-point soldering of electrical connections is more in its line. The result of using it on lead joints is an impatient dragging rather than an even flow of solder over the joints. The beginner compensates for this

SOLDERING IRONS

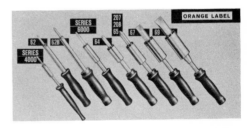

Fig. 3-7. A few different sizes of soldering irons, showing the different weight tips. Courtesy: Esico Co.

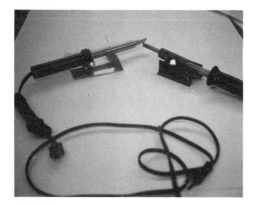

Fig. 3-8. On the left a Weller, on the right an Esico iron. Both are heavy duty tools of 100 watts or slightly more; both will do a satisfactory soldering job.

generally by pressing harder with his iron against the joints in an attempt to flatten them. Novel effects not originally planned for can be achieved in this manner, although none of them are particularly artistic. Users of such questionable devices that do not iron out their problems immediately, will find themselves led astray.

The Heavyweight

Here is the other extreme: an iron endowed with such overabundant electrical vivacity as to cleave through solder, lead and fingers, and crack the glass into the bargain. Usually it has a tip large enough to fry an egg. For some reason, people using such an iron invariably are attempting the most delicate joint work.

This iron gobbles solder at an alarming rate and generally spews it in absentminded dribbles over table top, floor and shoes, and only seldom on the work in progress. One can barely touch a joint with it, lest it evaporate. Great clouds of steam and a residual hacking cough mark its operator's position in the studio.

The Soldering Gun

If you must pack a weapon, a lead knife would be more practicable. Of all soldering equipment, this is the item most people have lying around the house and for convenience will attempt to use in stained glass work. Rarely have we seen excellent work done with a soldering gun, and that produced at an expense of time and effort that could have been halved by the use of an iron. While we have seen individuals become quite adept with such a tool, we feel that it is an expensive price to pay for developing a handicap. Use of a gun will always mark you as an amateur in the field.

There can be no changing of tips in such an instrument and therefore, no mobility in the soldering of different objects and different angles. It is also extremely difficult to solder wide joints in any large sort of work, as the soldering gun simply cannot cover the area involved in one swoop. As for "tinning" either lead or copper foil, that is, drawing solder along its length, it's pretty much out of the question. There's no fast draw with a soldering gun.

The Blow Torch

No one who has done even the slightest work with stained glass would consider using a blow torch on a lead joint. It is mentioned here only because the question is constantly raised. Use of a flame thrower, such as this, would simply burn the leads right off the panel, as well as crack the glass. For creative endeavors, such an instrument is better left in the hands of the plumber.

Since we have now covered a flotilla of wrong instruments, what tool would be best for use in the stained glass craft? Let's have a look.

Our Hero

This is a 100-watt, ⅜″ bore iron with a set screw for the tip. It comes straight or "hatchet shaped," whichever fits the hand best. Such an iron is designed and constructed to give constant production performance. It features a handle that does not get hot, and it has the latest in heating elements, with such elements being easily replaceable should one burn out. It is light enough to be easily held, heats up readily to a workable temperature, and maintains that temperature for long periods of time (Fig. 3-9). The tendency for an "uncontrolled" iron is to eventually get too hot for the lead cames, so a certain amount of plugging and unplugging of the iron into the electrical circuit becomes necessary. A "controlled" iron will save its operator excess wear and tear by maintaining the ideal heat, and allowing work to proceed unhindered by continual stooping and searching for the outlet. Such an iron employs the use of a rheostat (see below).

Fig. 3-9. Cutaway to show the wiring of a standard iron. Courtesy: Esico Co.

The set screw on the iron is particularly important. Irons that employ screw-in type tips tend to have such tips freeze into place with the continual expansion and contraction as the iron heats and cools. Then they cannot be removed, and this limits the mobility of the iron, since it is highly desirable to vary the size and shape of the tip depending on the type of soldering being done (Fig. 3-10).

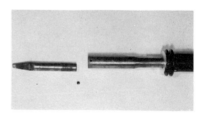

Fig. 3-10. Soldering iron with tip removed showing ease with which parts may be alternated. Tip slides into the barrel and is held by a set screw.

The hammering, oiling, squeezing, twisting and sweating that result when it is discovered that a tip cannot be removed from the iron, provides a colorful break in routine, but generally results in the purchase of another iron. The set screw in a new iron should be loosened after the first few uses. Once the iron has been broken in, you may rely on it to open and close readily. Even if you are careless and allow the set screw to freeze into place, it can still be drilled out and replaced. With a screw-in tip, however, once it freezes it is generally done for, as attempts to remove the tip forceably will very likely break the iron.

One method of avoiding the plugging and unplugging of your iron is to put a simple line switch on the cord (Fig. 3-11). This is easily accomplished and,

THE SWITCH

Fig. 3-11. Showing line cord switch approximated at the proper working distance from the iron.

THE STAND

Fig. 3-12. A few different soldering iron stands.

THE RHEOSTAT CONTROL UNIT

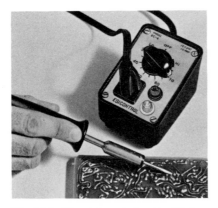

Fig. 3-13. Rheostat control unit with iron attached. Courtesy: Esico Co.

THE TIP CLEANER

providing you remember to use it, you won't wonder why your lead is melting or your solder isn't. Caution should be exercised in placing the switch. If you place it too close to the iron, it will clatter against your productive endeavors. If you place it too far away, it involves a lot of stooping and bending to find it. Putting it in the middle of the cord will probably have it catching the edge of the table and pulling the iron out of your hand. A fairly safe rule of thumb is to put the switch approximately 12 inches from the end of the iron and check it before cutting the cord to make sure that is where you want it.

Most good irons come equipped with a little stand to rest the iron on when it gets hot. It's a good habit to use your stand, even for a cold iron. There are occasional workers who don't seem to know the difference—charred wood is their specialty. Such individuals plug in their iron and leave it on the table top just for a moment to warm up while they arrange their equipment. Somehow the stand is the last thing they locate.

The stand is one of the easiest items to lose. If you misplace it, get another one. Trying to rest your iron on a hammer or a wrench or a pair of pliers as a temporary stand only results in the iron rolling off and burning either the table or yourself. There is no room for improvisation here.

For anyone doing serious work in stained glass, this item is a must. It effectively controls the amount of heat going through the iron and does away with the plugging and unplugging, switching on and switching off ritual that is the plague of beginners in the field. Such a unit provides manual control of soldering iron tip temperatures with automatic corrections for voltage fluctuations up to 80% of the full wattage of the heating element. It also allows operation without control at 100% of full wattage. There is a pilot light on the instrument which indicates cycling of the current. The unit we recommend is self-contained, pleasant to look at and small enough to fit unobtrusively on the work table, while being large enough to do the job. Rheostat control units are not inexpensive, but they last indefinitely. The only part that may need to be replaced is the small fuse.

This handy device is designed to clean a vitacote or copper soldering tip quickly and efficiently. A stroke across the wet vertical sponge removes undesirable residues, which fall into the tray at the base. Solder on the tip's working surface is not destroyed.

The top cover of this device lifts off to refill the water reservoir that keeps the sponge wet at all times. It is certainly a friendlier way of cleaning the tip than shaking the iron across the floor and across your neighbor's foot (Fig. 3-14).

Fig. 3-14. Tip cleaner.

SOLDERING TIPS

There are copper tips and ironclad tips. The copper tip is cheaper, more widespread in use and more difficult to maintain. The ironclad tip is coated with a surface of alloy, making it easier to work with than the copper tip.

Tinning the Copper Tip

This is a procedure that must be carried out from time to time with a copper tip. It involves first scraping off the dirt and oxides that have gathered on the surface from previous soldering operations. This is best done with a file. Be careful to maintain, while filing, the same shape the copper tip had before. If it is a chisel shape, you will want to keep it that way when the filing is done. Once you have filed your copper tip down to a point where it is again shiny and new looking on the surface, it should be heated and retinned. That is, the tip should be fluxed and solder run over its surface. It should accept this solder readily. If it does not, the iron is probably too hot and a certain amount of cooling should be allowed so that the solder will stick to the surface. The tip should be tinned on all its surfaces. As the surface then gathers up more and more oxides from use, the tinning process is necessary once more.

Ironclad Soldering Tips—Their Use and Care

Ironclad tips have a longer life than the plain copper tip. They require a minimum of attention and give maximum uninterrupted performance. They have a core of copper of high conductivity. The working surface and shank are ironplated to a controlled standard. The tips are pretinned and the entire shank is alloy plated and ready for immediate use. Such tips cost more than standard copper tips, but they last much longer. It is important that such a tip never be filed, as it will be ruined in this fashion by removal of its plated surface. To clean this tip, it is advised that it be simply run over a wet, cellulose sponge while hot. This should remove all oxides and dirt from the surface of the tip and allow a freshly cleaned surface for the next soldering operation. These tips come in a number of shapes. Many workers have a set of them which they interchange during a particular project, depending on the type

Fig. 3-15. A few of the varied shaped ironclad tips. From left to right—chisel, semi-chisel, pyramidal, conical. Courtesy: Esico Co.

of joint under fire. This not only cuts their soldering time physically, but makes the whole procedure an artistic pleasure.

SUMMATION

Fig. 3-16. A few different irons. At top are two industrial irons; next is one holding technique for a light pencil iron. Below is a "hatchet" shaped iron. This type is more popular among women, who prefer its lighter weight and more sharply focused balance.

The soldering process, including the use of the correct soldering iron, is an integral part of working in stained glass. Your finished product reflects the tools that you have used. While we do not recommend that beginners go out and immediately purchase professional soldering irons and a complete set of iron-coated tips, we do feel they owe themselves a debt to use equipment that will allow them to achieve results which they will find worthwhile. They should approach the entire matter of soldering cautiously at first. Initial attempts may be delightful, only to look second rate as critical appraisal develops. This in itself will lead to the urge to acquire the proper tools for the job (Fig. 3-16). To sum up:

1. Never use anything but 60/40 solid core solder. It makes a difference whether you call it 60/40 or 40/60, since the solder is composed of tin and lead and the percentage of tin is placed first in the equation. Any percentage other than this will make for more difficulty in the soldering process. If you use a "resin core" solder, you will have sloppy joints due to the resin oozing all over the glass and being almost impossible to get off. It will also eventually gum up your soldering tip.

2. Use an iron that is hot enough. Irons below 80 watts are not recommended, as they take too long to heat up and don't last. Also, the tips available for such irons are too small for use on large joints. There is no question that a small iron will eventually get the job done, but you will be spending more time on this one procedure than is necessary. Also, by the time you have gone through several small irons, you will have paid for a large one. So, if you intend doing any extensive work in glass, why not get the right iron to begin with?

3. Make sure your soldering tip is clean. If you are using an ironclad tip, wipe it every so often on its sponge to remove excess flux and solder. You will notice a considerable difference in solder flow if you do. If your preference is a copper tip, then check to see that it is properly tinned and fluxed. The tinning and retinning that is necessary with a copper tip is a nuisance, but more of a nuisance is solder that won't take to the lead because it keeps rolling off the soldering tip due to a barrier of dirt on its surface. Re-file the copper tip, flux and tin it with solder.

4. If your tip is clean and still won't pick up solder, the solder rolling off and away from the tip, then your iron is too hot and you must allow it to cool somewhat. Ideal heat is when the solder, touched by the soldering tip, instantly melts and clings or is "picked up" by the tip to be transported to the work in progress.

5. If your soldering leaves sharp pointed ends on your joints, you are "dragging" your solder and your iron is not hot enough. Solder properly applied should flow smoothly.

6. Use the right flux. A liquid works best.

CHAPTER 4

Aids or Band Aids— The Tools of the Trade

Fingers were made before forks, as children and hostesses at chicken dinners are fond of proclaiming. They were also made before picks and shovels, rivet buckets and stained glass tools. Nevertheless, their sole employment in such activities would lead to a prolific diminution in both their quality and quantity. Our purpose in this chapter is to describe some of the aids that spare the band-aids—and the fingers themselves—at least as far as stained glass is concerned. We will look first at that most basic of all tools, the glass cutter.

GLASS CUTTERS   There is a good bit of confusion as to exactly which glass cutter does what. In an attempt to establish some sort of universal language, the Fletcher-Terry Co. has published the following chart:

Number	Type of Glass Cutter
01	General purpose (boxed)
02	General Purpose Ball End (boxed)
01DC	General Purpose (in pouch)
02DC	General Purpose Ball End (in pouch)
04	Plate and Soft Glass
05	Plate and Soft Glass Ball End
06	Hard, Cathedral (thick or granite-backed) and Opalescent
07	Same with Ball End
08	Pattern Cutting
09	Pattern Cutting: Ball End

Number	*Turret and Wood Handle Cutters*
29	Turret Glass Cutter: 6 wheels
30	Wood Handle: Interchangeable: 3 wheels

Carbide Cutters

CO 1	General Purpose
CO 2	General Purpose Ball End
CO 4	For Plate and Soft Glass
CO 6	For Hard Glass (Opalescent especially)
CO 8	For Pattern Cutting

There are thus two major categories of glass cutters, the steel wheel and the carbide wheel cutter. The difference in price is quintupled from the former to the latter, but there is a good reason. Carbide cutters, if treated properly, will last about five times as long as steel cutters. It is recommended that beginners in stained glass supply themselves with at least two steel wheel cutters: an 08 pattern cutting, small wheel cutter and an 06 hard cutter. One of them should be ball ended. If, as a beginner, you really want to make things easy for yourself, you'll add a general purpose carbide cutter to these two.

Ball ended cutters are provided for tapping a "score line" into a "run line." We will go into the actual technique of cutting glass in Chapter 6. As we have said, only one of your cutters need be ball ended. This will leave you a hard straight end on your second cutter to use as a fulcrum for breaking a straight score in glass.

A word about turret and wood handle cutters. We have known some individuals to complain about the thinness of the metal handles on regulation cutters. If you find yourself among them, you may decide wood handle cutters are more to your liking. The handles are stouter and fill the fingers more securely. Such cutters are also lighter than the metal handle cutters. You must be careful how you hold your wood handle cutter or you are liable to end up with chafed fingers and a blistered web between the fingers. It is worthwhile experimenting with these lighter and thicker-handled cutters, just so you know they are available.

Turret, or multiple wheel glass cutters, really have no place in stained glass. The extra wheels in the turret get in the way of fine pattern cutting and by the time one of the wheels gets dull and needs changing, you probably will have misplaced the cutter anyway. They are fairly expensive, and our advice

Fig. 4-1. The original 1869 patented "Bristol diamond" steel wheel glass cutter. Courtesy: Fletcher Co.

Fig. 4-2. Present day glass cutters—one straight, one balled. Courtesy: Fletcher Co.

Fig. 4-3. A Fletcher "refill" style glass cutter wheel on U shaped axle.

Fig. 4-4. A Fletcher glass cutter wheel many times magnified.

is that if you are considering one, add a few dollars to the price and get yourself a carbide cutter.

What actually is a glass cutter? It is a very simple device, consisting of a handle of some type, with a hard steel wheel rotating on a bronze axle. As this instrument is pushed or pulled along the surface of glass, the wheel turns around and plows a groove in the glass, causing it to fracture the surface and creating a weak place throughout the length of the score you have made. When pressure is then applied in proper fashion to this score, the glass will fracture the rest of the way through and separate into two pieces. If pressure is not applied properly, the glass may well separate into 22 or 102 pieces. You should choose your cutters so as to be able to handle all kinds of glass easily. You will not break up glass so frequently if you use the right cutter for it. The following are some various things to note:

Size of the Wheel

The smaller the wheel, the easier it is to steer the cutter. With patterns to follow, a small wheel is necessary. A $5/32''$ wheel is the best size for stained glass work. Larger wheels are fine for straight lines, and while a larger wheel might last longer, it won't cut as easily as a small one, nor will it have that "feel" a small wheel gives your hand. In stained glass pattern cutting, developing a "feel" for both glass and cutter is important.

Angle of Bevel

The angle at which the wheel was sharpened is quite important as far as the kind of glass being cut is concerned. Broad beveled cutter wheels are designed to cut soft glass while the steep beveled are for hard glass.

Handles

As we have mentioned, most handles are metal and may be a little narrow for some people. A piece of rubber hose slipped over the handle will improve it in this dimension if it is necessary. Surgical tubing works best for this, although we have known individuals to wrap their cutters with tape. This, however, usually gets sticky from use and is not as desirable as the tubing. None of the wood or plastic handles has a ball attached.

Ball Ended Cutters

Balls are used to tap a score to cause it to run. This ball helps you fracture the cut and makes it easier to separate your glass once the score is made.

It is possible to tap glass with the tooth side, that is, the underside of the cutter. This does not work as well and requires more skill in tapping than does the ball. If the ball on your cutter is not smooth, sand or file it smooth for good tapping results. Some cutters have a small ridge around the ball that interferes with accurate tapping. This should be sanded down.

Grozzing Teeth

The three slots found on the underside of most cutters were used for grozzing. Grozzing is the act of chipping off small pieces of glass to get exactly the shape you want if the glass didn't follow your score line, or if the piece was a little too large, or just to smooth the edging (Fig. 4-5). These teeth are not of much use in stained glass work. Originally, they were cut into brass or soft iron. The soft metal would allow one to break off small pieces of glass without cracking the rest of the piece. Today, however, grozzing slats are of hard metal and their use causes more glass breakage than it saves. Forget about the grozzing teeth and buy yourself a good pair of glass or grozzing pliers which are made of special soft iron. The use of ordinary electrical pliers in this regard will also break up more glass than it saves. Be professional and use the right tools.

Carbide Glass Cutters

Some carbide cutters will say "carbide" on them. That is, they will have the word engraved on the cutter handle. However, in most instances they are color coded. Since a carbide cutter looks pretty much like any other cutter, it is a good idea to mark it in some fashion, so that you will be able to distinguish your carbide cutter from your regular cutters. Carbide cutter wheels are made of silicon carbide and can be resharpened by the manufacturer for a nominal charge. Good carbide glass cutters are a pleasure to use.

Changeable and Multiple Wheel Cutters

As mentioned previously, these are not much good for stained glass work, as the wheel wobbles on the axis and the turrets get in the way of the pattern.

Sharpening Glass Cutters

It is possible to resharpen a glass cutter, but it takes patience plus the proper type of stone. A white Arkansas stone is used. The cutter is then held at a slant to match the original angle of bevel of the wheel and run back and forth over the stone. Use a

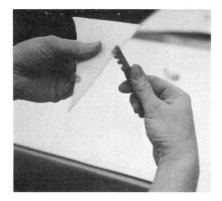

Fig. 4-5. Grozzing a piece of glass using the grozzing teeth on a glass cutter.

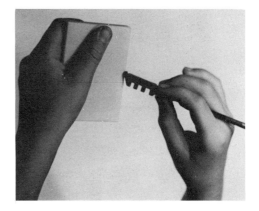

Fig. 4-6. Sharpening a cutter.

light oil on the stone. We generally do not recommend resharpening cutters. Once you sharpen a cutter, it seems to get dull very quickly again and you are forever fooling with it to keep it usable. Buy a new one when yours gets dull. It's well worth it. A dull cutter will only end up ruining pieces of glass instead of saving you money.

Lubrication

Lubricating your cutter correctly will make your cutting more successful and will keep your cutter sharp and useful. You can ruin your cutter in one stroke if you don't lubricate it. A small short jar or glass with a piece of fine steel wool or bit of cloth at the bottom containing ¼″ of kerosene is just right. Do not use oil or turpentine. Turpentine will gum up quickly from the heat of use, and soon the wheel will be stuck in its axle and refuse to turn. Once that happens and you continue to use the wheel, you'll burn a flat spot on it and the cutter is ruined. Remember to use only kerosene or specially prepared lubricants for your glass cutter. It is necessary to keep that axle well-lubricated. We have seen individuals buy a new cutter and in one week have it completely unusable, while others who have their cutters sitting in a jar of good lubricant are still cutting with it months later. If you can get a special lubricant for your glass cutter, it will be less volatile than kerosene and will therefore last longer.

Testing for Sharpness

You can test a glass cutter for sharpness by simply comparing the way it scores to a new cutter. As you learn the feel of your cutter, and as you cut more and more glass, you will be able to tell quite easily when a cutter is going dull. When your old cutter seems difficult and you don't get that "singing" from the glass when you use it across the surface, try a new one and see how that sounds. A dull cutter may make a score, but that doesn't mean the glass will separate easily. When your glass starts taking a great deal of your effort to separate it and when your score line looks very uneven and shallow, your cutter is probably getting dull. Always keep a few new cutters on hand. It's no fun trying to cut glass with a dull cutter and it's also expensive in terms of broken glass. A cutter can also get flat spots and dents in the wheel from cutting on dirty glass or from rough handling. Such a cutter will go "tic, tic, tic, tic," as you make a score. No matter how good the cutter is otherwise, it is useless with this defect. Such problems are generally caused by dropping the cutter on the wheel end or from poor lubrication as mentioned above. If you take care of your glass cutter, it will serve you well for a reasonable length of time.

Prices

It is not wise to try to cut stained glass with a cheap hardware store or ten-cent store cutter. A good cutter runs 85¢ and up, with carbide cutters now selling for approximately $4. Fletcher is one of the best-known American-made cutters. "Diamantor" is a good German made glass cutter.

Diamond Cutters

This is a completely different type of tool from the glass cutter we have been discussing. It is not generally used in stained glass work, since to follow a paper pattern with a diamond cutter is impractical. For straight lines, a diamond cutter works fine. There are different kinds of diamond cutters for different kinds of glass. Usually the handle is made of wood or plastic, without a ball, and prices range from $3 for an extremely questionable one up to $24 and more for a commercial highgrade one. A diamond cutter actually requires more skill to use than a wheel cutter, but of course it cuts much more easily. As in buying any other tools or supplies in this very unique art, it is best to buy a diamond cutter from someone who deals in such materials specifically, who knows his material and can help you select a tool of your choice.

Probably the most frequently requested piece of information on glass cutting is how to cut a circle out of glass. Circles may be cut freehand with a regular glass cutter as described above, or with a machine calculated to cut circles for you to any dimension you may wish. Circle cutters come in two styles, and cutting a circle in glass is quite simple with either one of them. For small circles, from ⅜" to 5" in diameter, a rather compact, rotating handle instrument may be employed, manufactured by the Fletcher-Terry Company. Once the circle is inscribed, it is "broken out" of the glass by scoring lines at right angles to it and pulling off the pieces with glass pliers. For larger circles, from 2" on up, a cup circle cutter is used. This has three pieces: a cup stand, a movable turret with a screw gauge, and a rod on which the turret travels. The further the turret is placed from the cup stand, the wider the diameter of the circle will be. The cup must be additionally braced by holding one hand on top of it to

CIRCLE CUTTERS

Fig. 4-7. A typical circle cutter mounted on a wooden stand. Courtesy: Fletcher Co.

make sure it doesn't move. The cutting wheel on circle cutters is the same type of cutting wheel available in the regular glass cutters, and must be cared for in the same manner. It should be lubricated and kept clean. When such wheels finally become dull, replacement wheels are available, and are put into position simply by loosening and tightening a single screw.

GLASS PLIERS

Glass pliers differ in jaw width, in handle length, and in shape. They are used to trim away pieces of glass too small or too thick or just too awkward to remove by hand. Since the jaws of glass pliers work parallel to each other, they do not pinch the glass, but rather overreach the edge to the desired clamping area. They are made both with and without grooves in the jaws; our own preference being for grooved pliers rather than without, as such a tool can also be used for rough grozzing. To be used in this fashion, the jaw of a grooved glass plier is run over a glass edge more or less like a file. Be careful —if too much pressure is applied, the glass will splinter, and the edge will be in worse shape than before. Grozzing takes practice and fine grozzing should never be attempted with glass pliers. Only the more obvious points and imbalances can be aligned with this instrument, but this it will do well (Fig. 4-9).

Fig. 4-8. Left to right: regular glass pliers, heavy glass pliers; running pliers; small grozzing pliers, large grozzing pliers.

Fig. 4-9. Our own preference.

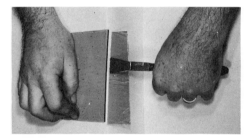

Fig. 4-10. Glass pliers in action; the two pieces of glass separated by use of this tool.

Glass pliers can also be used to break a piece of glass after it has been scored. Once the score is made, providing it is a straight cut, the glass is laid flat on the table surface with the score uppermost. It should be extended over the edge of the table until the score is directly in line with the table edge. Now, with the glass pliers, firmly grasp the nearest piece directly at the score line, so that the pliers' lower jaw is almost against the table's edge. With the left hand, press the furthermost section of glass against the table to keep the piece from moving. The pull on the pliers should be out and slightly down, and the two pieces will separate with a musical "ting" (Fig. 4-10). It's a good idea for the novice applying this technique to keep his feet out of the way, as occasionally the glass will break into more than two pieces, with the excess raining down like arrows. Glass pliers should not be employed in breaking sharp curves, unless you have a good deal of skill in their use, for here the width of their jaws makes the procedure somewhat chancey. It is better to use grozzing pliers in this instance.

Our own preference in glass pliers is either a 6″ or 8″ handle with a ¾″ or 1″ grooved jaw (Fig.

Fig. 4-11. Two types of glass pliers: above the more usual one; below a glass breaking pliers with a more acute lower jaw to give a more concentrated pressure below the score line.

4-11). This is an excellent beginner's pliers and will provide for those who have never used them an increased confidence as they find their score and break lines coinciding to a degree never previously achieved (Fig. 4-12).

These are pliers with much narrower jaws than glass pliers. Such jaws have very fine teeth and are used strictly for grozzing. They are made of soft metal, and any use other than glass grozzing will damage them. Unusual and difficult shapes can be literally carved out of glass with their help. They are, of course, a specialized tool, and are employed in nibbling the fine points and inconsistencies left on the glass from less than perfect cuts. Use of these pliers requires more practice than any other pliers, but they're worth the effort. It's a good idea to make sure your grozzing pliers are well oiled, so they will open and close with little work of the hand. It's best if they open with the weight of their bottom handle. If you hold the grozzing pliers with one handle up, the joint should be so limber that the lower handle will drop. It's a good idea to keep all your pliers this spry. It eliminates the tiring motion of constantly having to open them by hand.

The fine teeth of grozzing pliers wear down in time. When this happens, a fine file may be employed to recut them. With care and thoughtful use, such a pair of pliers will last for a very long period of time.

Probably the most difficult cut to break out of a piece of glass is a thin, long strip. Invariably, this strip runs off the score line somewhere along its length. The running pliers is a tool calculated to make just such cuts and do it right the first time. It is one of the more expensive of the pliers, in the $13 range.

The jaws of running pliers are so made that they curve into one another. The top jaw is concave and the lower convex. The lower jaw thus becomes a fulcrum for the two pressure points of the upper jaw (Fig. 4-15).

Such an arrangement allows an even pressure above and below the score line. To be certain that a strictly measured pressure is produced by the operator, a screw gauge is provided on top of the pliers. This screw is turned so that the pliers are only permitted to grasp the surfaces of the glass with the smallest amount of pressure—just enough to fracture the score, but not enough to crush the glass. The worker must spend a minute or two arranging the

GROZZING PLIERS

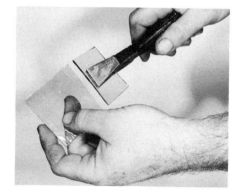

Fig. 4-12. Breaking a small diagonal line with glass pliers.

Fig. 4-13. Small grozzing pliers, a graceful instrument for graceful cuts.

RUNNING PLIERS

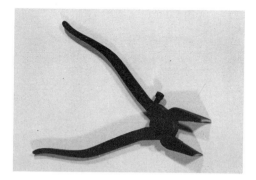

Fig. 4-14. Running pliers, two views. Note the curvatures of the jaws. The center line of the pliers should line up with the score of the glass.

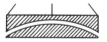

Fig. 4-15. Front view.

pliers at the score line, but he will get straight cuts. The procedure is as follows:

1. First score your glass in a straight cut.
2. Bring your glass over to the table edge so that the table edge is at right angles to the cut. Take your running pliers and line up the score on the glass with the line shown on the upper jaw of the pliers.
3. Turn the screw gauge so the jaws of the pliers are grasping the glass as lightly as can be without slipping. Then loosen the screw perhaps half a turn more; press firmly on the handles and the cut will travel along the score line.

PATTERN SCISSORS

These scissors come in two sizes, $\frac{1}{16}''$ and $\frac{1}{8}''$, the measurement referring to the amount of paper cut away between pieces. How do you judge which size you want? Easy. If you're using lead up to $\frac{3}{8}''$ you are probably better off with a $\frac{1}{16}''$ scissor. For anything over that you might want the larger size. Either size will do the job, however, since in the long run most individuals are not making large windows using very heavy lead. If, however, you happen to be doing just this, you should have both sizes of scissors, since you are probably varying lead sizes within the framework of your design. Pattern scissors consist of three blades, two below and one on top. The bottom two blades are joined to form a slight bend. The space between them is commensurate with the size of the paper they cut out. It is into this space that the top blade falls. Thus, the paper is cut precisely and with guillotine sharpness. This sharp edge on the paper pattern is important. A pattern with a poor memory for its horizons is a cloudy guide.

Fig. 4-16. Pattern scissors, two views. Note the double bottom blade.

Using the scissors for the first time is an experience. One's tendency is to cut with them as with ordinary scissors, that is, by taking a bite the length of the blade. This will be found to be more than you're able to chew off. The strip of paper that is being trimmed away will clog the progress of the cutting. It is therefore best, when using pattern scissors, to take small bites with the very back of the blades, inching up on the pattern with a crafty maneuverability. Turns and angles can be cut quite readily following a little practice.

Pattern scissors can be used either with the top blade up or with the double blade uppermost. If you use it with the top single blade up, you can sight along the blade against the line being cut. If you want to use it theoretically upside down, with the double blades on top, this may also be done. You would then sight between the two blades and make sure the line being cut falls in the middle. Remember that once the pattern is cut, you cannot trim with regular scissors, or your space between patterns will be off.

PATTERN KNIFE

This instrument is a compromise between the finished product and the pocketbook of the craftsman. It is also a compromise between the scissors and a razor blade/magic marker combination.

The simplest method of allowing space for lead lines in a pattern, is to go over the pattern lines with a medium size magic marker, and then simply cut these lines away with a razor blade. This, of course, takes time and a certain amount of precision. Even so, the line will not be exactly even doing it thus freehand, as a razor blade cannot be employed to a precise enough degree to satisfy critical measurements. The next best step, if the pattern scissors are not employed, is to use a pattern knife.

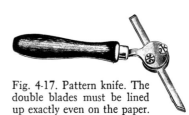

Fig. 4-17. Pattern knife. The double blades must be lined up exactly even on the paper.

This instrument consists of double blades in an angled handle. The width between the blades is variable. The tool functions well but it takes a bit of adjusting to get the blades even. There are minor disadvantages. You are, by the very nature of this tool, pulling it toward you, and so operating in your own shadow. This slows up the procedure. Also a fairly steady and heavy pressure must be exerted on the blades so they cut through the thick pattern paper. You can, of course, also operate the tool by pulling it away from you, reversing the handle in your hand. Now, however, you are working directly against the line you are cutting, and have to peak around the end in order to see where you're going.

While there is no doubt the cutting will be more precise than the razor blade method, there is still a good bit of time and effort involved. For those who do not wish immediately to incur the expense of pattern scissors, a pattern knife will improve their work and sharpen the accuracy of their leading process.

LEAD KNIFE

Here is one of the most essential of all tools in the stained glass armamentarium. This is an instrument for all purposes, being at once a cutter, fitter, hammer, flange, straight edge, bender and straightener of lead came. Its activities are such as to provide the operator with another set of fingers. While leading knives sold without the weighted handle are somewhat more cheaply priced, we do not recommend that you get one of these. It is possible to put

Fig. 4-18. Lead knife showing the weighted handle. One of the most useful of all tools.

your own weighted end on a knife by carving down the wood and melting lead into the space thus prepared. This is what many old-time workers in glass did before the knives began to be made commercially. It's easier, however, to let the factory do the work. The blade of the leading knife comes either straight or curved, and here individual preference takes over. The curved blade can be put to more uses, and can get into more crevices, in a far more cunning fashion.

Turned over, that is, with its sharp side uppermost, the flared edge with its point can be used to hook and position leads within a panel prior to soldering. As for cutting the leads, that is a technique in itself. With the soft leads, such as ⅛", ¹⁄₁₆", ³⁄₁₆", either "U" or "H", the danger is that by applying too much force your knife will heel over and crush the channel. You are then faced with the additional job of opening the crevice and re-straightening the lead. A variance in technique will easily obviate this extra work. Since a professional leading knife is made of the best steel and will keep its temper far longer than the operator who is inefficiently welding it, it is not necessary to come down with it like a guillotine against the lead, nor should you apply simple pressure hoping to slice through the came in that fashion. Let the knife do the work. The best way to cut lead came with it is simply to lay it on top of the came with the slightest pressure and wiggle it from side to side, that is, from left to right. It will cut through the channel with surprising dispatch, and the lead will hardly be bent at all. For cutting leads such as ¼" and up, the same principle is used, except that it is safer here to use more pressure on the knife. With very heavy leads, you may even have to use both hands, but wiggling it from left to right will enable the blade to gain purchase on each level of the came it is slicing through, and you will find you are making very neat, very able cuts when employing your knife in this manner.

A word of caution: A professional leading knife is a precision tool. It occasionally needs sharpening. Do not use a kitchen knife sharpener to do the job, since it will end up chipping your blade and making it look rather like a dissipated saw. An Arkansas whetstone will put an edge on your knife with ease, and it will then be ready for another year or so of use. Such a sharpening process involves strapping the knife across the stone, which is oiled with a very light machine oil. Don't be impatient with this process, and try to keep the angle at which you are strapping the knife the same with each stroke.

The leading knife is one of the basic tools. It ranks next to the glass cutter and soldering iron in importance.

This tool is used to widen and straighten the lead channels so that the glass will "seat." No advanced worker in stained glass would consider beginning a project without this convenient item at hand to act as an eleventh finger.

Metal lathkins come in two sizes, thick and thin, and they can either be pushed or pulled through the channel of the cames, depending on the convenience to the operator. If your desire is to push the lathkin through the came, you would hold the instrument with the rounded end within the channel as shown (Fig. 4-20), and wiggle it slowly through the came, using the force of your arm to push it along. You must keep the lead straight and braced behind the instrument as you go. If you would rather pull the lathkin through to straighten the channel, you would hold it as shown (Fig. 4-21), dipping the point into the channel, and pull it toward you. Don't pull it too hard, especially in a piece of came that is somewhat twisted, or you will tear the lead.

You can make your own lathkin out of wood, if you so desire. Many operators do just this, making personalized tools to fit their hand (Fig. 4-22). If you wish to make your own lathkin, be sure you start with a hard wood such as oak or walnut or maple, and sand it to the appropriate dimensions. A bench sander is best for this. Dipping it in a hot oil will serve to lubricate it, as well as acting as a sealer for the wood. It should be left in oil overnight. An old pool cue cut down will serve as an excellent base for a wooden lathkin. It is already almost entirely shaped for this purpose. Wooden lathkins, however, no matter how hard the wood, will wear out in time. They do not wear out evenly, but begin to chip and fault along the working surface. Both wood and metal lathkins are easily replaced when they begin to lose their function. They are both inexpensive and serve as another example of a tool which can give ease to the craftsman so that he may apply more of his energies to the creative process.

Here's a handy little device which, while not as essential to the finished product as the tools described above, will still save time and allow you to get on with the work in as rapid a manner as possible. This unit is really a little vise with grooved teeth that fits in unobtrusively against a beam in a corner of the room or on a shelf that is itself firmly

LATHKINS

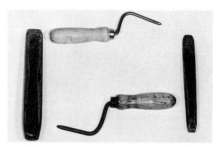

Fig. 4-19. Lathkins: two different sizes of metal ones—a thick and a thin; two different shaped wooden ones. The left wooden lathkin was originally a pool cue.

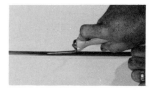

Fig. 4-20. Using the metal lathkin by pushing it through the channel . . .

Fig. 4-21. . . . and by pulling it. Note the position of the bracing hand.

Fig. 4-22. Using the wooden lathkin.

LEAD STRETCHER

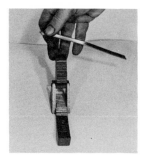

Fig. 4-23. The lead stretcher, open to receive a came.

Fig. 4-24. The lead stretcher, closed with a came in it, ready for stretching.

LEADING NAILS

Fig. 4-25. Leading nail, exact size.

GLASS DRILLS

placed against the wall. The top jaw opens so that the teeth may fit snugly against the lead came which is placed between them. The top is then put down and the lead is stretched, one end being pulled while the lead stretcher holds the other. The grooved teeth are so placed that when the lead came is pulled, they automatically lock against the end. To remove the lead, simply push it forward; the teeth will relax and the came may then be pulled out. A vise will work as well in the holding process, but the vise must be screwed open, and if you're stretching a lot of lead, you may find this process annoying; also the jaw of the vise tends to crush the ends of the came so they are quite useless for the leading process and will need to be cut off. People working in stained glass sooner or later end up getting a lead stretcher. It's such a convenient little item that it's simply annoying not to have one.

The special nails used for stained glass work are different from those used to build houses, hang pictures, or hold furniture together. We would like to drive this point home with some emphasis since it answers a constant query. For one thing, these nails have a specific taper, which allows exactly the right amount of pressure against the glass, while getting the right amount of purchase into the table or workboard. Nails that are too fat will split or chip the glass edges they are holding. Those that are too slim will not grip the glass at all. As will be discussed in Chapter 12, any movement of glass pieces while they are being leaded can be critical. If you take the time and effort to draw a design, cut a pattern, and then cut glass to match it, you are entitled to know the pieces will stay where you put them.

These nails are reusable; the points remain true no matter how often they are hammered. If you have been using common nails or finishing nails, you are bound to have noticed how eventually the points begin to turn up—ever so little at first—but enough to make them awkward to use as you continue to employ them. Further, leading nails are just the right height to hold the work together, and yet not interfere with the movement of your hands over them. All in all, they combine characteristics which, while not individually unique, together form a unit of convenience.

In order to drill a hole in a piece of glass, a special drill bit must be used. Such bits fit into any standard hand drill, and are generally used wet against the glass. They may also be used in an electric drill, providing a rheostat unit is in control to slow down the revolutions. If too much heat is generated by the drill, the entire piece of glass will crack. In wetting the glass, you can use either a fine machine oil or plain water. Don't use too much; if the surface is puddled over, the drill will be able to acquire very little purchase on the glass. It's best to go by sound. If you hear no sound at all from the glass, and the bit is turning in the hole with no perceptible progress, you are very likely using too much water or oil. You will hear, as the friction mounts, the "cry" of the glass, a mild grinding sound, and see the glass dust come up. Diminish the sound with lubricating material so that it is faint but still there. If maintained at that volume, your drill will guide you safely through the glass. The average hole should take no longer than two or three minutes to drill. Glass drills are available in different shapes, from spear-headed to triangular, and vary in price, depending on the size of the drill. They go from ⅛ inch up to ¼ inch, and are not inexpensive. The most frequently used size is ³⁄₁₆ inch. This generally serves the purpose for hanging small objects and will allow for a satisfactory drilling operation without breaking the drill or glass.

These instruments are not to be confused with flux brushes. They have a stiff copper bristled, fairly wide scrubbing area, and are used to scrub the oxidized surface off lead prior to soldering a joint. Their use is especially advised where joints have been allowed to sit for some weeks prior to soldering. The more oxidation formed on the surface of the lead, the more difficult a time you are going to have getting the solder to "take." Employing this sort of brush, with a little elbow grease, cuts the frustration factor considerably. Don't get a brush with tough steel bristles. This will scratch the glass, and probably tear the lead right away from it. An instrument more of the nature of a heavy suede brush will do. A few sweeping back and forth motions should give a nice shiny surface to your lead, which will then take the solder in a satisfactory manner.

If you've a large window to do, and a number of lead joints which are oxidized, it might be worth your while to use a round brush with a central axle that fits into an electric hand drill.

These brushes should be used with reasonable control and if you get a soft enough one, it will not mar the glass. A little cleaning and polishing powder placed over the glass will clean off oxidation even more speedily. Be sure when using a drill that the machine doesn't slip and run rampant over the glass.

Fig. 4-26. 3 types of glass drills. Upper, reamer type; middle, spear point; and lower, three corner types.

Fig. 4-27. Drill bit in brace.

WIRE BRUSHES

Fig. 4-28. Some wire brushes. Make sure the bristles aren't too rough for the lead.

MARKING PENCILS

These are specially formulated crayons which mark on glass. They come in various colors; white, red and black are the most popular. The beginner who wishes to lay out his pattern on a piece of glass before cutting, in order to get the most use out of the piece, should use a marking pencil to calculate his cuts. Such pencils are also useful to mark an edge for trimming. They should not be used in place of a paper pattern, however. Care should be taken to clean off all such pencil marks on any glass pieces going to be fired in the kiln, as these marks will bake right into the glass. Most studios involved in making a large piece of work, such as a window, will mark each piece of glass by number with one of these marking pencils to correspond to its paper pattern.

PATTERN, ABRASIVE, AND KRAFT PAPERS

Pattern paper is a heavy duty paper not quite as thick as cardboard. This dimension is critical. It must be thick enough to allow for a certain amount of wear and tear when used as a pattern, yet thin enough so that the glass cutter wheel can ride along its side without the paper lifting it by the axle. While pattern paper need not be white, it is easier to work with if it is of a light color, since it must be numbered and used against glass pieces, many of which will be dark. Beginners tend to employ the cardboard they receive from the laundry, backing their shirts. This is too thick and will not allow you to follow its outline with the glass cutter, since you can't press against the glass hard enough to score it. Pattern paper must also be able to be easily cut, either with a pattern knife or pattern scissors and leave a sharp edge to the pattern. Ordinary cardboard tends to fray. It is important to be as accurate as possible in pattern cutting. Any inaccuracy anywhere along the line will lead to a total disproportion as an end result.

Kraft paper is a brown rolled paper which is used for making the original drawing or cartoon from which all later efforts will evolve. It is used specifically for its rugged quality. This original cartoon will be with you throughout the entire procedure and will be subject to nail holes, spilled flux, hot solder and other types of torment. The brown kraft paper holds up quite well through it all. Any lesser strength paper is liable to disintegrate right out from under you, guide lines and all.

Abrasive paper is a special type of wet-dry sanding cloth which can be used to take rough edges off your pieces of glass. It is best used wet. Simply dip it in water, and placing your glass flat against the table edge with the portion you wish sanded sticking over the edge, rub it with the abrasive paper. You will find it works quite rapidly. Abrasive paper will last quite a while if properly taken care of. Let it dry after use and shake out the glass dust. You may also rinse it out in running water to get rid of the glass dust. If abrasive paper is used dry, its lifespan will be considerably shortened.

Stained glass windows or panels that are going to be exposed to the weather must be puttied. Any stained glass work larger than one square foot in size should also be puttied. The puttying not only weatherproofs the work, but adds strength to it by supporting the glass within the lead cames. Only linseed oil putty is used. This material is freely workable when it is fresh and tends to become very hard as the linseed oil evaporates from it. Linseed oil putty comes either white or black. Both work equally well. It is an esthetic question of your own whether you wish to see a white or black line following under the lead line. The puttying procedure will be gone into thoroughly in a later chapter.

Slab glass is a term for thick glass pieces also called "dalles," measuring usually 8″ x 12″ with a thickness of 1″. Dalles are too thick to be leaded or foiled as they are and are too heavy to be used with regular stained glass pieces in full measure. They can be used as small pieces or "chunks" of unequal sizes and shapes, which then furnish enough surface to be foiled into an existing stained glass piece for a three-dimensional or other unusual effect. Dalles are imbedded in cement or epoxy in heavy walls or large embrasures. They are not always used full size and their shaping is done with a slab glass wedge. This wedge is placed underneath a piece of slab glass below the desired cut line. The glass is tapped directly above the wedge with a slab glass hammer; the force of the tap carries through the glass to the sharp edge of the wedge beneath at which point the impact fractures the glass cleanly. There is a notion that this procedure involves a lot of flying pieces. This is not the case. It might be so if the slab glass wedge were not used. It is the slab glass wedge that provides the guiding line for any designing in this medium and allows for planned figurations in this heavy glass.

This is the tool used with the slab glass wedge. It provides the impetus for fracturing the slab. This hammer comes in two sizes—small and large—and is shaped like a mason's hammer. It comes to a sharp

PUTTY

SLAB GLASS WEDGE

Fig. 4-29. Slab glass wedge; one method of holding it. This wedge was imbedded by its handle in a wooden block, a form built around it and melted lead poured into the form. The form was then removed, leaving a solid base for the wedge.

SLAB GLASS HAMMER

angle at either side of the head; thus, the force of the blow is concentrated into a narrow line, allowing for a fairly gentle tap to be highly effective at the point of impact.

ANTIQUING PATINA

Fig. 4-30. Two sizes of slab glass hammers.

This solution changes the color of soldered joints from a bright, shiny surface to a coppery, aged look. Our antiquing patina will not work directly on the lead came itself. In order for the proper effect to be achieved, the reaction must occur in the presence of tin. Therefore, if one would desire an entire length of came to be "antiqued," it would be necessary to "tin" the entire length of lead. Following this procedure, the antiquing solution may be applied, and the desired effect attained. Antiquing solution works best when it is warm, or if the joint is warm, such as one that has been freshly soldered. It will, however, work cold, in a slower fashion, and should be rubbed on with a flux brush, wiped off, and then re-applied. Do not use the same brush both for flux and antiquing, as the antiquing solution will dirty the flux and interfere with its activity.

CHAPTER 5

Baubles, Bangles and Beads

Ancillary devices to add character to stained glass objects do well when employed with discrimination. Used to point up a whimsical creation, brighten a window, or balance off in width by adding a third dimension to flatly stated schemes, such fillips serve as punctuation marks in the grammar of design. With the art of stained glass becoming ever more popular, these supplements are acquiring an inventive use which seems to have no limit.

Such supplements are not all themselves made of glass. Many are of materials which complement the glass they ornament. Others are glass objects which have been formed, shaped or pressed into three-dimensional form and which may be applied to a finished work to add that little extra touch that gives it definitive charm.

Glass jewels were made, for the most part, by the Heidt Company of Brooklyn and were known as "Heidt jewels." Their manufacture commenced with a solid glass rod of chosen color. The end of this rod was heated to molten state in a beehive furnace, then quickly placed into a mold press. The molds, themselves, were of Swedish steel. The glass jewel was pressed out, then placed into a lehr and allowed to slowly cool. While many of these old molds have been lost to us, enough of them do remain so that some of these jewels could still be processed. There are a number of such jewels in old windows and in private collections. They have rather a charming, antique look about them. We have found that many

GLASS JEWELS, OLD AND NEW

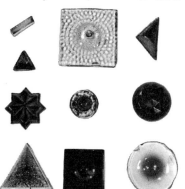

Fig. 5-1. Selections of jewels, old and new.

53

Fig. 5-2. Glass jewels (continued).

Fig. 5-3. And more glass jewels.

ROUNDELS

Fig. 5-4. Roundels—different texture, different sizes.

of them go together in combinations very nicely. A little imagination is all it takes.

We have used them as well in new windows of abstract and modern free-flowing design and found that their effect here is equally as effective as in the old, more classically designed window. They give a heightened impetus, a sense of sudden emphasis to a portion of the work where such emphasis may be highly desirable. They also may be used in free-form hanging objects as the central portion of a glass arrangement. Intriguing mobiles may be achieved with their use.

Such jewels are much in demand—reds, golds and yellows are particularly sought after. We have found many old windows in antique shops which though pretty well in tatters from mistreatment over the years, still yielded up a handful or so of old jewels.

New jewels are not nearly as expensive. They don't have the filigree you find impressed into the older ones, but they are still lovely as ornamental fillips. Many new jewels are clearer in color than the older jewels.

Roundels are circles of glass which have been spun by hand or pressed by machine. They come in all colors and sizes from two inches on up to twelve inches or even larger.

It is not always easy to tell the difference between a spun and a pressed roundel. Both types are beautiful and both types are equally effective used within panels or free form mobiles, or even just leaded up as is and hung. A spun roundel will generally show more whirls within it than one that is pressed by machine. These whirls of color within the surface of the object give it a soft and beguiling appearance that, added to its geometric shape, makes it one of the more popular among the stained glass jewels. Since roundels come with a rounded edge, there is very little difficulty in leading them with the usual type leads. You cannot use too narrow a lead or the rounded flange simply will not go into it. Roundels need not be used as whole pieces. They can be cut and used in part. The present vogue of "peace signs" is a natural for the roundel, which can be broken at the proper lead lines and simply releaded into such a symbol. One or more roundels may be used to mix the colors. Designing a window or panel with roundels is a tricky task, as it is only too easy to get carried away and use too many. These colorful circles may then take over the figuration of the window, overwhelming rather than intriguing the viewer.

Roundels are fairly expensive and are individually

made for decorative purposes, as are the other jewels we have spoken of so far. There are as well glass circles which resemble roundels, but really are not thus specifically made. They also have swirls of color within them. These are not true roundels, but "bottle bottoms"—in reality, the bottoms of the cylinders which are blown as a primary process in the making of a sheet of stained glass. These bottoms are then cut off and can be used as decorative pieces. Because of their production, they are irregular in shape to some degree, with rough edges and may need further trimming when they come into the hands of craftsmen. For all that, they are impressive and outstanding effects can be gotten with them equal to and in some cases, surpassing the qualities of roundels. Added to this is the fact that they are much, much less expensive than roundels.

Bottle bottoms generally are eight inches in diameter and can be cut across the center with minimum difficulty and broken into two equal halves. They make beautiful peace signs and other decorative objects and may be leaded into abstract shapes and forms. Bottle bottoms tend to be more opalescent than roundels. In fact, roundels of certain tones may be too clear for the taste of some individuals, who would perhaps find bottle bottoms of similar hues more to their liking.

Fig. 5-5. Some larger roundels of different colors.

MILLIFIORE

These are tiny cylinders, also known as Venetian beads or tube beads. Peeking down at a random few seen on end, one is reminded of diminutive pizza pies. Designs vary from stars to fleur de lis. Many just have rings of color. When these beads are heated in a kiln. the pizza pie parallel becomes even more evident. Each melts into a flat radius of multi-color whirls almost kaleidoscopic in nature.

When one of these beads is placed atop a piece of glass and heat is applied, it melts through into the glass base forming what may well appear to be a technicolor ink blot.

Millifiore does not have to be heated, however, to be effective. Used as eyes for small glass animals or grouped in patterns and glued in abstract designs, it forms unusual three-dimensional effects with two-dimensional free-form glass mobiles. While millifiore is fairly expensive, a little bit will go a long way.

GLASS GLOBS

As the name implies, these are marble-like humps of solid glass varying in color and varying as well in shape to some degree. Unlike the types of jewelry discussed above, they are not individually molded, but are produced in free-form fashion in a kiln. They are transparent and are available in several sizes, usually from ⅜″ to 1″. While not as instantly captivating as millifiore, they have character of their own. They can be foiled, leaded or glued, depending on the choice of the craftsman and the occasion. Stunning and unusual variations in design can be created with them.

Globs have at least one fairly flat surface which can be used for gluing. This surface is where the glob itself rested while it was being formed in the kiln. Occasionally, one will find twinned globs or globs of interesting deformities among a particular batch. Such unusual configurations may, themselves, be put to good use with the imagination of the craftsman.

Globs can be employed as eyes, the petals of flowers, decoration for glassware, bottles or jars, to make candleholders, or as lamp ornaments. If you have enough different sizes and colors, you can create patterns with them alone in a mosaic effect. Spaces between the globs may be grouted or filled with liquid lead. Special glues are available for this type of work, which dry to a transparent rapid finish and which will not shrink so that the globs loosen after a period of time. Beware the general all-purpose hardware-store glue which, like a bank president's smile, will diminish in intensity as its stickiness evaporates.

Glass globs are also extensively used in stained glass jewelry, as will be discussed in Chapter 18.

Fig. 5-6. Illustrating use of roundels and odd jewels within a new window. Courtesy: Edward Martin.

METALS

Heavy copper sheeting may be used to cut leaves, wings or other filigree items. This material is so wonderfully malleable that designs may be embossed on it with gratifying ease. It also cuts very easily with an ordinary pair of scissors. Of course it solders beautifully. Brass is another interesting and obedient entity. While somewhat more difficult to work with than copper, it will impart more rigidity and as an axial skeleton for a glass work, it's second only to galvanized steel.

Some workers have used parts of wire hangers for skeletal structures. That is to say, stems of flowers or backbones of animals which must stand to a certain height. The use of metal or wire hangers for this purpose involves a certain amount of fuss, as the metal must first be sanded clean of paint and then fluxed vigorously with an inorganic acid flux (such as hydrochloric acid in glycerin) and then tinned. Tinning is impossible if a strong flux is not used, as the solder will simply roll off this metal. Once the metal is tinned, soldering can take place with little trouble and the hanger becomes a convenient stem, wand, spike, handle or body in its re-incarnation within the world of creative design. One has occasional nightmarish visions of closets piled full of limp clothing whose hangers have been ravished away for use in an uncompleted esthetic.

Probably the commonest metal, other than lead, in use in stained glass windows is the galvanized steel bar. This is used for bracing windows, which need more strength than what the lead and putty can provide. Older windows used plain steel bars for bracing. Since steel cannot be soldered, copper loops were wound around these bars at juncture areas and these loops were then soldered to the window. Coating the bracing rods with zinc did more than make the bar itself solderable. In the process the rod became a metal strap, averaging ½″ wide by ⅛″ thick. Larger spans, involving heavier areas, take a heavier bar. But for purposes of this discussion, the slimmer bar is the one used in free-form stained glass design. It is much easier to employ than hanger parts, since no preparation really is necessary. Besides it bends more easily.

Pieces of galvanized steel scraps cut to size make wonderful cross bars for the tops of lanterns to support the underlying socket and the hanging ring above. If this is what you have in mind, be sure to get a wide enough piece of metal to allow for the hole you must drill through it for the socket to penetrate. If you'd rather not take the trouble to drill through one of these metal straps, simply cut two of them to size, leaving room between them for the socket nipple, and rely on the pressure of the hanging ring to maintain stability. This process works quite nicely.

Zinc cames are also used in stained glass work (Fig. 5-7). They have little if any flexibility and cannot be used within a window to follow a curve. However, for outside edges, where strict rigidity is a must, they do the job quite well. They're also used in very long windows or panels for straight side-to-side supports, instead of bracing rods being used. However, the design of the window must allow for them. We mention them here as another adjunct to stained glass design in free-form pattern. They are generally H cames with quite wide channels and will accommodate English streaky or very thick French glass very nicely. The width of the channels enables the glass to be tipped one way or another, having first been foiled and then fixed against the zinc came with solder. This gives an intriguing three-dimensional quality to mobiles, butterflies, coronets or whatever you may have in mind.

Fig. 5-7. Glass sample rack made from zinc cames.

GLASS RODS   These are available in odd sizes and thicknesses and can be cut to size with a glass cutter by scoring round the rod and breaking it, or more easily and with far less waste, by simply sawing through it with a special carborundum blade that fits any hacksaw. Such glass rods can be melted in the kiln to interesting shapes and designs (the heat must go way up here, since you are dealing with a solid glass core), but they may be also used for a more obvious purpose, that is, support. Such support is evidenced in mobiles where multi-colored balancing rods add tremendously to the effect. Fishline, which is all but invisible, can be purchased in any sporting goods store to bear the mobile and it may be attached to the proper balancing point on the glass rod by making a deep score around the rod at that area and wrapping the fishline into the groove. To smooth the ends of the rods, polish them down with abrasive paper.

BOTTLES   Bottles don't have to be heated to be used in stained glass work. The bottoms of many wine bottles make wonderful roundels and can be cut away from the rest of the bottle with that same carborundum blade. The tops of such bottles can also prove interesting, and a number of them strung together make wonderful wind chimes.

Fig. 5-8. Hanging owl 10" x 6". Bottle bottoms cut with a carborundum blade were used for the eyes.

PART II · Procedure

CHAPTER 6

The Art of Cutting Glass

The average inexperienced worker will find himself all thumbs when it comes to dealing with glass cutting for the first time. While a certain awkwardness may have to be overcome, it is essential that correct work habits be scrupulously observed. The end result depends on initial control of the material. It is best to make an effort right at the beginning and cut correctly, rather than develop habit patterns that will provide handicaps later on.

Choice of a cutter is an all important first procedure. There is no sense in fighting the instruments you use. If you are attempting to cut opalescent glass with a cutter calculated for soft glass, you will have to use more force, more pressure and more downright labor than if you chose the cutter meant for such a glass. As we stated in Chapter 4, cutters are labeled according to the type of wheel they possess and what this wheel will do in the way of cutting specific glasses. For general, all-purpose cutting, a carbide cutter is best. This cutter will do equally well on opalescent as on cathedral, on plate glass as on window glass and you need not worry about picking up the wrong cutter for the wrong piece of glass. Carbide cutters, however, are expensive and you may not wish to invest immediately in such an item. On the other hand, stay away from the dime-store variety glass cutters. They are useless for stained glass. Get a reputable cutter, a Fletcher, and make sure your choice is guided by the type of glass you are going to cut. Ask your dealer; he will know the number cutter you require.

WHAT TYPE OF CUTTER TO CHOOSE

Fig. 6-1. The correct position for holding the cutter. Courtesy: Fletcher Co.

59

60

PROPER METHOD OF
HOLDING THE CUTTER

Fig. 6-2. Wrong cutting position. The handle of the cutter is too far back. This extreme tipping does not allow the wheel to ride fully on the glass. It also may irritate the skin of the hand. With the elbow resting on the table the wrist motion is extremely limited.

Fig. 6-3. Correct cutting position. The elbow is off the table and alongside the body allowing free wrist motion. Note the position of the cutter handle.

It is possible to cut glass holding the cutter any number of ways. One may grip it in the fist, hold it like a pen or pencil, grasp it grozzing teeth uppermost as though squeezing a tube of toothpaste, or even grab it with both hands and slash away. All of these methods will score a piece of glass. The problem lies not in scoring glass per se, but in learning to score it in such a manner as to be able to do it with ease and to follow a pattern.

Individuals who have never held cutters correctly when attempting to cut around stained glass patterns, are forced to place their body in contortions to allow for their lack of wrist mobility. It is much wiser, even though it may appear at first unnecessarily fussy, to apply the proper rules of glass cutting at the beginning. A fledgling pianist stumbling over a fingering guide shortly learns that it is in the long run the easiest method of getting from one note to another. So, in glass cutting, the correct position of the hand on the cutter is the simplest way of getting from one part of the glass to another.

The proper way to hold a glass cutter is to place the cutter between the first and second fingers as shown. The thumb supports the cutter on the underside. Use a free wrist motion. The usual mistake is to hold the cutter as you would a pencil. As we have said, this limits the wrist motion and leaves the cutter unstable in your hand. Make sure that the cutter is not leaning backwards against the web of your fingers, or you will end up with a blister in this area and a very painful one at that. The cutter should not be leaning backwards at all. It should be straight up and down or even tipped slightly forward. The wrist should be able to move up and down or side to side with ease. Pressure should come from the shoulder, not from the wrist. Pressure from the wrist is an immediately tiring process and will end up giving you a stiff joint. Let the weight of your body apply to the cutter through your shoulder, almost as though you were leaning directly on the glass cutter. The grozzing teeth should be pointed down toward the glass being cut. It is possible, of course, to cut with the grozzing teeth up. But since this throws the cutter off balance by making it top heavy, it is just one more thing for your fingers to fight. Make it easy for yourself and use the cutter properly.

THE CORRECT STANCE

If you're right handed, you should be standing with your left foot slightly forward and your right foot turned not quite at right angles to it. This will automatically shift the weight of your balance over toward your right arm and allow the weight of your body to apply directly toward the cutter. It also angles your body so that you are not pulling the cutter directly into your abdomen and leaves as well a free space for your wrist to move smoothly from the initial point of the cut to the end of the cut line on the glass. Left handed individuals should, of course, reverse the process. Do not cut glass while sitting down. You cannot achieve a proper amount of body strength against the cutter in this position. You will end up using more wrist pressure and rather quickly get a tired arm. It is also difficult to follow a pattern accurately while sitting. We have seen rather frail, elderly women learn to cut glass using the correct cutter and the correct stance in an hour.

Glass cutting, like any other trained skill, requires practice. The more cutting you do, the more adept you will become—especially if you follow the simple rules laid down in this chapter.

MAKING THE SCORE

Before actually running your glass cutter over a piece of stained glass, there are two processes to be attended to. The first is to be sure that your glass is clean. Any lint, dust, or other debris which accumulates so readily in any working area may interfere with the line of your cut. Be certain, also, that the material you use on the glass to clean it is a good liquid cleaner, not something which in itself will cause problems. Anything, for instance, that would make the glass slippery would lead to difficulty with the cutting.

The second procedure, before actually scoring your piece of glass, is to examine it carefully to make sure that you are cutting on the right side. Unlike window glass, stained glass has a right and a wrong side for cutting purposes. In some cases, it is perfectly obvious. For instance, granite-backed or very rough, bumpy stained glass surfaces, call clearly to be avoided.

It is a good rule of thumb that the smoother side is generally best for cutting, but it is sometimes difficult for beginners to decide which side is the smoother. In cases where this happens, it is best to make a small score on each side of the glass before making any major cut, to determine which side provides the best cutting surface. On sheets of flashed stained glass, that is, where one color is laid on top of another, one must always cut on the white, or clear side, of the glass. This side may be discovered by holding the glass up to the light on end and looking to see where the layers of color are. If you still cannot tell by this method, chip away a small corner and you will soon see which layer has had the color applied to it and which surface is clear. It is on the clear, or white surface, that the cutting should transpire.

It is essential that the glass to be cut be placed on a flat surface, preferably one with a slight amount of "give" to it. An old carpet, especially made cutting mats, or even a newspaper will furnish the requisite fullness. This is a particular necessity with certain sheets of antique glass, since due to the nature of their production, the pieces do not always lie flat.

This slight rock in the glass, when cut against so stern a surface as bare wood, is caught between the pressure of the cutter and the unyielding pressure below and may shatter. The carpet or newspaper will allow for the discrepancies in the surface of the glass.

Be certain that no crumbs of glass remain on the cutting surface from previous cuttings. Shake out your mat fiercely and religiously. These leftover tiny pieces will cause an unevenness in your cutting surface, and will act as little levers. Press down on them and your glass will shatter.

To make a straight cut, draw the cutter along a straight edge once, and only once. Do not repeat a cut. Going over a score line will ruin your cutter. It may also fracture the score irregularly right through the glass. If your score line wavers, it would be best to forget it and try another some distance away. Start your cut at the top edge of the glass, or as close to the top edge as possible, and allow the cutter to run off the bottom edge. Do not let it run off with such force as to break the glass. Then go back to the top edge, pick up the line, and run it backwards over the top edge. Again, do not let it bounce off the glass with unnecessary severity.

Use only enough pressure to make the score. If small slivers of glass begin to shower from your cut, you are pressing too hard. On the other hand, if you cannot hear the "cry" of the glass, your score is inadequate. The cutter should move along the glass evenly, not wavering from side to side. If the handle wavers, it means the cutting wheel is not plowing an exact groove. This will make your score line much more difficult to break. Only practice can stabilize your technique.

Again, it is not the pressure of your wrist that counts, but the pressure of your shoulder and body. Naturally, your cut will also be guided by the thickness or thinness of the glass under hand. If you are dealing with a thin antique tint, you would apply less force than with a thick English streaky. As you begin to deal more and more with the various types of glasses, you will learn their tolerances very quickly.

Some individuals draw a line of lubricant over the surface to be cut prior to cutting. Providing you keep your glass cutter itself well lubricated, this is scarcely necessary. Remember to break each score as you make it and before making another score.

There are a number of ways of doing this. Each has its virtues, depending on the size and type of glass under consideration, as well as the type of score—whether it be a straight line, outside curve, or inside curve. We will discuss each in detail, as follows:

1. *The Tapping Method*

Tapping the glass is usually done (and taught) incorrectly. There is only one right way of doing it, and that is to hold the glass securely on both sides of the score, and with this line uppermost, tap along its length from the bottom (Figs. 6-4, 6-5). Glass is always broken from the bottom, never from the top. Tapping should be accomplished with a ball-ended glass cutter; that is what the ball is provided for. But don't swing at the glass as though it were a piece of steel. A splinter in the eye is the logical termination of a trajectory impelled by a blow from beneath while staring at the top of a piece of glass. It really isn't necessary to tap that hard. The ball is purposely provided to give an inordinate force to a gentle tap. Furthermore, the ball should not be swung wildly. Balance the glass cutter in the hand and guide the ball with a finger against the handle. The object is not to break the score, but to "run it," that is, to fracture the initial score line further through the surface of the glass. As you tap along, you should hold your piece of glass up to the light to see if the score is "running" or not. You will see a deepening line appear and start to progress along the surface of your score line. Once this line reaches the end of the score line, you can snap the piece of glass by hand. This is a difficult concept to communicate, many beginners having the notion that tapping alone brings the end result. With this in mind, they tap blindly until the pieces suddenly separate, one or both perhaps exuberantly dropping to the floor. If you hold both pieces, neither one can fall away from the other, and you will save yourself a lot of glass and a lot of frustration.

Tapping need not always be done with the ball-ended cutter. Some individuals tap with the front of the glass cutter, that is, with the grozzing teeth.

BREAKING THE SCORE

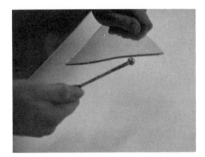

Fig. 6-4. Wrong way to tap a score. The glass cutter is being swung wildly and the piece of glass is supported on only one side of the score line. As the glass is struck it will move upwards with the blow and most of the sharp force will be lost. There is also the strong possibility that should the score run the glass will split in two so rapidly that the unsupported piece will fall to the table or floor and shatter.

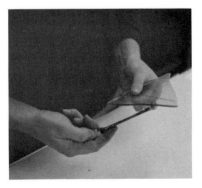

Fig. 6-5. The right way to tap a score. The left hand holds the glass so as to support both sides of the score line. The right hand guides the tapper. Note the index finger positioned along the handle of the glass cutter. A slight movement here is enough to bring the ball end of the cutter against the score with a sharp, decisive tap.

Fig. 6-6. Tapping a large piece of glass. The sheet is supported on the tabletop and one hand holds the scored pieces from separating too abruptly. This procedure takes practice.

Fig. 6-7. The fulcrum method. Only gentle pressure is needed.

Fig. 6-8. Oops.

Fig. 6-9. The correct way to hold glass for breaking a score. The pull of both hands is out and down.

This furnishes less force, but may be used where very fragile taps are desired, such as in very thin, delicate pieces of glass with rather tricky cuts. On large pieces of glass we don't recommend tapping at all. It is too difficult to hold the glass with one hand, and you're very liable to cut yourself if the two pieces fall apart suddenly (Fig. 6-6).

2. *The Fulcrum Method*

Here is a procedure which is equally useful on large pieces and small pieces of glass. Once the score is made—and it must either be a straight line or very gentle curve in order for this method to work—the piece of glass is lifted on one end and a fulcrum, such as the straight end of a glass cutter, is placed directly under the score line (Fig 6-7)—not much of it, only enough to provide a lever about ¼″. The glass is then pressed down on either side by hand, and the score should run true across the length of the glass. Do not use the ball-ended cutter as a fulcrum. It is too high and will not transmit an even pressure. For very long scores, use an even thinner fulcrum than the glass cutter handle. A leading nail or an unrolled paper clip will do. Occasionally, with this method, you will hear a crack and find that your score has run, but not all the way across. This happens usually with large sheets of glass. You'll find, perhaps, that the score has run only half way. Turn the glass around very carefully and apply the same procedure at the other end of the score line. Your glass will then score right across evenly and true.

Occasionally, you will find you place your fulcrum under the glass, press on either side, and the glass shatters. You have either pressed too hard, placed too much of your cutter under the score (generally the tip is quite enough), or your glass had a crack in it to begin with. Many pieces of glass are ruined by the craftsman overlooking a small crack which should be run out before any work is attempted. As we have pointed out, it may also be that thin as the end of your cutter is, it still provides too much leverage. Antique tints, for instance, can best be broken with no larger fulcrum than a paper clip. Anything stouter shatters them.

3. *Breaking by Hand*

Breaking by hand involves two procedures. The first is to snap the glass, holding it with a thumb on either side of the score line (Fig. 6-9). You must keep as much of the glass away from your hands as possible. Too often we have seen individuals grabbing a piece of glass as though it were wood, disregarding the sharp points ogling their palms. To snap a piece in this position would drive points of glass directly into your flesh (Fig. 6-10). Stay behind your glass. Keep your hands in fists and only use your thumbs braced against your closed fists when you are breaking glass by hand. In this manner, even if the glass breaks badly, you will not get cut. The pull is out and down. You can actually let your closed fists roll one against the other which will give almost the precise pull that you want to achieve.

If the glass will not break this way, despite the amount of force you are applying, it might be best to try the second method of breaking by hand and that is to use the table top as a breaking wedge. Lead the glass over the edge of the table until the score line is parallel to the table edge. Then raise the glass and snap it smartly downward, so that the piece you are holding in your hand will come free as the leverage of the table snaps the score line (Fig. 6-11). Keep your feet out of the way when using this method. Very large sheets of glass may be broken in this fashion and broken cleanly. It takes a bit of practice, and courage, to apply this method the first time, but it will not be long before you find yourself in control of the material. Then you will have no qualms about breaking any size sheet of glass to a guided dimension. Naturally, the procedure can be used only for straight line cuts.

4. *The Running Pliers*

Running pliers are used for specialized cuts where long, thin pieces are required. This tool is placed so that it lines up with the score, a certain amount of pressure is placed on the handles, and the score will run automatically. Again, this is only used for straight cuts (Fig. 6-12). (See Chapter 4.)

5. *The Glass Pliers*

Glass pliers are used to break score lines where the pieces to be broken are too small to be broken by hand. They may also be applied to break off small irregular edges, whether the score is straight or curved. Hold the glass in one hand and the pliers with the other and carefully grip and pull out and down (Fig. 6-13). You may prefer using the table top as a working surface instead of holding the piece in the air. Do not snap downward too abruptly here or the sudden force may break your glass. When using the table top, always keep one hand firmly on the glass to stabilize it. You may use your glass pliers also to some degree as grozzing pliers. Both jaws should be grooved with fine teeth, which may

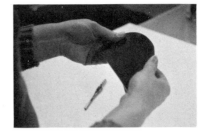

Fig. 6-10. The wrong way to hold glass for breaking a score. As the glass snaps, the pointed ends on either side will drive themselves into the palms.

Fig. 6-11. Snapping the glass along the table edge. Both pieces are supported.

Fig. 6-12. Using the running pliers.

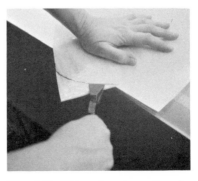

Fig. 6-13. Using the glass pliers by stabilizing the piece of glass on the table top.

MAKING CIRCLES

Fig. 6-14. Cutting a circle using the circle cutter.

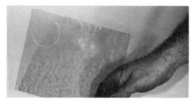

Fig. 6-15. The piece of glass scored for a circle.

Fig. 6-16. Showing tangential cut lines.

Fig. 6-17. Circle turned over and pressed from behind.

INNER CURVES

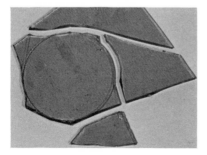

Fig. 6-18. The circle partly broken out.

be used carefully to file away small out-croppings of glass from the score line. (See Chapter 4.)

Circles may be cut out of stained glass by using a freehand method with a paper pattern, or by using a small machine known as a circle cutter. Circle cutters are of two basic types. There are those that use a central pivot, with a variable arm, and those that use a stand with a limited arm but provide compactness and extra stability (see Chapter 4). Either will cut circles up to certain dimensions accurately and without fail each time.

Scoring the circle is not difficult, but it is only half the battle. The major procedure is breaking the circle out of the glass. Here your glass pliers will once again come in handy. The procedure is as follows (Figs. 6-14 to 6-20): (1) Cut your circle, using either circle cutters or pattern and straight glass cutter. (2) Cut lines tangential to the circle which reach from the circle to the edge of the glass. You can make as many of these lines as you wish. (3) Break these lines away, using the glass pliers. Pliers will allow you sufficient purchase to break the required amount of glass without breaking into the circle itself. Use caution that you don't nip off too much waste at one time. Better to score a few extra lines than to try to get too much in one bite and break the piece of glass right across. In this regard, it is good to keep in mind that in cutting glass you cannot entirely save both pieces —the piece you want to use and the piece of waste you are breaking away. Be frugal and get as much as possible out of your glass, but be willing to sacrifice your waste piece to save the piece for the pattern. To try to salvage both usually results in both being wasted.

As you become more adept in using the glass pliers, you will find you can break circles out of glass with an ease and dispatch that will amaze you.

Probably the most difficult cuts to make in glass are inner curves. Whereas outer curves, such as circles, allow for the tension of the glass that is being broken to run freely to the right and to the left, the glass being broken from an inner curve must have its tensions well under control, or else it will simply run right into and through the piece of glass that is being cut out. Inner curves must, therefore, be cut in small pieces. They cannot be broken out in one entire piece, unless they are of a very gradual shape. Sometimes an entire section of such a curve may be achieved in tapping, but very often in a sharp curve the tap line may run right off the score and break.

The best procedure to follow in breaking out inner curves is to cut duplicates of the inner curve several times within the hollow of the curve itself (Fig. 6-21). Run these extra curves into one another, so that when you are through you will have a pattern looking like the illustration (Fig. 6-22). Then begin to break out each of the mini-curves that you have made, using your glass pliers to do the job (Fig. 6-23). When breaking out such a curve, grasp it at its narrowest portion and allow the tension to flow into the wider part, which can handle it better (Fig. 6-24). This will give a far more controlled break. Whatever you do, don't grasp the glass in the center and just pull out and down any which way, as your piece will tend to fly all apart. Break each little curve out separately with more and more care as you get farther into the hollow of the major curve. When you finally get to a point where you are quite close to the original score line, proceed even more cautiously (Fig. 6-25). You may even want to start grozzing out the final piece, almost as though you were carving it. Only in this fashion, will you be able to break out the more severely shaped inner curves.

For more gentle inner curves, the same procedure is applied, but it is not necessary to make quite so many inside cuts. They may also be larger and you may break them out right up to the actual score line without fear. Of course, a lot depends on the glass you are using and how well it breaks. Greens and reds and yellows tend to follow a score line poorly, especially in inner curves, and must be treated quite literally with kid gloves. On the other hand, certain French antique glasses will break perfectly at a touch along the inner curve line. Beginning craftsmen should make it easy for themselves by placing as few inner curves as possible in their designs. As you become more familiar with glass and glass cutting, there will be plenty of time for you to practice on inner curves.

Long strips, as we have discussed, are best cut with a running pliers, or a small fulcrum under the edge of the glass surface. To attempt to tap out a long strip of glass almost invariably leads to disaster, as the run line leaves the score line to travel its own way across the piece of glass you wish to save. Generally, this doesn't happen until you have traveled safely a considerable portion of the distance.

Fig. 6-19. Breaking out the remainder of the circle, using glass pliers.

Fig. 6-20. Final circle completed.

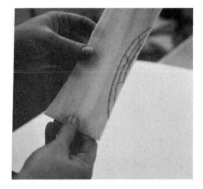

Fig. 6-21. An inner curve to be cut out of a piece of glass. The major curve is to be cut in two prior sections leading up to it. To attempt to cut the extreme inner curve as one piece would probably shatter the glass.

LONG STRIPS

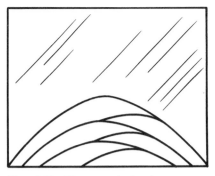

Fig. 6-22. Diagram of the inner curve noted in Fig. 6-21. Note how each mini-curve runs into the one behind it. This is to equalize the pressure of breaking so the entire piece will not shatter.

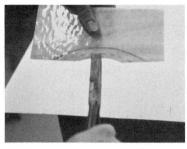

Fig. 6-23. Breaking out the first mini-curve.

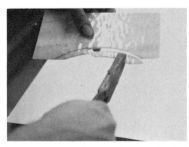

Fig. 6-24. Breaking out half of the last mini-curve. Large grozzing pliers are being used.

Fig. 6-25. Breaking out the last mini-curve right next to the final score line.

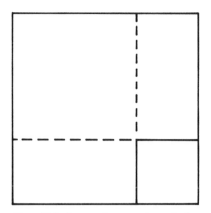

Fig. 6-26. Incomplete scoring of the surface. You cannot cut the rectangle out of the piece of glass as such. You must continue your score along either of the dotted lines before making the second cut.

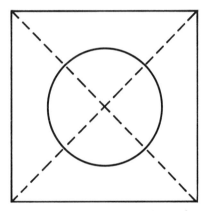

Fig. 6-27. Cutting an inside circle. The glass is cut along the diagonal lines and the comparatively mild inside curves are cut away from the ends of the remaining triangles. The four truncated triangles are then leaded back together and the circle is established as a negative space.

Fig. 6-28. Points meeting in a veritable explosion of lead lines—all discrete and unconfused radiating from a central focus.

There are certain cuts which cannot be made in glass. To design a panel with angles and possibilities which look good on paper, but which cannot be cut is simply to violate the medium. Let's look at a few of these impossible dreams.

Incomplete Scoring of the Surface

Remember that each score must run two edges. You cannot make a score and stop in the middle of the glass. You must continue to an opposing side. Obvious, of course, but in the heat and passion of designing an original glass panel, beginners tend to forget that the medium in which they are working has its own specific rules and regulations.

The Cut Within a Cut

This is a nice trick if you can do it, but we don't know anyone who can. We suppose it is eventually possible to cut a square as shown and then cut a circle out of the middle of it. With paper, of course, it's easy enough; you simply cut a hole in the center and then put your scissors in that hole and cut around the inside circle. With glass, it's not quite the same. You cannot control the tensions and ripples of pressure set up within the glass substance once you start chipping away. The easiest way out of this particular nightmare is to break the square at each corner with a lead line and cut four triangles.

Points

Probably the commonest error for beginning designers is points. Don't have three or four lines congregating at a specific point and expect to lead them up and have them all remain discrete and obvious. What you'll get is one big blob of solder covering the multiple lead lines. Instead of the delicate effect you hoped for, you'll end up with an area looking as though an elephant had passed by and left his footprint. There are ways to design around this problem. If you must have points meeting, be sure to leave enough space between them so that there will be room for each of the lead lines to be clearly visible (Fig. 6-28). The same is true if you are going to make a compass design, which is a very popular initial attempt. Don't make your points so thin in the glass that when you come to lead the surfaces you lose the points. (Fig. 6-30).

The Three-Ring Sign

This is a very famous impossible cut which has been intriguing glass cutters since the time of the Middle Ages. Was it ever actually done? Can it be

Fig. 6-29. Overall view of compass window.

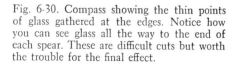

Fig. 6-30. Compass showing the thin points of glass gathered at the edges. Notice how you can see glass all the way to the end of each spear. These are difficult cuts but worth the trouble for the final effect.

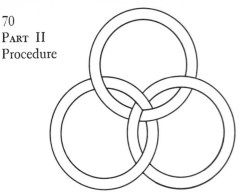

Fig. 6-31. The three ring sign—an old medieval glass cutter's challenge.

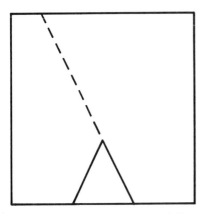

Fig. 6-32. The V cut. The dotted line shows the recommended score.

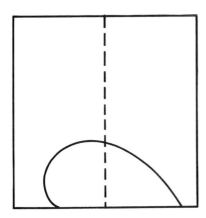

Fig. 6-33. The C cut. Note the acute undercut on the left. You might cut this by establishing a number of mini-curves that run into each other up to the major score line (as in cutting inside curves), but in the long run it's easier to follow the suggested score along the dotted line and then cut the two remaining inside curves.

SAFETY MEASURES

done? We, ourselves, have never tried it, but we offer it as an extreme example of what impossible cuts might look like. If you care to try it, make sure that you use rather inexpensive glass, as you will undoubtedly be using quite a bit of it.

V-Shaped Cuts

Cutting V's out of a piece of glass is considered impossible, although it is not entirely so. We have produced this cut ourselves, although only in instances where, due to the pattern of the design, we were unable to get away from it. The V cut usually goes along very well until you are approximately half way into the V, at which point the entire piece of glass splits, right along one of the arms of the V. It's a good exercise in grozzing technique, as each little bit of glass must be crumbled out of the hollow of the V with a sharp pair of grozzing pliers, a sharper eye, and infinite patience. Almost invariably, the piece splits as you are congratulating yourself at how far you have come. It is much easier to split it by design and lead the V, instead of cutting it. It looks just as good; in fact, it looks better, and even if you should succeed in cutting this particular impossible cut, it may not hold up very long in the window, since the strain on the glass is such that any jarring will probably carry that V in its natural break along one arm.

C Cuts

This is the example of the inside curve in extreme. The tension set up in the glass, even by grozzing gently into this tremendously acute inside curve, will almost immediately split the glass right across either arm of the C. Better to just cut the C in half, split out the two inside curves remaining and lead it back together.

Thin Cuts

Although these are not truly impossible cuts, they may be useless ones, since the glass tends to disappear when leaded. Remember that the lead does have to take up a certain amount of room. To cut and struggle over a piece of glass, perhaps ¼″ in breadth, and then see it disappear in the panel as the leading process commences, can be discouraging. Avoid such tiny cuts, unless you have well calculated them for extremely thin lead or copper foil.

Oddly enough, one very rarely gets cut when working on glass. It's when you let the glass work on you that problems occur. Many people have an innate fear of glass which is really unjustified. Though glass is sharp and can inflict damage, if you let it, it's easy enough not to let it. It's absentmindedness that causes most of the nicks and cuts in glass studios. Workers get so involved in what they are doing, they tend to forget about the simplest precautions. Just brushing glass crumbs off the work table with one's hand, rather than using a cloth or brush, is one of the commonest ways to cut yourself. We have seen students who simply could not resist running their finger around an edge of glass to see if it was smooth. Invariably, it wasn't. Piling one piece of glass on top of another to a dangerous level, while frantically looking for the right color to use, also presents a hazard. Such a stack is rather unstable and tends to tip over at the slightest nudge, usually in the direction of an innocent victim. Lifting large sheets of glass from the glass bin can present a danger. If the glass has a crack in it, it is liable to fall apart before you get it very far. Any large piece of glass, before it is brought any distance across a room, should be tapped lightly with a knuckle while it is still resting on the floor to make sure it is not cracked. If a crack is present, you will hear the rattle of the vibration in the cracked area. If the glass is entire, it will give a solid sounding ring back at you and it is then safe to handle. No large piece of glass should ever be transferred from one part of the room to another without this test. Smaller pieces also should be looked at for cracks, though they are not heavy enough to have their weight pull them apart just from the motion of carrying them. They should, however, be checked before cutting, not so much for any danger to the fingers, but because the crack in the glass may well run right across your score line. Don't hold a sheet of glass over your face to look for cracks by an overhead light. If there is a crack in the glass you may have the piece shatter all over you.

Many cuts come about because the individuals involved are too lazy to move glass out of their way. While hunting for a particular piece of glass in the scrap bin they may see a hidden corner that looks intriguing. They're in too much of a hurry to move the glass on top and simply plunge their hand into the bin to try to pull out the piece they're after. They often don't get that far before looking around for the band-aids.

Glass should never be stored in bins higher than one's head. Though space is at a premium in most glass studios and hobbyists' basements and attics, it is still a wise decision to put something other than glass in areas that need a step ladder. No matter how

Fig. 6-34. Storage of glass in studio bins.

habitual you may be at getting that ladder, there will come that one time when you're in a hurry and will reach for a piece of glass in a bin over your head, pull it out and possibly find glass falling out of the bin on top of you. This is sheer carelessness and can be avoided simply by keeping your bins nearer the floor (Fig. 6-34). Step ladders, in addition, get wobbly and should not be used to transfer glass from one level to another.

It's not only glass that presents problems in the stained glass art. The soldering iron also must be treated with respect. It does get hot and should not be left in an area where the pattern paper you are using will somehow creep up on it and start smoldering. We have seen this happen. We have also seen individuals reach for their soldering iron without looking and grasp it by the hot barrel. If you wish to operate successfully in the stained glass craft and not be operated on, you must always watch where your hands go.

Many individuals come into our studio and act quite impressed with the fact that we work with glass, which to them seems to be such a dangerous commodity. In fact, glass is no more dangerous than the individual who is using it. Glass does not act, it reacts. The only times we have cut ourselves is when we have been overtired and not concentrating properly, or through sheer carelessness and haste. Otherwise, we have found glass to be one of the safest and most rewarding materials that can be worked with.

CHAPTER 7

Cutting Patterns

Pattern cutting begins the stained glass process. Here is the guide from which all further efforts will extend. If there is an error here, it will be compounded throughout the other steps. It therefore behooves the student to check his patterns carefully and make sure that they are cut precisely. It is also wise to design them so that they can be cut effectively in glass. Remember that it is easy enough to cut a pattern out of pattern paper. Cutting it out of glass may present different problems entirely.

Every stained glass piece takes its origin as a drawing. When you make your drawing, don't worry about the fact that you're eventually going to transfer it into glass. Draw it as you see it in your mind's eye and as you would like it to be seen by others. Put everything down on paper: perspective, the shadowing, the different type of linear qualities it may have, even color, if you wish. Use pastels to match as closely as possible the colors you have in mind. This will give you a rough idea as to how the colors will blend. Once you have your sketch or sketches down on paper, you may select from them the one which best suits your purpose as far as glass is concerned. Your sketch then must be transformed into what is called a cartoon. This is the transformation of a piece of artwork into a beginning blueprint for a piece of work in stained glass (Fig. 7-1). The cartoon is, in fact, the guiding line drawing for what the finished stained glass piece will look like. It shows all cut lines and all lead lines in their final dimension (Figs. 7-2, 7-3, 7-4). If large and thin lead

DESIGNING THE PATTERN

Fig. 7-1. A paper pattern ready to be cut. Each line is a cutline drawn to scale. The next step is to number each piece to correspond with the work drawing.

lines are to be used, the cartoon must indicate that. The only thing the cartoon does not have to show is color, and if you wish to, you may indicate that on your cartoon as well. Remember to keep your pieces wide enough to show themselves as stained glass items. Don't squeeze them together with tiny lead lines that will throw your whole panel off balance. Keep your lines easy and flowing and try to give the linear quality of your cartoon an interesting pattern.

USE OF THE PATTERN KNIFE OR THE PATTERN SCISSORS

Fig. 7-2. Preliminary sketch for the Pirate Window. Concentration on background detail with outline only of the central figure.

Fig. 7-3. Sketch concentrating on the pirate figure with color possibilities beginning to be worked in pastels.

FREEHAND CUTTING

Once you have designed your pattern, the next step is to cut it, making sure you leave enough room between the pieces of pattern for the intermediate line of lead. The best instrument to use for this purpose is a pair of pattern shears. As previously described, this instrument consists of three blades, two lower and one upper, with the upper fitting snugly into the two lower blades to give a sharp edge to the cut piece. The excess piece comes out in a thin strip below the scissors, in one continuous piece (Fig. 7-5). If a cut is made the entire length of the scissors, this excess strip will clog the further operation of the cutting, as it will then double up in the lower blades. It is best, therefore, to cut using only the very back portion of the scissors which then can take curves, as well as straight lines. Don't be afraid to bend a piece of pattern in order to get into a difficult angle for cutting. The piece will straighten out. When cutting pattern, be sure to go exactly along the planned lines (Fig. 7-6). Any swerving to right or left will end up giving your glass this same effect. Some beginners feel they can make a mistake in the pattern and fix it later when it comes to cutting the glass piece. This ad lib method is mentioned only to be condemned, as it invariably leads to sloppiness later on. If you make a mistake in cutting your pattern, a new piece must be substituted or everything will be thrown off.

The pattern knife is another instrument (Figs. 7-7, 7-8) which will cut leaving an intermediate strip for the lead came. It is somewhat more difficult to use than the pattern scissors and does not give as satisfactory a cut. Many individuals buying a pattern knife usually end up purchasing a pair of pattern scissors anyway.

This is the way most beginners in stained glass start. They trace over the lines of their cartoon with a heavy marking pencil, being careful to trace exactly over the lines, so that a thick mark now takes the place of the thin pencil or pen lines that existed previously. Once this is done, they take either a razor

Fig. 7-4. Final work drawing of Pirate Window. All cutlines were then transferred to pattern paper, numbered and cut.

Fig. 7-5. Using the pattern scissors. Note the strip of paper below feeding through the scissors as the cutting proceeds.

Fig. 7-6. Cutting pattern seen from the top. The single upper blade of the pattern scissors is lined up to follow the cartoon line having just come around a sharp bend. Note the space left between the cut pieces of pattern.

Fig. 7-7. Using the pattern knife. It is pulled toward the operator along the cutline.

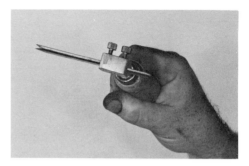

Fig. 7-8. The pattern knife.

Fig. 7-9. Cutting pattern. The piece of pattern is placed on top of the glass and the cutter is run along its side.

Fig. 7-10. One side cut to pattern.

Fig. 7-11. The piece of glass almost cut to pattern size.

blade or an ordinary pair of scissors and cut their pattern on either side of this black line—literally cutting the black line away. This leaves an empty space where the black line was, which is the space approximated for the leading to fill. This is the least precise of the three methods of cutting pattern and is not recommended for any critical work, that is, any work that is going into existing dimensions such as a window, panel for a door, shutters, etc. As an introduction for cutting patterns for free-form objects, it works fairly well. You must remember, however, that not all magic markers are the same in width, and even those that are the same in width wear down as they are used, presenting a variable line which, perhaps, may be thicker at the end of the pattern than it was at the beginning. Also, the mechanics of cutting out the line furnish another area for error, and this cut must be done twice, which doubles the possibilities for mistakes.

All in all, this is an amateurish way to cut patterns and is mentioned only as an introductory method to the field.

USE OF THE PATTERN

Once you have your pattern cut to the proper dimensions, with sharp edges all around, put each piece back on the cartoon. They should be placed so that the cartoon piece shows as slightly larger than the pattern piece. It is important to do this as there are occasions when the pattern will somehow seem to shrink; either the worker has misjudged his lines and is cutting too closely within them, or the lines were never made dark enough for him to see properly and he's gone off them. In any event, one piece of pattern imperfectly cut will lead to an imperfectly cut piece of glass. If the pattern pieces placed back on the cartoon seem to match correctly, your next step is to cut a piece of glass to match each of your pattern pieces.

Cutting glass from a pattern is a very specific activity (Figs. 7-9, 7-10, 7-11, 7-12). The pattern is placed on top of, not below, the piece of glass and the glass cutter is then run around the edges of the pattern to make the cut. Make each cut individually and then break it before going on to the next. To cut pattern by putting the piece of pattern under the piece of glass and looking through the glass to follow the lines, is a very imprecise and amateurish way of cutting patterns. It will never work properly. This is to say nothing of the fact that there are opalescent glasses and glasses which are quite dark which cannot be seen through. It is impossible to cut accurately without putting the pattern on top. For

Fig. 7-12. Pattern on the left, matching piece of glass on the right.

precise pattern cutting, the glass cutter follows the edges directly.

The average piece of pattern will last for five or ten cuts should you desire to make that many of this one piece. It is suggested that if you are cutting a pattern for multiple cuts, such as a lamp panel or skirt, that you transfer your pattern to a thin piece of sheet metal instead of using the pattern paper. Even pattern paper will tend to fray and change dimensions as the glass cutter rides against it after repeated cuttings. Be sure in transferring your pattern to a piece of sheet metal that the sheet metal is thin enough to allow the axle of the glass cutter to run along its edge.

All pattern pieces must be numbered to correspond with numbers on the cartoon. Only in this way will you be able to find your pieces quickly. In a small window or panel there is no major problem in finding the pieces of pattern; but numbering them is a good habit to get into, so that when you make a larger piece of work, you will be able to tell exactly by number where your pattern fits. It can be very confusing to have nervous little pieces of paper fluttering all over your work table while you pick each one up by hand to try to find its place in the jigsaw puzzle.

CHAPTER 8

Designing for
Stained Glass

ARTIST: *"One day, I was carrying a large sheet of stained glass across the room. It slipped out of my hands and shattered on the floor. It was beautiful.*

INTERVIEWER: *"And?"*

ARTIST: *"I leaded it up just as it was. Well, not quite. I had to step on one or two of the larger pieces. The effect was breathtaking."*

—THE GLASS WORKSHOP

Weird as the above may sound, there are people who take this type of designing for stained glass seriously, especially in abstracts. Not long ago we had some visitors in our studio, who inquired in all frankness why we spent so much time designing abstract windows when the lines were only there to hold the different pieces of glass together. To their mind, a stained glass creation is simply that, the lead lines being there solely for a functional purpose. Stained glass is such a new art form to many people that this sort of idea, naive though it sounded to us, is likely to be more widespread than we care to think. We would like to rectify, or at least diminish, this impression in these pages.

In fact, stained glass design involves a feeling for line and linear quality that is present in no other art form. This inheritance has come down through the centuries. Of course, the lines are there to hold the different colors of glass together, just as notes in a musical composition are there to hold the counter-

Figure 1. Pirate window by Anita Isenberg.

Figure 2. German streaky glass.

Figure 3. Transom window by Anita
Isenberg.

Figure 4. Diamond flower by Anita
Isenberg.

Figure 5. Tiffany-style lamp by Anita Isenberg, private collection.

Figure 6. Mediterranean-style lamp by Anita Isenberg.

points and melodies together. It's how the notes are arranged that makes all the difference, and the same holds true for the leaded aspect of stained glass. To the untutored eye, lead lines may not seem to make any difference to the work as a whole; just as to the untutored ear, all chamber music sounds alike. Nonetheless, differences do exist and they are not lessened by the fact that they may not be recognized.

For anyone interested in working in the stained glass medium, design is an essential function—not only in preparation for a finished project of his own, but as an understanding of what the stained glass art is all about. Every craft has its secret little ways which may be barely apparent on the surface, but which expand enormously once one becomes a devotee of the process. Designing for stained glass, therefore, involves choice of linear quality as well as choice of color. Color is something that we have all been brought up with and of which at least we can say, "This pleases me; that does not." Line quality is something else again, and the eye must be tutored in its subtleties before an opinion can be even considered.

A composition in stained glass combines a number of entities in relationship to one another. We have color, line, space, texture; each element an entity in its own right and each acting upon the other for good or ill, depending on the choice of the craftsman. Certain colors as well as certain lines will take away from one another. A heavy blue next to a light green, for instance, may tend to wash out the green and give it a pallid look. An extremely heavy lead line next to a very thin one may tend to overpower the lesser and more delicate leading.

Almost all stained glass windows, unless they are done in silhouette of a single character or feature, contain a foreground where the attention is basically directed and a background which fills in lesser detail and completes the totality of the space. This is true whether the window is pictorial or abstract. In this regard, the linear quality is most important. Obviously, you don't want your heavier lead lines in the background, as that would emphasize this portion of the work too strongly. At the same time, you cannot disregard the background entirely; like music faintly heard against the major theme, it orchestrates the overall projection.

Be careful in designing your windows, that your background does not grow so complicated and so busy that it detracts from your foreground aspiration. This is probably the commonest mistake in stained

BACKGROUND AND FOREGROUND

Fig. 8-1. A "porthole" giving an example of designing for a limited space. The mountains and sky form the background with the water below. The rope effect is painted and baked onto the border glass giving a tightly knit design concept.

A UNIQUE DESIGNING EXPERIENCE

HOW TO BALANCE LEAD LINES

glass designing. A good rule of thumb here is to make the background as simple as possible and save your complexities in colors, cuts and leading for the foreground. You must, of course, decide which is which and not just lead up indiscriminately, or what you will have at the end is a piece that resembles a sheet of stained glass dropped on the floor and put back together again any which way. While there have been painters who made a great deal of money standing above a canvas and throwing gobs of paint at it, it takes a certain amount of gall and publicity for success here. If you feel that your stained glass can promulgate the same effects, more power to you. We concentrate, however, on the greater audience which prefers a planned, rather than an accidental, artistic effect. Certain individuals in this category come to stained glass from other art fields, such as sculpture, painting or music, and hope to apply principles gained therein to stained glass. To a certain extent, this can be done, as an overall feeling for an artistic expression, but as far as technique is concerned, there is just no similarity.

Designing for stained glass is not like designing for any other art form. For one thing, no matter how ornate or how simple your sketch, always in the back of your mind must be the question, "Can these pieces be cut out of glass?" We have seen many beautiful designs brought forth by individuals in our classes who were artists in other fields. Unfortunately, these designs were useless as far as stained glass was concerned. This is not to say that artists from other media cannot learn to design for stained glass. It's a good idea, however, to park the habits gained in other modalities by the way and enter the glass craft with an open mind and a willingness to learn its particular regulations.

There are several aspects of balancing lead lines which may be gone over without too much elaboration. Remember that the lead lines act as guides for the eye. They move the eye either across the entire composition, or to a certain feature, allowing then another line to take over. It is important not to design so that the eye roams into areas which are deadends. Such breaks, or snags, in the overall pattern disrupt the entire viewing enjoyment. There should be a smooth and rhythmic quality to any good stained glass work, not a staccato, uncertain jumble of lines. You can get headaches from too much exposure to this sort of thing. The eye tends to read a stained glass window pretty much the same way it reads the pages in a book guided by the lines of type. That is, with little jumping motions. For the eye to suddenly jump as it were into space and come down nowhere is very disconcerting. And while it is strictly subliminal, enough of these little jumps into confusion can end up giving the viewer a feeling of distress and dislike, even though he may not really be aware just why.

To strengthen the flow of line within a composition, the artist should engage himself in the following rules:

1. Try to avoid having too many lines meeting in one place. This effect acts on the nervous system pretty much the same as a traffic snarl on a busy afternoon. There is simply no place to go to get out of it, and the brain of the viewer eventually begins to overheat.

2. Try to mix your leads. Don't use only one type all the way through the panel unless it's a very small panel. Too much of the same in stained glass as in any art can lead to monotony and tiring of the viewing eye. An eye that begins to get a little bored never recovers the animated sparkle with which it first began investigating. Try to keep the eye intrigued by a creative linear quality as well as a colorful one.

3. The lead lines must be a unifying force over the composition, contributing to its meaning either in terms of geometric beauty or whatever abstract meaning you may want to express. Lead lines used hesitantly, instead of unifying, will fragment the composition just as a voice defect may interrupt vocal ideas no matter how brilliant in their inception.

4. Avoid passing your lead lines through areas where they obviously don't belong, such as through painted areas or through pieces of glass that have intricate line cuts. Doing the latter makes it look as though you could not cut the glass as a unit and had to cheat by cutting it in pieces. While this may be the case, you don't want to advertise it. It would be better to redesign your drawing to work your way out of this with a pencil, rather than cut the glass any old way because it challenges your skill as a cutter. In stained glass, technique and artistry ever go hand in hand. As for painted areas, to run lead lines helter-skelter through these will make the piece look as though it were broken and badly

Fig. 8-2. A second "porthole" in a series of four designed to fit into shutters in a boy's room. Chunk glass is used for the sun with radiating rays of lead lines. A whale sports in the waves below. All lead lines are worked in as part of the design.

Fig. 8-3. A panel hung in a window as a decorative piece. Lead lines flow out from the central focus and carry the eye along. The symmetry is pleasing even without knowing the colors.

repaired. We will have more to say on this subject in the chapter on glass painting. Enough here to simply state that leading painted areas is a technique of its own.

MIXING VARIOUS SIZES
OF LEADS FOR EFFECT

Mixing leads should be a graded process. Don't juxtapose a ⅛″ lead immediately to a ¾″ unless you have a very good reason for doing so. Go instead from your ⅛″ to perhaps a ³⁄₁₆″ or at most a ¼″ lead and thus mount to larger sizes in a stepwise fashion. This rule is a general one; it is quite possible to get some magnificent effects by leaping across the lead sizes in a quick, emphatic manner. But be sure that your design and your ideas call for it; otherwise, you can end up overpowering the smaller leads by the larger ones and losing that portion of your work entirely to the casual viewer.

Don't use large leads on one small area of the window and tiny leads through the rest of the work or you'll get an unbalanced effect. The line quality should be well thought out and designed into the cartoon, not decided upon when the leading procedure is already in full swing.

Fig. 8-4. Another panel in symmetrical design, demonstrating how simple geometrical patterns may be employed to artistic advantage. In this instance the central flower has three-dimensional leaves jutting out from the ruby jewel. The severe border complements this rather ornate interior.

There is a general rule that small pieces of glass take small leads and larger pieces of glass take larger leads. This is not only a good rule design-wise, but for the physical safety and strength of the window, it applies equally well. Like many rules, however, this one may also be broken and you may decide that your large pieces of glass should take small leads as well as large. Naturally, you cannot be so cavalier with the small pieces of glass for, if you use large leads on them, you will show only lead. The smaller glass pieces will sink into the channels to such an extent that they will disappear entirely.

WATCH THOSE CORNERS

If you're going to have a number of lead lines meeting at one area point, you will create a trap for the eye and a soldering area that when you are done will resemble an ancient tar pool. The more leads that you have meeting this way, the more space you will take up with leads and the less there will be for glass. In a pencil sketch it may look as if there is no problem. The lines here are all discrete enough and carry very little thickness, so that the spaces between show up as enclosed areas of the overall design. Not so when it comes to putting it into glass. We have emphasized this in other portions of this book but since it is such a common designing mistake, we feel that we should mention it here once again. If you want to have a number of lead lines meeting, try to arrange it in the design stage, so that they don't all meet at exactly the same point. Let them meet either a little further up or a little further down along the line they are traveling towards. Just an inch or so will make all the difference in the world.

One of the more popular stained glass panels is a compass type of design showing spikes radiating from a central hub. Such spikes may be cut to needle point sharpness in glass, but when it comes to leading them up you will find that the end of your spike has suddenly moved two or even three inches into the panel itself and all you have toward the border are two leads cramped close together so that solder must be applied to their surfaces. This is not a particularly lovely effect. To avoid this sort of thing just don't cut your glass to these needle point edges. Leave enough thickness even at the point of such a glass spike so that the leads have room to grip the glass and still show glass between them. A good way to check for this, even while making the design, is to cut such a piece of glass and check two pieces of lead against the end of it. This will show you what width of glass is necessary to allow for. This is a technique that will stand you in good stead throughout your stained glass designing.

Remember that these leads do not bend well and, therefore, do not take curves well. Keep in mind also that they have a much thicker heart than all other leads, to allow for the steel rod running through their center. The best way to see how wide a space is necessary for their application is to take such a lead and look at it in cross section. You will easily be able to see the lead heart with the rod inside of it. Mark off this dimension on a piece of paper. This will give you the exact amount of room that you must cut out of your pattern to allow this particular lead to seat properly. It's about the size cut by a large pattern scissors—approximately $\frac{1}{8}$ of an inch. When we design for reinforced leads, we make certain that we have the line for the heart running the entire length of the lead line so that we know exactly in our initial drawing how much room we have for the design border.

Remember at the beginning to consider the end. If your stained glass window is going to be above three feet by three feet, reinforcing rods will be necessary at every two feet to brace the window. Such rods must be cut with a hacksaw and if possible designed into the window. If, however, this is not possible, try to modify your design somewhat so that the rods will not go through an area where

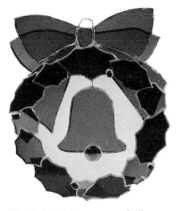

Fig. 8-5. Christmas wreath showing overlapping of the circular leaves as well as the bow above. The bell hangs supported by copper wire.

DESIGNING FOR REINFORCED LEADS

Fig. 8-6. Cornucopia. The design shows a crowding of the elements composing the horn of plenty without a crowding of the structural design.

USE OF REINFORCING RODS

their line will overlie an important part of the design. Such rods can be bent and will follow simple curves if you think it necessary. This is really only done in free form hanging objects of large size which must be braced along their borders. In these instances, reinforcing rods may be bent right around following the bordering came to give it a very stiff and sturdy support. There are artists making such large free form sculpture stained glass works and a method used by them to support these pieces is to employ flexible reinforcing rods to follow the curvatures. In a window we do not have this much leeway, and the amount of curving we can do with our reinforcing rods is limited. So try to keep the reinforcing rods in mind when designing out your original window, but still without compromising any of the artistic integrity going into the design.

HOW TO TRAIN YOUR COLOR SENSE

The use of colored glass as a medium for composition implies a knowledge of the interchange of colors on the artist's part, together with an appreciation of such interchange on the part of his audience. Unfortunately, this is not always the case on either side. To employ such a medium in all its force one should have an idea how colors blend just as in listening to symphonic music the enjoyment is enhanced the more one is aware of the interplays of harmony.

A good color wheel is mandatory for anyone working in stained glass. Such a wheel should always be at your side when choosing glass so that you can study which colors go together and which do not. A study of other people's stained glass work will also help in this respect. The more modern works will help more than the medieval, where the color spectrum was somewhat limited. Remember that it is not just a choice of red or orange or yellow or blue. The individual colors, especially in antique glass, have such modifications of hues and tones that choosing among them can be a real problem and can end disastrously if the choice is poor. There are a number of books which go into this subject at some length, and it would be wise for the beginner to study them (see Bibliography). You can never have your color sense sharp enough and it is not only the ability to pick and choose among colors that counts. It's the ability to recognize what color in a window will suddenly blur out or be overemphasized by the interplay of another tone elsewhere. Constant practice and constant self-criticism is the only way to sharpen your color sense. Very few windows, even when they are all finished, are so well balanced colorwise that they could not have substitutions made for a better effect.

Take your finished design and lay it over the light table. You will see that the light penetrates it fairly readily. Then take colors of glass that you would like to employ and place them over those respective areas of the design without cutting the glass to size, simply to see how the colors will mesh (Fig. 8-7). Keep in mind that looking at colors on the light table is not the same as seeing them by true light (daylight) (Fig. 8-8). You should try to lay out as many colors of your choice as possible in their general areas. Then stand over the design on a chair or small ladder, as far away as possible, and study the color pattern. You may find that what you thought was a good balance before laying it out now looks pretty bad and will have to be changed. It is easier to change the color scheme now, than when the pieces are already cut. Take as much time as you like in studying the color design of your window and don't be afraid to change all the pieces if you think the colors are not promoting themselves properly. Hold a few of them up to the daylight if you're unsure of them and see what the quality is with this light. This will also give you some idea of the modification between daylight and the light table for all your colors.

A stained glass composition is, like all artistic compositions, a relationship of certain design elements, each acting by itself and interacting with the others. How effectively this interaction takes place will determine how unified the composition appears. It makes no difference what the subject matter is. This is an entirely different proposal, and one which is judged separately. The artistic endeavor may be noted either in the composition or the subject selected, or both. Where artistic expression is most valid, naturally, is where the subject and the composition complement each other and present a finished and professional appearance.

Whether a composition in the stained glass medium is good or bad depends upon the textural elements involved. We have endeavored to go over such elements and point out briefly the methods by which they may be put to use in a fashion which employs their best features. Because stained glass is such a new medium, the tendency among beginners is just to turn out something, the novelty of which will engender attention and admiration. In the long run, as most beginners who stay with the art will find, this is not enough.

USE OF THE
LIGHT TABLE
IN DESIGNING

Fig. 8-7. Balancing colors on the light table. The pieces are not cut to pattern, but placing the colors next to each other gives an idea how they will relate.

SUMMARY

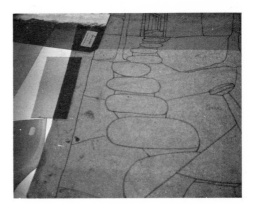

Fig. 8-8. The work drawing is on the light table and colors are being balanced against it in a final decision. This final placement of hues is most important and should not be rushed.

CHAPTER 9

The Copper Foil Method

The inclusion of copper foil in the stained glass armamentarium came about in the Tiffany era, and for this reason work involving its use has been categorized as the "Tiffany Foil Method." Whether Tiffany actually invented the method is questionable. What is certain is that he wrought with it some of the most delicate effects imaginable, effects not possible with the bulkier, less nimble lead came (Fig. 9-1).

The flow of any design is dependent on the quality of line involved. A work of intricate pattern almost mosaic in form presupposes a linear movement that will exhibit, not obscure the workmanship. To this must be added when dealing with glass, a rigidity sufficient to skeletonize the piece, so that what you have planned as a line will not in time provoke itself into a curve. What is demanded, therefore, is a material which is at once mobile, inexpensive, adhesive, easily solderable and one that can be induced to become rigid on demand. In short, copper foil.

Fig. 9-1. Two types of copper foil for use with stained glass. On the left is the 6″ wide roll foil, which is cut into strips prior to use. On the right is a roll of ¼″ wide adhesive backed foil pre-cut for use.

THE TIFFANY METHOD

The pieces of glass are each wrapped in the copper foil; the ends are soldered together, and these pieces are placed over a pattern (or mold in the case of a lamp) and soldered together. The process itself is simple enough. Where the procedure raises difficulties is in exactly cutting the small pieces of glass and so wrapping them with foil that they will lie as flat as possible against one another.

86

Three types of foil are used in stained glass work: hard, soft and medium. The degree of rigidity depends on the thickness of the sheeting. "Hard" foil is .002 inches thick, twice as thick as the .001 inches of the "soft" foil. "Medium" foil has a thickness of .0015 inches. Choice of foil is rather dependent on the type of work being done. Very small pieces of glass require only a thin foil to hold them together; such a foil is also easier to manipulate over their smaller surfaces. Since foil is sold by weight, it is also less expensive. However, the final decision is up to the artist and the effect he wishes to create. For a bulky, rough effect with small pieces, a thick foil can be used.

Not so much choice is possible where truly large panels of glass are involved, as in lamps for instance. Here, a heavy foil is almost mandatory, simply for reasons of support and ease of manipulation.

Foil is supplied in 6-inch wide lengths in the thicknesses given. From this width, strands are cut with either scissors or razor blade to the width demanded by the work in progress and consistent with the skill and design of the craftsman (Fig. 9-2). Ideally, the thinner the strip the better, since the effect produced will be more delicate the less the foil overlaps the glass. At the same time, there is a point of no return which is helpful to keep in mind where the foil is clipped to such a cleverly thin degree that the work falls apart due to insufficient bracing of the pieces. Such an effect is guaranteed to draw attention to your product, but only from one audience.

Since it is likely that not all the glass you are working with will be the same in thickness, it is a good idea to cut only a few strands of foil at a time. Each strand is then wrapped around its glass portion and the ends cut and soldered. Remember that since each piece of glass is going to butt one against the other, your amount of visible foil (the amount overlapping the glass) will, in effect, be doubled by the time you are done. It is an unthinking neglect of this fact that necessitates the use of so much solder later on.

Copper foil is limber enough so that there is generally no problem about its adhering to the glass, providing it has been pressed tightly before the ends are soldered. It will fold nicely into all crevices and against all curves if it is given half a chance. Fingers are the best instruments to produce this tight edging since a finger can press down and around at the same time.

TYPES OF FOIL

Fig. 9-2. A piece of roll foil being cut into strips. The width of the strips may vary according to the discretion of the worker.

USE OF FOIL

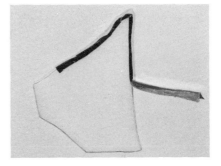

Fig. 9-3. A piece of glass being edged with foil.

Fig. 9-4. Two pieces of glass showing foil wrapping.

ADHESION

Should there be difficulty in getting the foil to lie against the glass, however, the use of a small amount of vaseline around the glass edge should facilitate the operation. Glues and other types of gummy material brought into play to produce a bond are to be avoided, as during the soldering process the heat will tend to melt them over the glass, from whence they are very loath to depart. (Exception: see Adhesive-Backed Foil.) The presence of such residues not only clouds the glass but makes the surface tacky. The only advantage to this sort of thing is the allowance it provides the maker to boast that people simply can't lay his things down.

TO TIN OR NOT TO TIN

The Tiffany Foil Technique has generally been used with pre-tinned copper foil, that is to say, foil which has been covered on one side with a thin layer of solder. The rationale for this is that it is easier to solder together metal which has been so treated. Working with this type of foil, one would press the untinned side against the glass and face each tinned surface, therefore, to each other. In theory this works fine; practically, however, the method is cumbersome for several reasons.

In the first place, tinning the foil—no matter what thickness it may be—makes it less flexible and therefore more difficult to work.

It also adds another procedure which, while not overly time consuming, is yet another thing to do. Further, it uses quite a bit of solder which adds to the expense. And, lastly, if the tinning is not meticulously done, it may ruin the piece of foil altogether, as you will end up with hills and valleys of solder from uneven applications of heat; bumps and pits from pressure against the wrong tinning surface; or actual folds and tears in the copper from dragging the iron across it.

If you prefer to work with tinned foil, it is important that you take time to do the tinning procedure properly. This involves use of a tinning board—a heavy piece of flat cardboard will do—that you use for nothing else. It should be propped at a 45° angle during the work. This presents a flat, constant surface with enough tilt to allow the excess hot solder to run off instead of pooling in areas over the foil. Needless to say, the foil should be pressed and held as flat as possible; thumb tacks at the corners will do (Fig. 9-5). A very wide-tipped iron should be used, at least an inch across, which should be employed for nothing else. This will preserve its shape. On no account use a corrosive flux, since in time this will end up pitting the soldering tip and providing

Fig. 9-5. A length of roll foil on the tinning board prior to being tinned.

areas of inconstant heat and consequent dragging of the solder.

If you would prefer to side-step all of this procedure, you may do so and still work successfully with foil. Untinned copper is easily soldered if it is cleaned and fluxed properly. True, it doesn't go together with the alacrity of its tinned brothers, but increased skill of the operator will in time provide a rapidity that will dispel any lag. It is also far friendlier to the glass in its untinned state and will take acquaintance with even the most grotesquely-cut pieces with a less labored introduction on the part of the craftsman.

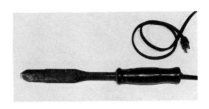

Fig. 9-6. A tinning iron. Notice the wide, flat tip.

FOILING TIPS

Although any soldering tip that you can use with lead can be used with copper foil, many craftsmen prefer a thin tip for foiling. This gives them a control of the solder which is not possible with the fatter tip and allows them to see what they are doing as they bead the solder over the thin widths of copper foil. The same iron is used as in the leading process. The copper will not burn as will the lead came, but the heat must still be controlled (see below). Make sure the copper is fluxed. The same flux is used as in the leading process.

The size of the tips vary with the individual operator's preference. Many, ourselves included, prefer for foiling a ¾₁₆-inch or ¼-inch semichisel iron-clad tip, which gets into the smaller crevices easily, and copper foiled pieces of glass do have innumerable crevices to get into. This is at once their pride and their challenge (Fig. 9-7.)

Some individuals tin each piece of copper foil after it is wrapped around the individual pieces of glass. We do not find this necessary, as long as the two ends of the foil are soldered together. Make sure that the foil is pressed as tightly as possible against the glass so that it fills every cranny. The solder will then flow easily into these areas when the pieces of glass are tacked together.

Fig. 9-7. Four tips commonly used with copper foil. Top to bottom: cylinder, chisel, ¾₁₆" chisel, half chisel. All of these are steel coated.

Pick up a piece of glass from your design (a simple shape at first), and notice the thickness of the edge. Now cut a strip of foil with scissors or razor blade, approximately three times that thickness and wrap it around the glass (Fig. 9-8). It will be easiest to bend a little tab over where you start, so that when you get to the end you can trim off even and still have a closed corner. Now fold the foil around and solder the open joint (Fig. 9-11). Just the tiniest bit of solder is necessary. Flux the area first. It is perhaps easier to touch the glass and foil to the iron at the

THE FOILING PROCEDURE

Fig. 9-8. Wrapping a piece of foil around a glass edge. It is crimped to the glass as you go along.

Fig. 9-9. The same process wrapping from the bottom. Your choice.

Fig. 9-10. A piece of glass rimmed with copper foil. The upper right-hand edge has not yet been turned down for soldering.

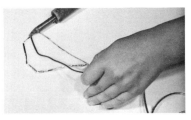

Fig. 9-11. Soldering the rim of foil together. A touch of the iron is all that is needed.

BEADING

joint, rather than pick up the iron and touch the foil. However, you may do it either way. If you have any trouble soldering this overlapped joint, scrub it gently with a wire brush and reflux it. By soldering the joint, it is now possible to put the piece down without the foil popping out of position. It is also easier to press each portion of the foil down firmly without it coming off the glass. Go through this procedure with each piece of glass, and then place each piece in its proper position on the work drawing or cartoon. You should be able to see the ink line around each piece of glass on the work drawing when the glass is put in place.

After all the pieces are properly foiled and placed in position, take some stained glass nails and place them around the outside of your pieces so that all of the pieces are held together according to the lines of your design. If they do not come together according to these lines, something is wrong. It is best to find this out before soldering the individual pieces of glass together, because it is almost impossible to unsolder them without stripping off all the foil you have so industriously put down. Very often the pieces do not come together according to the design, because the foil on one or more is not pressed tightly. This will take up room and extend your glass over the original cartoon lines.

When all the pieces are in order, take your soldering iron and solder them at the corners, or any place that will hold them together. Once they are thus tacked, you may take out the nails and more easily solder up the entire panel. Do not let your iron get too hot during this procedure. If the iron does get too hot, your solder will flow completely through the joints to the other side. It does no harm, except that when you come to do the other side, the procedure will re-occur and you will spend time chasing solder. It's best to flux all visible copper to make it solder more easily. When your panel is finished, there should be no evidence of foil showing underneath the solder.

This is the final step in the production of a copper foiled piece of work. It occurs after all the pieces are firmly soldered together and is a decorative fillip, which adds the last bit of character to the product. This process consists of running solder over all the joints to produce a rounded ridge. It is a process that can be both frustrating and tricky for the inexperienced worker, who will find his solder flattening out as before over the same roadbeds and running from there onto the table. If he is particularly inept at this finishing touch, he will also manage, perhaps, to loosen some of his previously firm joints in the process. Beading is not a simple, last minute icing on the cake. It is an integral part of the entire work, and time for its direct application must be allowed. A cool hand with a cool iron is imperative. The idea is to keep the rheostat control reading about one-half to three-fourths line voltage. If no rheostat is available, use a line switch and keep your iron as cool as possible, while still able to melt the solder. Try to keep the solder plastic, rather than liquid. This will allow it to build up on the previous solder bed and give an esthetically pleasing rounded line to the two-dimensional linear quality of the work.

It is best after a panel is completed to put a "U" shaped lead came, or a flat strip of metal around the outside edge to finish it off. This, too, should be soldered in place and made strong by tacking it to each foiled line running into it. You may also want to solder a loop to it, so as to hang the panel. A copper loop should be "tinned" at least where it will be connected to the panel. For easy attachment of the loop, it must be cleaned just like the foil before soldering it.

(a) The Tiffany type lamp shades were made on round, wooden forms the shape of the lamp, starting at the top of the form and working down to the bottom (Fig. 9-12). They may still be made by use of such forms. Purchase of these forms involves a great deal of expense. You may find ready-made ones in the shape of upturned salad bowls, or even plastic forms for lamp shades, which may be purchased in many hobby shops (Fig. 9-13). We will have more to say about this in Chapter 13 on lampshades.

(b) Chunks of glass, stones, sea shells, etc. can easily be foiled into unusually beautiful things, even jewelry. They may also be foiled into small hanging objects, or indeed, into larger windows. The foil is especially useful here, as it is such a nimble medium that it will grasp almost any irregular edge and hold it firmly into place once the solder is applied (Fig. 9-14). Chunks are usually from dalles, the large glass slabs, which are broken up and shaped into designs for the epoxy technique. The chips and edges from these dalles make wonderful multi-colored prisms, which may be used with copper foil.

(c) In foiling, different thicknesses of glass do not make any difference. Simply calculate your foil to be slightly wider, to take the additional width.

Fig. 9-12. A rock maple wood mold for a Tiffany-type lamp. Such large wooden molds are expensive and are, of course, good for only one style lamp. (See color section for lamp made from this mold.)

FINISHING THE PROCESS

Fig. 9-13. Two plastic molds for Tiffany shades.

ANSWERS TO COMMONLY
ASKED QUESTIONS

Fig. 9-14. A foiled Christmas star. The ribs of the star angle out toward the viewer—a technique more easily accomplished with foil than with lead. In addition the center is a small glass "glob" clutched into place by foil.

(d) Shapes can be built up by soldering as you go along. In fact, three-dimensional objects may be made with the use of copper foil, simply by soldering one to another in the form of an abstract sculpture. We will have more to say about this, also, in a later chapter.

(e) The width of foil which shows as a joint can be very narrow or very wide, as the operator desires. Many workers prefer a joint which shows a minimum of lipping of the copper foil. Remember that the end result will show double this amount of lipping, because you will have two pieces of glass together, one butting against another. A good rule of thumb is to have as little copper showing as possible that will still hold the piece of glass in place. Don't be afraid that the glass will move away. The foil becomes very stiff and solid once it is tinned. At the same time, a certain amount of purchase is necessary for the copper to grasp the edges of the glass. Practice will soon give you an idea of what can and what cannot be done with foil, and how much grasp it needs to thoroughly sustain the object it is holding (Figs. 9-15, 9-16, 9-17, 9-18).

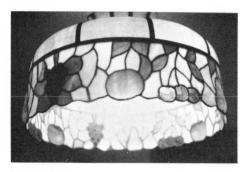

Fig. 9-15. A "fruit" lamp showing the intricate foiling of the border. While the copper is malleable when it is being worked, once it is "tinned" with solder it becomes very stiff and holds the glass quite firmly.

TROUBLESHOOTING

Here are the most likely reasons for having problems with the Tiffany Foil Method:

(a) The tinning not done smoothly enough. This will make bumps on the surface and not allow the pieces of glass to butt against each other as closely as possible. If you are using pre-tinned foil, the chances are that you used too much solder when you were tinning it. This not only makes the foil stiff, but gives an additional thickness to the copper that you can well do without.

(b) Unclean copper foil. Copper will not take solder if it has an oxide coat on it, or if it is in any way dirty. If you are using sheet copper and cutting it in strips, it is best to go over the entire sheet quickly with a wire brush and make sure it is unoxidized and clean before even cutting off the strips. It is easier to clean it in its sheet state than after it is wrapped around the glass, as then you have all those crevices to try and dig into with your wire brush.

(c) Not enough flux, or the wrong type of flux. Don't be afraid of using flux to excess. All it can do is flow over the glass, and you're going to clean this off later anyway. If you're using the wrong type of flux, that is, an inorganic acid flux, it may prove to be simply too strong to bond the solder and will do

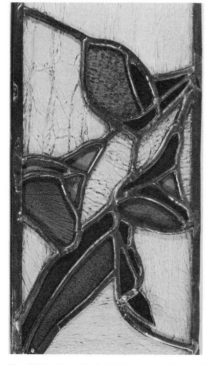

Fig. 9-16. Detail of side door panel owned by Dr. and Mrs. A. Lazar, Teaneck, N.J. Artist working in foil: Anita Isenberg.

nothing but create a foul odor and dangerous fumes in the workroom.

(d) Check the heat of your iron. If you're having trouble tinning the foil, your iron is probably too cold. If the solder, on the other hand, is running all over the place, it's probably too hot.

(e) If you're having trouble getting into the joints, you are probably using the wrong shaped tip. Your best bet is a flat, thin, chisel shape, such as a $\frac{3}{16}$ inch or a flat $\frac{1}{4}$ inch.

(f) Poorly cut glass, of course, presents problems of its own. If the glass does not conform to the pattern to begin with, the foil will follow this ad libbing, and you will end up with a design that has no relationship to your pattern. If the glass is cut basically to the correct shape, but still is full of little splintery edges, not grozzed smooth, your foil will not have a flat surface against which to cling and will keep coming off. Further, you will show a chipped edge of glass right alongside the edge of foil. This looks unprofessional and sloppy. Glass cutting, especially when using an element as delicate and as thin as copper foil, must be absolutely precise. Light coming through where neither glass nor foil meet is poor workmanship. When using copper foil, as with using very thin lead, the glass must be cut and possibly sanded to an extent where it shows no discrepancies in the edges whatsoever. There is no margin for hiding poorly cut or poorly grozzed edges under copper foil.

(g) Make sure that your foil is pressed down and around the glass tightly. No matter how well the glass may be cut, if the foil is not emphatically introduced to the surfaces, your edges will show.

This is a comparatively new item in the stained glass armamentarium. Its use follows all the regulations and possibilities so far observed with the additional advantage of convenience.

It comes in pre-cut rolls of thirty-six yards, and is equipped with a glue backing which, in turn, is backed by a strip of paper from which the foil peels away as it is used. The glue allows the foil to grip the glass firmly and remain adherent during the entire foiling operation. This allows for an ease and rapidity that cannot be approached with the older technique. The pre-trimmed edge, furthermore, gives a much neater and more finished look to each piece of glass. Both $\frac{1}{4}$-inch and $\frac{3}{8}$-inch sizes are available as well

Fig. 9-17. Lampshade demonstrating ornate foiling in the "Tiffany" method. Such an intricate pattern could only be foiled and still have its delicacy preserved.

Fig. 9-18. Hallway light using chunk glass foiled into the bottom panel. The light is lit, seen from below.

ADHESIVE-BACKED COPPER FOIL (TAPE)

as ³⁄₁₆″, and the size should be selected to allow enough overlap so that the tape will grip and allow the entire piece to be neatly rimmed with copper. The size tape you are using, of course, depends upon the thickness of the glass you are employing. With some of the thicker glasses, as with English streakies, the width requires the ⅜-inch tape. It would also be required in foiling stones or chunks into a piece of work where more grip is required for such thicker items.

Using the foil is simplicity itself. Let the roll rest on the table in front of you. Strip away the paper backing from a piece of it, and foil away. It can be done almost like knitting, with the foil in your lap while watching television. After a while, your fingers simply take over and wrap. We have found a great amount of time is saved in using such adhesive-backed foil in rolls.

There are several different makes of this foil on the market, and they do not all have the same amount of success in stained glass work. A low melting glue backing, when touched with a hot soldering iron, will tend to "weep" from under the foil onto the surface of the glass. You may well weep, too, as the glue will not come off, and the glass becomes cloudy and tacky. Be sure you are working with a high temperature adhesive before wrapping your glass in it.

COPPER VERSUS LEAD CAMING

Not everything that can be done with lead can be done in copper, and vice versa. The two techniques, while not mutually exclusive by any means, at the same time carry rules and regulations of their own, which call their usage into play quite clearly.

Essentially, the difference is one of size. Copper foil has its usefulness mainly where small pieces of glass are to be used, either in a panel, or in a lamp. Here, bends may be produced by use of such pieces over a form. The smaller the pieces of glass used, the greater the bend that can be made. To make bends in large pieces of glass, usually to be leaded, the glass itself must be physically bent in a kiln. While leading gives a bolder, more emphatic look to a piece of work, copper foil provides more of a delicate, lacy intonation. This is achieved through the intricate linear quality.

On the other hand, copper foil is not really meant to take the long spans of glass that lead can handle with ease. There are stained glass lamp shades which may have comparatively long panels held together by copper foil, where a very delicate effect is re-

Fig. 9-19. Lead came and copper foil in combinations. The central portion of the flower is foiled, while the outside skein is all caming.

quired, but this is a question of taste. The foil will hold as well as the lead, though a different technique must be applied in forming the lamp, and the entire shade will be much lighter for it. Many people, however, prefer a more substantial look to their leaded shades, where large pieces of glass are involved.

Both the leading procedure and the copper foil technique may be used together, either in a window or a panel where small and large pieces of glass are combined, or where the design involves foiling into the basic pattern old jewels, chunks, globs, stones, sea shells, or what have you. These can be wrapped with foil and brought into the decor as added delights to the eye.

The inclusion of the copper foil technique into the stained glass field opens up an entirely new facet to the art form. Its use is being constantly explored by experimentors, with effects running from the bizarre to the most intriguing and beautiful. The introduction, as well, of the adhesive-backed copper foil, pre-cut in rolls, allows for a finshed professional look for even the most inexperienced worker with this medium.

Fig. 9-20. Detail from the Pirate Window showing the tiny stained glass windows in the background. Ninety-eight pieces of glass were cut and foiled for this section alone.

CHAPTER 10

Finishing Techniques

In order to end up with a product that is professional in appearance, it is necessary to apply a final effort. This will make all the difference between a saleable or unsaleable item, even though equal technique up to this point has gone into both.

Enthusiasm usually begins at fever pitch with the design and the ambition to provide oneself with a finished work. This ambition may be sustained through the fabrication of the object but, humanly, can slip a bit when the project is completed and the nitty gritty of cleanup must begin. There are people who are starters and people who are maintainers. But the people who are finishers are a rarer breed. Final touches that one must apply to any stained glass work are not creative and tend to be skimped; partly for this reason and partly because many workers feel that it won't make much difference. This is not true. Any stained glass which is not thoroughly cleaned and puttied is a ghost that remains forever unfinished, and one which can come back to haunt you later on should you sell it. So try to pay as much attention to the finishing processes as you have to the designing and the fabrication of your work. Only in this manner will you develop the necessary work habits to carry you through a successful and satisfying project.

CLEANING THE GLASS   Once your stained glass project is completed and the soldering has all been done, it is necessary to clean the piece as soon as possible. Many individuals consider it finished as soon as it's soldered and anything thereafter as icing on the cake. They may let it

96

sit and start something else. The longer you allow your finished piece to sit before cleaning, the more difficult it will be to get it clean. The flux residues and the general grime that has accumulated during the fluxing and soldering operation will form a crust over the lead and the glass which will be more difficult to remove the longer it remains. So, no matter how tired you may be upon completion, you had better start cleaning immediately. A simple rinsing in soapy water will not do; although the object may appear clean while it is wet, especially opposed to how it looked before, you will find when the water and soap are wiped off that the panel is smudgy, tacky and probably still weeping flux from the joints. Rather like an individual whose teeth are not brushed, nothing is more scruffy looking than an uncleaned stained glass object. Why labor for hours to complete a thing of beauty and dress it in rags? We have seen lamps and mobiles offered for sale that were absolutely filthy. Your chances of selling any object are certainly better if it is clean and it should be more satisfying to you, the artist, to present a neat and clean offering no matter how complicated the design. Beauty of design cannot make up for a sloppy final effect.

Cleaning the glass is the first step. The panel should be laid flat on the table and cleaning and polishing powder sprinkled over it. Best to get yourself a small strainer and sift the cleaning and polishing powder over the glass as lumps and other debris may get into the powder, and if they are rubbed against the glass pieces will either scratch or possibly even break them. Sift the powder over the glass in a fairly even manner so that you cover the surface (Fig. 10-1). Then get hold of a floor scrubbing brush with bristles that are flexible enough to ride over the leads without tearing them loose. You can use a great deal of force pressing straight down providing your glass object is on a flat surface. Rub the powder with the brush all over the glass trying to get into every nook and cranny. Don't be afraid to use too much of the powder. We suggest that you work in an enclosed area, and possibly even with a handkerchief over your nose, because the powder does fly about and you may find yourself sneezing it onto the work.

Once you are satisfied that the surface is clean, turn the panel over and apply powder to the other side. When this is done, either with a vacuum or with a rag, take the powder off the panel. This powder is not to be reused. Tap your panel against the table to remove the remaining powder from under the cames and hold it up to the light. You

Fig. 10-1. Cleaning the completed panel. The cleaning and polishing powder is rubbed dry against all surfaces of lead and glass. A fine steel wool pad or floor scrubbing brush may be used.

will find that you might still have a few pieces of glass that look smudgy or that feel tacky. Repeat the process for their benefit. Once you are satisfied that your panel is neat and clean and the leads are uniformly shiny, you may use soapy water to further clean off the surfaces or you may prefer a routine glass cleanser like Windex. Following cleaning, your panel will have a sparkling look.

USE OF PUTTY

Putty used in stained glass work is of a linseed oil base. Use of any other type will lead to problems. Linseed oil putty hardens after a certain amount of time and provides a stiff lining between the lead came and the glass in the channels. Use of a putty that does not harden will defeat the purpose of the entire operation.

Almost everything you make should be puttied with the exception of small hanging objects and lamp shades. In some instances even lamp shades will have to be so treated if their panels seem to rattle in the lead channels, or if the panel angle is so acute that you can see the edge of it within the lead came.

Putty is used as follows: First get yourself an old pair of kid gloves or coat your hands with a protective glove coating such as Pro-Tek. This is a DuPont product which protects the hands and arms against paints, oils, grease, printing ink, etc., and it washes off easily with water when the job is done taking all the dirt with it. It's a lot easier to use this than to have the putty stick to the fingers and have to scrub like mad later. The Pro-Tek is greaseless and within a few moments after applying it to your skin, you will not even know it's there.

Once this is done, take a handful of putty from the can. Rub it into a ball between your palms. If it is too sticky or too moist, add a little cleaning and polishing compound to it to stiffen it up a bit because if it is too adherent, it will be unusable. It will simply come out of the came as fast as you push it under, preferring to stick to your fingers.

Fig. 10-2. Puttying the panel. Putty is pushed under all lead flanges.

After getting the putty to the right consistency, snip off a bit with your fingers and start pushing it under the cames with your thumb (Fig. 10-2). Each and every piece of lead should have putty under it. This is not as painstaking a procedure as it may sound. In fact, many individuals find it quite relaxing, because no thinking is necessary and all that is required is a slight pushing motion of the hand. Be careful that you do not crack any pieces of glass by getting *too* relaxed. The border leads should also have putty underneath them. Be careful when pushing the putty under them that you do not push them away from the glass.

When you are done you will have a pretty sloppy looking object in front of you, covered as it is with gobs of putty. Don't worry about it. Take a bent putty knife or even your lead knife, and turn down all the lead cames, pushing them as firmly as possible against the glass surfaces. More putty will ooze out from beneath them (Fig. 10-3). With a nail or an ice pick go around each surface of lead (Fig. 10-4). The putty will easily be cut loose from the lead. Save your excess putty; just scoop it up with your hand, roll it into a ball, and pop it back into the can. Remember to seal the can tightly if you wish the putty to remain soft and pliable. If you leave the lid even slightly ajar, the putty will harden up.

There are two types of putty which may be used: black or white. They are both linseed oil putty and the choice is completely up to you. Black putty will leave a black line under the lead; white putty, a white one. It is especially important if you are using black putty to use some sort of protective covering on your hands. The carbon particles that furnish the color are very difficult to get rid of once the job is over, and you may end up wearing putty for quite a while.

Puttying the object, of course, weatherproofs it as well as helps stiffen it. You should warn whoever is buying your stained glass, if the puttying has only been done within the past several days, that the work will continue to ooze putty for at least another week. Warn them not to clean it. If they let it alone for about that length of time the putty will be pretty well set within the channels and they may then go around the leads with a knife or a sharp object, being careful not to dig under the leads, clean away the putty and clean the panel with Windex.

After puttying, cleaning and polishing is again necessary. You may avoid repeating this operation by waiting until you putty the panel to employ the cleaning and polishing powder. It is sometimes more difficult, however, to putty directly after soldering, as little puddles of flux will still remain and will be carried back under the lead by the putty. The putty will then become liquified and unusable. But you might find it worthwhile to go over a few areas twice rather than do two complete operations over the whole surface.

Not only the glass must be cleaned but the leads as well. This should be done both as a general cleaning when the glass is brushed with the cleaning and

Fig. 10-3. Turning down the leads in a panel after puttying. Be careful how much force you apply.

Fig. 10-4. Removing excess putty using an ice-pick. The point is passed around the surfaces of the lead.

BRUSHING THE LEADS

polishing powder and as a specific cleaning either before or after cleaning the glass. The leads are best brushed with steel wool of a very fine nature (3 ought will do). The steel wool is dipped in the cleaning and polishing powder and then scrubbed along the lead surfaces. You will find a bright and shiny appearance coming up as you strip away not only the grime and soldering breakdown residues, but the oxide coat as well. Don't worry about the shiny surface and the new looking appearance of the leads. They will immediately start to darken again once the cleaning process is over, but this time they will all darken evenly. The soldered joints will also darken in time, though they take longer than the lead.

AGING THE LEADS

For those who don't want to wait for the leads to age naturally, a chemical is available which will hurry the process along. This is an antiquing patina which, when brushed over treated lead surfaces, will change the color from a bright silver to a dark, copper look. In order for this process to take place, the lead came must be tinned; that is, solder must be run along its entire length. This procedure is not only time consuming, but costly because of the great amount of material that must be used. But it will give your final product an entirely different look.

We advise cleaning the entire panel before starting to age the leads. If you try to age them when they are still covered by oxides and flux residues, you will have a very difficult time tinning them. Once you have them ready to be tinned, be very careful that you do not drop further flux over the glass as you will then have to reclean. This process, unless gently done, may remove from the leads some of the antiquing patina that you have been at such great pains to apply. This is not to say that the leads cannot be cleaned at all after the antiquing patina is applied to them, but they certainly cannot be cleaned with the force you used before. To use steel wool and cleaning and polishing powder on them now would once again give them a shiny appearance. So use the flux sparingly when you tin the leads and if any should spill on the glass wipe it off immediately with a rag so it doesn't stain. Keep in mind that if you are making a commissioned object on which antiquing was specifically requested, you consider this in the price, both for the extra materials and especially for the extra amount of labor.

FILING SOLDERED JOINTS

In our opinion there is no reason why this should ever have to be done. Your soldering procedure should be so calculated as not to necessitate this extra and awkward procedure. Your joints should be smooth enough from the iron to present a finished appearance. However, if in the beginning they do not, instead appearing ragged and even dangerous to the hand passing near them, perhaps instead of further spreading solder wildly around with the iron and getting excited, you might be better off to file them smooth. For this purpose a small flat, fine file is used which must be employed very carefully so that it does not scratch the glass. It is best not to try and make a masterpiece of each joint but to just file away the rough edges which you were unable to smooth out with the iron. You will find this a thoroughly painstaking operation, and just going through it once will probably convince you of the wisdom of doing the soldering procedure correctly the next time.

Copper loops are used for one purpose only: to hold stained glass panels or free form objects to a supporting string or wire in a window. It seems, however, many workers don't understand just how copper loops function. First of all, the loops must be tinned. This may lead to problems in some instances, as the copper can form a fairly inpenetrable coat from which the solder will run. Since the loops are of necessity fairly small, they are difficult to work with. We have seen students take a wire brush and try to go over the loop with it to make it nice and shiny. This can be awkward, as holding the loop in your fingers during the process may tend to flesh away some of their meatier parts. Using a vise to hold such a small item is impractical. A pair of needle-nose pliers generally works out best, but if you relax your grip during the brushing even slightly, you more than likely will find yourself on your knees on the floor looking for your loop. The best method for preparing your loop for the soldering process, therefore, is to dip it, held by the same needle-nose pliers, into a small jar of muriatic acid. This will clean the oxide coat off it almost instantly. Muriatic is a very strong, inorganic acid and should be treated with respect. Please keep it away from children.

Once your loop has had its acid bath, it should be dried, fluxed and tinned immediately. Do not attempt to tin it without using flux or without drying off the muriatic acid, since this acid will pit all soldering tips quite readily and will cause dangerous fumes at the same time.

A copper loop ready for tinning will accept the solder in almost a grateful fashion, allowing it to run full circle with one application. Please remember to

APPLYING THE HANGING LOOPS

Fig. 10-5. Applying a loop to a panel. First the corner is tinned . . .

Fig. 10-6. Then the loop is soldered in place, held in position by needle-nose pliers.

hold the loop with the needle-nose pliers, since copper transmits heat readily to unwary fingers. As far as the placement of your loop on your stained glass object is concerned, always make it a rule to apply a single loop to the strongest balancing point. This is usually where two or more lead lines meet. If this is not possible, use two or more loops to attain the balance and the strength. They may go at either corner or one may have to go behind the panel in order to support it from the bottom or mid portion. By pre-tinning the loops, you will find it a simple task to solder them to your object, which usually you will find yourself supporting one handed, one elbowed or even with your chin during this activity. It is no time to find solder rolling off an untinned loop.

CHAPTER 11

Using Slab Glass

In another portion of this book (Chapter 4) we have described what slab glass is and how it is cut with the slab glass wedge. Our purpose in this chapter is to demonstrate what slab glass may be used for and some of the techniques involved in its use.

Slab glass, or *dalles-de-verre*, is becoming more and more popular for decorative windows in large buildings such as churches and auditoriums. These large panels are made using either dalles as entire pieces, that is, as even rectangles of color, or by using parts of them cut to imaginative shapes imbedded in a holding material of some sort. Two such holding materials are cement and epoxy. Making such a panel involves the following procedure.

Work up a design into a cartoon similar to what is used in a regular stained glass window. Trace it onto pattern paper and cut the patterns. Use these as templates from which to cut the thick slab glass to shape. The shapes should be simple, rough hewn and fairly large. Don't try, at least in your initial attempts, to produce a delicate effect. A pretty good mastery of the material is required to accomplish this. If you have broken edges of the dalle chunks that you want to stand away from the holding material, fill them in with plasticene or clay. This will prevent the holding material from going into these crevices. If you are going to use a cement mix, it is best to place reinforcing wires on top of your basic work drawing before even putting the chunks into place. Holes may then be cut in the reinforcing wires

THE SLAB GLASS WINDOW

Fig. 11-1. Shaping a piece of slab glass using the slab glass hammer and wedge.

103

Fig. 11-2. A wooden form for use in the epoxy technique.

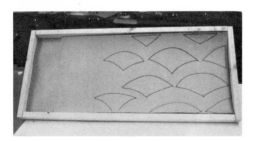

Fig. 11-3. The pattern placed in the bottom of the wooden frame.

to allow the chunks of glass to fit within them. The epoxy technique needs no such reinforcing wires.

The use of the cement method in this country has not proved very satisfactory because of the weather and the fact that buildings are heated during the cold weather. Therefore, the outside temperature might be zero degrees with an inside temperature of 80 degrees. With only one inch or so of cement separating these temperatures, the cement as a holding material soon develops hairline cracks that begin to leak. We do not run into this problem with the epoxy.

Once you have the design completed to your satisfaction and have selected the chunks that you are going to use, then you must build a frame around your work drawing, the edges of which will correspond to the borders of the drawing (Fig. 11-2). If the frame is made of wood, which most of them are, the sides should be greased with some sort of mold release. You may wrap waxed paper around the wood frame as a separator. If you do be certain it is tight. Waxed paper may also be used on the underlying cartoon if you wish. We generally don't bother with this, as the rubber cement we use to hold the slab glass in place sticks better to the brown Kraft work-drawing paper. We just rip this away afterwards. The purpose of the separator against the wood is so that the holding material will not dry against the raw surface of the wood and prevent removal of the frame. This can prove somewhat embarrassing when it happens. Make the frame as strong as possible and the inside surface—that is, the surface facing the holding material—as smooth as possible, as every indentation will appear in the border of the finished work. As these panels become very heavy, it is not advisable to make them any larger than roughly 2½ feet by 3 feet. For your beginning panel, you may want to make it considerably smaller than that.

Once your frame is made and you have tested it as being strong enough, place your pattern on the bottom of it (Fig. 11-3). Use a flat surface for the bottom. You should have enough overlap of paper around your pattern to allow the frame to sit securely on the pattern, with no curling of the pattern beneath. Make sure the paper is flat and free of wrinkles. Panels should be cast less than 1 inch in thickness so you may judge the width of your frame accordingly.

You are now ready to place your preformed chunks of glass on top of your work drawing. Make sure they are clean or the resin will not "take" to them. We wipe each piece with alcohol. Care must be taken to see that no epoxy can run under these pieces when you are pouring. Rubber cement coated on the bottom of each will hold them fairly firmly to the underlying work drawing, and this material can be easily removed later (Fig. 11-4). Remember to keep your chunks large enough so that they will provide enough surface coming through the panel to allow light to penetrate. A small piece that gets lost in the holding material will simply be covered over. Remember to fill with plasticene all broken edges of the chunks that you do not want to be covered.

Acquire some very fine sand and fill and brush the fine sand all around the mold and into all the crevices if you wish a textured surface on the underside.

Mix your epoxy, which usually comes in two cans, one a monomer and the other a polymer. Once the monomer and polymer are mixed, they will begin to harden. We like to pour our epoxy from a brown paper funnel. This acts almost as a sort of squeeze bag and allows us to regulate the flow of the material (Fig. 11-5). It also solves any cleaning problem later on as we simply throw the brown paper away. Epoxy sets up rapidly, so don't waste time once you have it mixed. Cover the surfaces of the chunks with beeswax or contact paper to prevent them from getting splashed by the epoxy.

Pour the epoxy to the requisite thickness and once it is poured, you may seed the top surface with coarse or fine sand or you can leave it smooth, whichever you choose.

Let your panel sit until the epoxy hardens (about a day); then turn it over, take away the work paper and the plasticene clay that you've used to fill in the edges you wanted to keep intact, and knock away the frame. With a knife you may scrape the rubber cement away from the glass chunks and acetone will clean off whatever surfaces remain tacky from this material. Keep in mind that you can pour your epoxy quite thin and make decorative hanging window objects of chunk glass arranged in imaginative form within it (Fig. 11-7). We have poured epoxy less than $\frac{1}{8}$ of an inch thick, allowed it to set and held chunks within it with no trouble at all. Such free form objects are not particularly heavy.

There are certain drawbacks to this technique. The major one is the fact that it does make quite a mess. The beginner in his haste, may end up spilling sand and epoxy all over the floor. The sand can be swept up, but the epoxy generally clings to whatever it hits and must be worked on before it will give way. There is also the somewhat laborious process

Fig. 11-4. Rubber cement is used to hold the pieces of chunk glass to the work drawing so they will not move out of place when the epoxy is poured.

Fig. 11-5. Pouring the epoxy. The heavy paper funnel controls the speed of flow with pressure by either hand.

Fig. 11-6. A finished product.

Fig. 11-7. Pieces of stained glass designed into a pattern and held together with epoxy. This material binds well even these ⅛" surfaces.

SLAB GLASS SCULPTURE

FURTHER EFFECTS WITH SLAB GLASS

Fig. 11-8. A decorative disk of chunk glass and epoxy. This side has been seeded with sand and the chunks are almost level with the epoxy.

of cleaning off the rubber cement and the paper afterwards from the pieces of chunk glass. All the same, these are minor items when compared to the beautiful objects that can be produced with this method.

Cement cannot be poured as thin as epoxy without developing stresses and strains within it that will bring forth unsightly cracks which can eventually crumble. Epoxy can be poured thin enough to accommodate stained glass pieces instead of chunks. It is a good idea when doing this, remember, to cover the surfaces of the glass that are to be poured upon with a protective material, so that it will not be covered by the epoxy splashing on it. Epoxy poured thin between the pieces of glass will bind them together quite well. Again, fine or coarse sand may be used to seed the surfaces to give a textured effect.

Because of their irregular appearance and faceted edges, slab glass chunks are a popular material for stained glass sculptures. Such objects are in truth three-dimensional projects, involving many chunks either cut to size or chosen at random and cemented together with epoxy to a more or less prepatterned design. The drawback here is that you cannot involve yourself in too many thicknesses without eventually blocking out all the light coming through and ending up with an object that reflects rather than refracts the light coming at it. All the same, we have seen a number of beautiful three-dimensional objects of this material, though among students the slab glass panel seems to exceed them in popularity.

Chunks may also be used as decorative breaks, interspersed between pieces of stained glass. They may be glued to an underlying piece of plate glass to add dimension to such a panel (see Chapter 16). They may also be used individually when small enough and when they are polished by a wet belt so that all surfaces are smooth, as a gem in a ring, being cemented to the underlying metal.

As for the use of such chunks in the foiling procedure by incorporating them into a window for three-dimensional effect, this has been covered in a preceding chapter.

For very small chunks there is no necessity to use the resin epoxy that is used in making large panels or windows. A simple epoxy glue will do here and will lock the smooth surfaces of the chunks into place very nicely.

As was mentioned in Chapter 4, slab glass is usually cut on the slab glass wedge with a special hammer. Most hobbyists, however, do not buy slab glass in full size, but rather as irregularly sized chunks. You may want to break even such pieces down further to provide a necessary fit in the surface of your panel. Get hold of a cold chisel and place it in a vise with the sharp side uppermost. Make sure the vise is a strong one and is holding the chisel securely. Then place the edge of the chunk on top of the chisel and with a hammer tap gently on the top surface of the chunk. You should be able to fracture the chunk along the line of cleavage you require. This is not by any means a foolproof method, but working with chunks is not like working with patterned stained glass. The same precision is not expected, nor can it be assumed. In fact, if you get your piece of chunk carved to approximately 75 per cent of where you want it, consider yourself lucky and fill in around it, either with epoxy or, if you are foiling it into place, with solder.

TRIMMING
SLAB GLASS
CHUNKS

Fig. 11-9. The same disc turned over. This side is smooth and the chunks stand out from the epoxy. A more dramatic effect is thus produced.

CHAPTER 12

The Traditional Leading Procedure: Making a Window

Fig. 12-1. A diamond window. Basic leading procedure. The work drawing is underneath, flanked by the right angle formed by the wood strips. The border leads are against them; the glass fits into these leads and lead is placed against them. Note that a separate pattern is cut for each diamond and each is numbered.

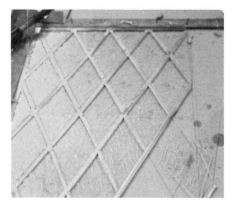

Fig. 12-2. As the work progresses the process is repeated many times, always building from the starting corner in the upper left and fanning outwards. Not seen for purposes of clarity are the leading nails, which ordinarily would be holding the end leads against the glass until new pieces can be fitted.

We intend to show in this chapter exactly how a stained glass window is made. To do so, we shall go step by step through the entire procedure, first using a simple panel as a guide. The stained glass window is a stained glass panel, though larger and more complicated. The same techniques are used in both productions. It is suggested that beginners on their first project follow the steps given here along with the designs that are proposed. We have found such particular patterns work well as teaching tools. They are projects which will allow the beginner to come away with work he may be proud of, as well as permitting the more advanced student to pick up information about procedure which he may have been lacking.

At first glance, the designs may appear to be simple enough, but you will be surprised when you begin work on them how complexities can suddenly arise, especially if you've not cut glass before. If you have cut glass before, or if you have done some work in stained glass and still wish to know the correct procedure, it is suggested that you also follow the mechanics as here laid down, so that you will be able to carry out the entire process as it is done in professional studios. Once you have acquired the basic techniques, you may apply them to a design of your own.

Remember that stained glass is a craft, as well as an art. Don't be ashamed to find the artistic impulse initially playing second fiddle to technique. There can be no marriage between the two until both are

108

thoroughly assimilated by the fledgling artist-craftsman.

1. *The Design*

Designing for stained glass involves a willingness to submit oneself to the rules and regulations of the material. Remember, above all else, that no matter how beautiful the design may be, if it cannot eventually be cut out of glass, it is useless. Even so straight-faced a design as a square panel, divided into quarters, thirds, or even simply in half, involves difficulties and procedures which are not apparent to the uninitiated. We make it a point in our classes to insist that all beginners start with as simple a panel as possible. That student who came into her very first class with a design of a pineapple consisting of 86 small pieces was quietly but firmly dissuaded. She thanked us afterwards.

Where do you get ideas for designs? Artists in other fields—Mondrian, for example—are worth studying. There are also many books with pictures of stained glass old and new, which will give you ideas of line flow. Geometric figurations in themselves have a charm and substance that will balance a beginning panel, i.e., triangles, diamonds, squares, rectangles, to say nothing of rhomboids, and trapezoids—all make linear statements and qualify as grist for your mill. There are also pattern books put out specifically for beginners and somewhat more advanced students who are looking for more specific ideas and stimulations in the free-form mobile-type stained glass object. As you progress, you will find yourself depending less and less on the work of others and on specific technical concentration, and allowing your imagination to begin to roam.

Sketch, draw, and erase until you have something on paper that looks good to you. Don't be afraid to detail your sketch to whatever degree suits you, providing you keep in mind that such detailing may have to be summarized in the cartoon by two or three lead lines. Exact and precise detailing on glass can only be done by painting it in. This is a technique of its own (see Chapter 17) which should only be used to complement the basically leaded end result, not to supplant it.

The design should be initially sketched in charcoal so that extraneous lines may be easily erased. It need not be drawn to scale or exactly to size. Once you have found something that looks as though it might do, concentrate on it, and when you think it is satisfactory, ink it in with a magic marker. Don't

A. BASIC PROCEDURE

Fig. 12-3. The finished window.

Fig. 12-4. Diamond window with center break. The basic pattern is thus modified.

worry about designing pieces too small or avoiding curves which look to be especially difficult to cut and fit. The idea is to get down on paper some formalized statement you can work with which will advance your thinking in the direction you wish to go. A good design starts as a preliminary survey and becomes more and more specific as it progresses. Once the design is set on paper in its entirety, you will have in front of you a beginning, middle, and ending to the progression as you conceived it.

Remember that color choice is going to affect your design strongly. You should be thinking in terms of color as well as linear quality. Study those pictures of stained glass windows to get a feel for line flow and color choice as done by professionals. Don't be afraid to keep changing your design until it's exactly what you want.

Once you have the design formulated, you are ready for the second step, which is making the cartoon.

2. The Cartoon

The cartoon is the stained glass blueprint. It is the design transposed for glass. It is drawn precisely to size. Every line in it is either a paint line or a lead line, and every space between lead lines is a piece of glass which must be cut. Many designers make it a point to draw lead lines in one color and paint lines in another, so that the two may be easily distinguished. Only the lead lines, of course, are to be cut. All extraneous lines from the original design are removed or condensed, while contiguous spaces are divided into individual cuts of glass. Lead lines are indicated as being wide or narrow. Joints are clearly marked.

Occasionally, the design must suffer some radical changes during this procedure. The extent to which it does not depends upon the craftsman's ability to design for glass. You will soon find the more obvious facets of this becoming second nature.

All background pieces from the original design involving sloppy cutting or impossible cuts when transposed to the cartoon must be completely redesigned, as they will only detract from your basic foreground statement. Remember to balance your lead lines even in the background as best you can, and make them attractive to the eye in a geometric flow, which no other art form can project.

Once you have your cartoon ready and inked in, you can begin "laying it out" to make, first, your work drawing, and second, your patterns. Remember to number each piece in your cartoon, even though

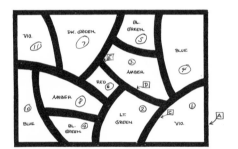

Fig. 12-5. A typical cartoon for a stained glass panel.

Figure 7. Garden scene, second window by Anita Isenberg, from the collection of Mr. & Mrs. Jerry Schlossberg, Englewood, N.J.

Figure 8. Garden scene by Anita Isenberg, from the collection of Mr. & Mrs. Jerry Schlossberg, Englewood, N.J.

Figure 9. Portholes by Anita Isenberg.

Figure 10. Stained glass box by Rik Heidloff.

Figure 11. Stained glass sculpture by Greta Vardi.

Figure 12. Three-dimensional
sunflower by Anita Isenberg.

Figure 14. Flower burst
by Anita Isenberg, from
the collection of Dr. &
Mrs. Allan Lazar,
Teaneck, N.J.

Figure 13. Kitchen window,
from the collection of Dr. &
Mrs. Allan Lazar, Teaneck, N.J.

Figure 15. Tiffany window.

it may be a very simple cartoon and have only a few pieces that are easily recognizable.

The work habits you learn here will stand you in good stead throughout more complicated projects in stained glass. Be patient and follow the directions precisely.

3. *The Layout*

The layout involves first, the cartoon; second, the work drawing; and third, the patterns. The work drawing, which is made on brown Kraft paper, will be used as a guide to lead up the panel. It should be an exact replica of the cartoon. Once you have transferred your cartoon to the work drawing, you should have the cartoon itself hanging somewhere in front of you, so you can consult it throughout the procedure. The work drawing will show where each piece of glass goes, as does the cartoon, but the work drawing will be on the work table covered with the pieces of glass placed on top of it. Having the cartoon in front of you will help give you a quick check on exactly where the lead lines are during the working process. The cartoon may be used to check against the work drawing during the procedure, should the work drawing tear or become obscured in any aspect from flux or solder spilling on it. Patterns, themselves, are made of a stiff, white pattern paper and will be used as templates for cutting each selected piece of glass to the correct size and shape.

The method of laying out the work is as follows: On your work table, place the piece of white pattern paper cut larger than the cartoon. We particularly like white pattern paper, because it shows up much more easily against the darker glass. Place on top of the pattern paper a piece of carbon paper, dark side down. You should use a special, heavy, re-usable carbon paper, and not an office stationery carbon paper, which is not able to take the wear and tear of the stained glass work. If your carbon paper tears or gives way in any fashion, either through lack of ink or simply because it is too fragile, you will have spent all your time in vain and will have to take all the papers apart to replace it. Use a heavy carbon paper to begin with and avoid a lot of difficulty through the working procedure.

On top of the white pattern paper, therefore, place your carbon paper. Over the carbon paper, place a piece of brown kraft paper, with much wider margins than the cartoon, then another piece of carbon paper, dark side down. Then place your cartoon on the very top. Having done all this, tack all four corners down on the board or table firmly, with no air

CARBON —
BROWN PAPER —
CARBON —
PATTERN PAPER →

Fig. 12-6. The layout.

Fig. 12-7. Production of a stained glass panel. This is the original sketch for a commissioned window for the Eisenstein family. Their initial was to appear in the center of the window. The lines were first drawn in charcoal and reworked until the artist was satisfied. The lines were then inked in and the design transferred to . . .

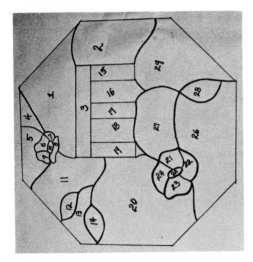

Fig. 12-8. . . . a larger piece of paper where only the drawing in its final stage would show. Since this panel was to fit a window in the home, strict attention to the given measurements was necessary. Notice every piece has been numbered.

spaces between them. Now, trace firmly with a pencil right down the lines of the cartoon so that it comes through to the underlying white pattern paper. If you have inked in your cartoon with a magic marker, trace down the middle of the wide lines. Next, number each piece that represents a piece of glass. If you have already numbered them on your cartoon, simply go over the numbers with a heavy pressure so that they will appear through to the underlying pattern paper. Take out two of the tacks and lift the papers at one end to see if all the lines and all the numbers have come through. If you remove all your tacks beforehand, you will have a very difficult time getting everything back together again in case you discover there are lines missing or illegible. If all is in order on the pattern paper and everything has come through, then all the tacks may be removed and you may start making your patterns.

Remember, in order to cut your glass accurately, you must use patterns. There is no such thing as freehand work in stained glass windows or panels. As we have previously stated, you must also allow for the heart of the lead came when cutting out your patterns (see Chapter 7). Whether you use pattern scissors or pattern knife or the freehand method, be sure that you have left as equal an amount of space as possible between all your pieces of pattern. If you intend to use very wide leads, either around the panel or through it, you must be certain that you leave an additional $\frac{1}{16}$-inch space between these pieces of pattern.

When you have your patterns cut, check them against the original cartoon. Each pattern should fit within its predetermined space on the cartoon, so that you can easily see the inked line around it. If you do not see this line, either in part or in toto, you must recut your pattern so that the line does show. If you think your pattern is accurate and yet a portion of the cartoon line does not show, go back and check your original design. The pattern must fit exactly. If you skip this step, you will find when you cut your glass that the piece will be oversized in this one area, which will cause it to butt too strongly against its neighbor, and if you simply disregard that, you will find that your total measurement will be off, because each piece will push against the other right over the border of the panel.

4. Cutting the Glass

We have gone over this in previous chapters and wish only to re-emphasize here that you must (1) hold the glass cutter properly, (2) work on a flat and steady surface—either a number of thicknesses of newspaper on a firm table, or a small piece of carpet will provide the proper give beneath your cutting edge, (3) remember not to tilt the cutter to the left or the right, but always hold the handle as close to vertical as you can (the handle of the cutter should not be resting against the web of your hand), and (4) always cut standing up and remember the pressure you put on the glass should be pressure from the weight of your body and not from the muscle of your arm.

You must try to cut your glass so that it matches the pattern exactly. If the glass breaks improperly and leaves a space where the pattern insists there is no space, you will have to recut the glass. It is difficult to get beginners to realize that while they may cut five, six, or seven facets on one piece of glass as accurately as possible, and then cut the eighth so that it looks nothing like the pattern, they will have to re-do the entire piece of glass. This is the sad truth, however. There is no room for partial perfection in this craft.

5. *Fitting the Glass*

Once you have all your glass pieces cut, they should be re-sized once again against the individual patterns. This is a procedure which is too often overlooked. You will be surprised to find how much off measurement a piece of glass can be once you re-size it, even though it looked pretty good when you cut it initially. It is easier to be somewhat more objective about a cut piece after you've let it sit for a while and then come back to it. If the pieces are to be critically close (as with copper foil), it is necessary to sand off all pinhead edges and small chips with abrasive paper. Keep in mind that all excess pains taken at this point will achieve far better end results and will make your entire job easier as you progress. So grozze the pieces as best you can, and if the fit is not good enough, sand them.

Once you have the pieces of glass where you think they are about as good as you can get them, place them all back on the work drawing and see how they fit. If you have large spaces between them where small leads are going, you may either have to revise your leading design or re-cut the pieces. The mistake was probably in cutting the initial pattern. No matter how well the pieces of pattern may have seemed to fit, the glass pieces are thicker than the paper and errors can creep in here as well. You may have edges of glass which are slanted toward one another. This, of course, will cut down on the space between them

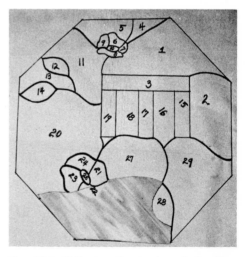

Fig. 12-9. Following the tracing of the lines from the work drawing onto pattern paper, the glass pieces cut from that pattern are re-checked on the work drawing. Here the first piece is being placed in position. It is also being checked for size against one of the borders.

Fig. 12-10. All the background pieces have now been fitted against the work drawing.

for the leading. In addition, you may have chipped edges of glass or even small indentations in the glass pieces, which may seem unimportant when looking at each individual piece, but which can become quite cavernous when they are put together. This is especially true if the fault matches across the two pieces so that the lead between them cannot cover both flaws. If you do not size your pieces back onto the work drawing but go ahead and directly lead up, you will come to these portions of the work and be faced with a difficult situation. In order to rectify it, you may either have to cut both pieces over again, or you might even have to take apart the entire panel at that point in order to re-work the design. It is much less frustrating to find out if your glass is going to fit before you do any leading at all.

6. Leading the Panel

If all your glass matches perfectly and all the spaces between them seem quite adequate for the lead and if the thicknesses of glass are not such that the lead you have planned for them will be too narrow, then remove all pieces of glass from the work drawing and place them within easy reach. You are now ready for the "leading-up" operation.

If your lead cames are bent, they may be straightened out by placing one end in a vise or lead stretcher and pulling slowly at the other end with a pair of pliers. This will stretch the lead slightly and make it straight again. All unstretched lead, even if it is straight, should be stretched. (See Chapter 2.)

Open up your lead cames with the lathkin to allow the glass to fit into the groove as easily as possible. Learn to use a lathkin often and always use it before employing any strip of lead came.

Cutting lead came is a procedure which is too often taken for granted. There are ways of cutting came which can absolutely butcher your work, or even yourself. We have seen individuals go to extreme lengths to cut their glass as perfectly as possible, sand it so that all edges are smooth, replace it on the cartoon and make certain that the lines for the cames are exact, and then go ahead and chop up the cames to an extent where the final product is a complete and utter exercise in futility.

There are a number of ways in which almost anyone can end up making a mess of the leading procedure. The major method is not to use a lead knife. A popular instrument for cutting came is a razor blade. One of the problems with this tool is the ease with which a corner of it can fly off when used on a fairly heavy came and get a fellow student in the

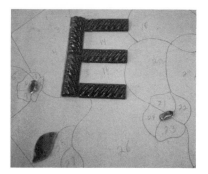

Fig. 12-11. The foreground pieces are selected and checked against the work drawing. It was decided to use five old jewels for the initial and small glass globs as the centers of the flowers. The leaves would be of the same general type opalescent glass as the blue background but, of course, of a green color. The flower centers would be foiled into place.

Fig. 12-12. Checking the border leads for size and placement against the given border of the panel. H leads were used here to allow for trim, if necessary, when the window is fitted.

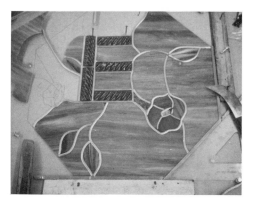

Fig. 12-13. "Leading up" the window. Because of the panel's octagonal shape, side braces had to be employed which would interlock as securely as possible along the outside angles. Note the plastic triangle employed as a brace. Leading nails maintain pressure above the initial, holding the panel together while additional leads are cut and measured. The panel is being put together from the lower right hand corner fanning outward.

Fig. 12-14. The panel is completely leaded except for the upper border leads. A few of the inner joints are being tacked with solder, and the brushing and fluxing of these areas are now being accomplished.

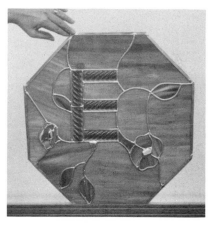

Fig. 12-15. The finished panel. The flower on the left is 3-dimensional.

Fig. 12-16. Close up of that 3-dimensional flower. The space behind it is, of course, filled in with clear glass.

eye. There is a possibility you may get cornered yourself by it, or, more likely, the thin blade may twist and suddenly break against the lead, mitering your fingers. This same inefficient activity holds true for X-Acto knives, wood carving tools, cheese slicers, hacksaw blades, stilettos, utility knives, and bayonets. Of all of these, and we have seen a great many of them employed in cutting leads, a utility knife at least offers the best possibilities. It still hasn't the curved blade of the leading knife which is so wondrously adept at nudging the cames into place, but at least it functions. That's more than can be said for most of the other items.

If you do have a leading knife, you should use it correctly. Don't pretend it's a machete and come down with it on the came with short, chopping motions which generally hack the lead up pretty well, but never cut it. The correct procedure is given in Chapter 4. The lead came is cut best by placing the leading knife on top of the came and rocking it against the surface with a side-to-side motion which only needs a minimum downward pressure to cut through the came. The came should be marked with a slight notch where it is to fit and how it is to be mitred. Measure it directly over the space it is to fill in the panel; then remove it to the table and cut accordingly.

Leading-up is begun by taking your finished work drawing of brown paper and laying it out flat on your board or table (Fig. 12-17). Acquire two wooden strips about two inches wide and somewhat longer than your work drawing. Nail them at right angles to each other along the lower right corner of the work drawing so that you can just see the outside line of the border. You must have enough margin on your work drawing to allow it to show outside the wood. Now take a piece of 3⁄16 inch "U" lead, cut it to size so that it is slightly longer than the work drawing, and place it along one edge of the wood strip on the inside, facing the work drawing. Put a leading nail through the excess end to hold it in place. Take another strip of this same lead, slightly longer in the other dimension than the work drawing, and fit it at a right angle to the first along the other strip of wood. Place a nail through the end. The corners where these two pieces of lead meet may be mitred to fit at an angle, or one may fit inside the other, or you may cut the top away from one of the lead cames and the bottom away from the other so the two interlock in the corner. This is perhaps the method giving the most strength (Fig. 12-18).

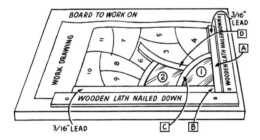

Fig. 12-17. The leading procedure.

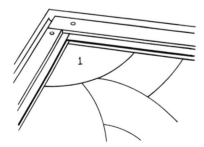

Fig. 12-18. Interlocking the corner leads. They are flush against the bordering strips of wood.

Now pick up your first piece of glass, the righthand corner piece, and place it into the groove of the leads at their corner juncture and along the sides. Tap it gently with the leaded end of your leading knife to be certain that it is seated properly within the channel (Fig. 12-19). The line on the work drawing should be visible around the edge of the glass. If it is not, it means that either the glass is not seated in the lead groove correctly, or that there is an inadequate cut somewhere on the glass surfaces. The reason for the ill-fitting of this piece of glass should be found out at once and not shrugged off with hopes of making up the difference in the next piece.

Each piece of lead came will be measured, marked, and cut exactly to fit into its proper space as we go along. Each must be not quite as long as its glass piece. Cutting it slightly shorter allows the next lead came room to seat. As you work on, you will see what is meant. If your leads are too long, they will interfere one with the other. If they are too short, you will have a gap between them to bridge with solder. Enough of these will make your entire panel look distressed. Be sure you understand the leading procedure before going on with it. It is a matter of placing each piece of lead came, properly cut to size and mitred, with the edges of the glass surface or surfaces inside the channel.

We will describe the method now in detail. Look at the cartoon we have included (Fig. 12-5) and follow along. You have put in place leads A and B and glass piece #1. Next comes the first inside piece of lead (Fig. 12-20). You will be using ¼-inch "H" shaped lead for this. Carefully bend the lead to shape against the glass edge, and cut it off at the proper angle at one end. Measure it again along the glass and cut it off at the other end. You should make the cuts on both sides correspond with the straight leads that are running up each side. In other words, the leads should be mitred so as to fit as snugly as possible against the opposing surfaces. If they are not so mitred, you will have a gap in the leads which will have to be filled with solder. This is a difficult process at best, especially for beginners, and one which indicates poor technique on the part of the worker. Place the lead, now cut and mitred, around the exposed edge of glass and fit it into place as is shown in the figure. Next, #2 piece of glass is put into the lead groove. If you can see the lines around it in the work drawing, then it is in the right place. If you do not see the lines around it, again check your piece of glass to make sure it is not an ill-cut piece standing away from

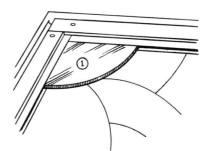

Fig. 12-19. The first piece of glass fitted into the corner leads. A few taps should seat it properly.

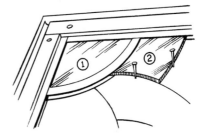

Fig. 12-20. The first inside piece of lead cut and placed and the second piece of glass placed and held with leading nails.

seating within the lead. Usually, the most difficult point of entry to the came is at either end where the lead has been cut. Slight bending down of the end of the channels here will narrow the width of the came and prevent the glass from properly seating itself. It's a good idea when cutting any came to get into the habit of taking your lead knife and automatically going to each end of the came and smoothing back the pointed end of the cut channel. This will allow the glass to seat without any difficulty whatsoever. It is easier to do this after you cut the lead with the pieces in your hand, than to do it with a lathkin when the piece is already seated against another piece of glass on the table.

Once your glass is seated, place two nails as shown to hold it in place. Remember when a glass piece has more than one exposed edge, it should always be nailed in place with leading nails. Do not use other nails if you can help it, or you are liable to experience a lot of glass breakage and a lot of sore fingers pulling them back up out of the board. The special leading nails are tapered so as not to press too strongly against the glass, yet so they may be removed easily from the wood surface into which they are tapped with the end of the leading knife. If you are going to use regular nails, bright steel common nails are probably the best. Do not use finishing nails, and especially *do not* use carpet tacks, which need only be looked at to have their points start bending up. If you use a carpet tack in this condition, its bent point will press against the glass and probably crack it.

Next measure and cut lead "D" as shown, remembering to cut the one end short at the proper angle at point "E." Notice that this lead goes past the piece of glass just placed, that is, piece #2. It may do this because it is continuing the line of the design directly to the line of piece #7. You could, of course, cut the lead between pieces #3 and #6, and simply put a new lead in, but that would give you three separate pieces of lead and more labor than if you used the single lead to sweep by this particular joint directly to piece #7.

Glass #3 goes into the groove next, again with a nail at each end to hold it in place tightly against glass piece #2. You would next fit and form the piece of lead going between pieces #3 and #4, and then place piece #4, tapping it into place from above with the handle of your leading knife, being certain that all other pieces are secured with leading nails, else they will fly apart. It is now just a matter of building up the rest of the pieces in their

proper places and cutting the leads to fit as you go
along. Remember that the pieces must be placed
consecutively and in a manner which allows maximum pressure, one against the other, to hold them
in place. Obviously, you would not place piece #6
or piece #8 before placing piece #3 and piece
#4. As you continue to fit your pieces of glass in
position, remove the leading nails one at a time
(Fig. 12-21). To insure that the lead cames fit under
the glass already positioned, it will help to slightly
lift the leads already in place with the point of
your leading knife. This will raise the glass. You
may prefer to just slide the knife blade under the
glass itself to raise it from the table. Remember to
use the lathkin often to insure that the cames are
open to receive the glass.

When all the pieces are in place, check your
border lines to make sure that they show. If they
do not, something is wrong somewhere. Possibly
the glass pieces are not seated firmly. Pieces should
all be tapped into place with the weighted end of
the leading knife to make sure they are fitted
securely. Do not get carried away with this, however, and tap them too hard, or you will start
chipping the edges, or worse still, break the piece of
glass entirely. Once you are satisfied that all your
glass is seated properly and that the borders are
even, take two pieces of wood similar to the two
you have already used and fit them securely against
the other two sides first applying U leads and cutting all U leads to size. Tap these boards firmly into
position so that they are at 90 degree angles with
the two that were already in place. Then make sure
that the outside borders of the panels are flush
against the pieces of wood. If they are not, then
push the U leads slightly against them with the
leading knife, so that they do line up exactly.
There may be a slight space thus left between the
channel of U lead and the piece of glass seated
within it, but it is better to have an even border
with a few pieces of glass not seated all the way to
the edge, than to have glass seated well but the
border uneven.

When the boards are securely fastened so that
all four sides of the panel are secure, you are ready
for the soldering procedure (Fig. 12-22). Before
soldering, if the panel is to fit into a predetermined
space, recheck all measurements to make certain
that you have not exceeded them. If you have, you
must trim down to the requisite dimensions. If you
have made your window or panel too small for
these dimensions, then you must build up where

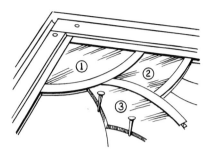

Fig. 12-21. The pieces of glass and lead
fit together like the pieces of a picture
puzzle.

Fig. 12-22. Prior to soldering the leads should
be tight fitting and the panel bordered by a
wood frame held in place with leading nails.

necessary. If you have followed the lines of your work drawing and if your work drawing was correctly measured to begin with, you should have absolutely no trouble with final dimensions.

7. *Soldering the Joints*

Check all your lead joints; make sure they are neat and fit well together. A loose joint or one with a large space will be difficult to solder. It may be necessary to clean the joints with a fine wire brush such as a suede brush or with steel wool. Remember that lead that is not clean will not solder. If you are not using an iron-clad tip, be certain that your copper tip is well tinned or it will not work properly.

Remember to flux each joint well with the stiff flux brush. Then lay about ⅛ inch of solder directly to the joint and apply the iron to it. It will immediately melt and form a puddle at the joint. You don't have to cut the solder into pieces. Just hold a roll of it in your hand, with the end resting on the joint, and melt it directly as it sits. Don't hold the iron to the joint any longer than is necessary or you may, of course, melt right through the lead to the underlying glass. Don't lift the iron too quickly, either, or the solder will drag after it, and you will have a messy looking joint. As you progress in the craft, you will learn exactly how much pressure to put on the soldering iron to get the solder to puddle and spread exactly evenly over the area. Solder all joints and check the panel over very carefully for flaws or missed joints before removing your pieces of wood. Then, turn the panel over and do the same to all the joints on the other side. Both sides must be soldered securely.

8. *Puttying*

Once you have soldered all the joints on both sides of your panel, you must putty it. Either black or white putty may be used, depending on whether you want a black or a white line showing beneath the lead came. Puttying is done by hand. It is best done by taking a small amount of putty from the can and softening it by rolling it between the hands. Then push pieces of it beneath the lead came between the lead and the glass. All the caming must be so treated. Don't worry how sloppy this looks. The main thing is to get it done.

It will help your hands if you get a pair of thin gloves (not rubber) to protect your fingers while puttying, as the lead came against bare flesh can be somewhat bruising. Push the putty well under the caming with your thumb and pull it under from the other side of the caming with three fingers. The entire panel must be puttied. Don't be afraid of overusing the putty, just slap it into place as rapidly as possible. This is one of the less enjoyable techniques involved in the craft, but an essential one.

Once the puttying is completed on one side, do not turn the panel over. Take a bent putty knife or even your lead knife and now turn down all the lead directly against the surfaces of the glass. You will find more putty will squeeze out from underneath the lead as you do this. When you have all the lead turned down, then take a sharp nail or ice pick and run the point around the edges of the lead caming. This will effectively free the putty from the lead and you may gather it up into a small ball as you go. Don't be afraid of scratching the glass. Of course, do not press so hard with the putty knife that you crack a piece of glass. The activity of turning the lead cames down is sometimes carried to excess by over-enthusiastic students and it is at this point that a piece of glass may crack, especially if you have a thick piece and a thin piece and use the same amount of force to push against the thin piece as you do with the thick one. If a piece of glass is cracked at this point, it must of course be replaced and this can lead to a lot of extra labor. So be careful. Once you have the putty all cleaned off the panel and the lead turned down, it is time for the final step, cleaning the panel.

9. *The Cleaning Process*

Take cleaning and polishing compound and sprinkle it dry over the surface of the panel. Then take a piece of steel wool, dip it in some of this powder and go over all the leads until they are bright and shiny. This removes all gummy oxides from the soldering process and exposes the leads equally to the air so they can all darken at the same time. Once the leads are done, take a floor scrubbing brush and apply a goodly amount of force to cleaning the glass itself. Don't be afraid to overuse the cleaning and polishing powder. It is advised, however, that you close all the doors as the powder does tend to fly about the room. Scrub the glass with the scrubbing brush or with the steel wool and then tip your panel up on end and tap it against the table top. This will knock off most of the remaining powder. The rest can be wiped off with a clean rag. If you find one or two pieces of glass still cloudy, go over them again with the powder. The panel should then be turned on its other side, laying it on a clean area of the table or a clean piece of paper. That area should then be puttied and cleaned. Once both sides are cleaned, hold your panel up to the light, look for any further smudgy surfaces and if there are any, treat them with the cleaning and polishing powder as before. An additional touch can be added by the use of a liquid cleaner such as Windex, which will remove ordinary dirt and grime from the surfaces, but which will not touch the soldering residues.

Now that your panel is finished, you may want to hang it in a window to brighten up a corner of the room. To do so, take two loops of moderately heavy copper wire and tin the loops with solder. Then solder one to each corner of your panel and string fish line through these loops. The fish line is colorless and will not be seen from any distance. It is also quite strong and will support your stained glass panel very nicely. Fishing line comes in different tensile strengths, and if you end up with an exceptionally heavy piece of work, you may want to check the amount of weight the line can bear before using it.

Your first stained glass panel is now finished.

B. ADVANCED PROCEDURE

As you continue your work in the stained glass field, word will get around and friends and relatives will doubtless begin to ask you to make things for them: "Just a little something out of stained glass." Many beginners, flattered by such requests, give these "little somethings" away as fast as they can turn them out. We feel this is essentially a mistake. Not that we are against giving gifts where the occasion is suitable and proper; but continually and indiscriminately to give away the products of your time and labor makes them worth exactly their purchase price—nothing. People do not tend to treasure what they do not pay for, and since they have no idea what the materials are costing you nor how much work is involved, they may regard your products as casual creations easily accomplished. Most individuals who come to our studio to buy supplies and who began by giving their finished products away now put at least a minimum price on them, if only to cover the cost of materials. It invests their objects with a psychologic, if not monetary value, that increases admiration and respect. To add to the amount charged a quotient for time and artistry is to begin to have people take what you are doing seriously enough to request pieces made to order. From this, it may be only a small step to a commission for a window.

While a stained glass window uses the same general techniques as we have just discussed in making a stained glass panel, the complications do tend to multiply, and before you know it, can appear to be overwhelming unless you are in command of each step. Making such a window is a responsible procedure, and responsibility must be directed primarily toward the dimensions into which it is to fit, the colors to be employed, and the individual who commissions the work.

It is important to remember when making a stained glass window on commission that you owe it to the individual who has put his trust in you to do the best possible job. You may find in many instances that your commissioner does not really know exactly what he wants, stained glass being a new field to him. Be prepared, therefore, to offer honest advice without compromising your artistic opinion in the process. A stained glass window generally comes into being through this interplay between artist and customer.

1. *Guiding the Customer*

As we have said, most people who come to a stained glass craftsman for a window to be done for their home really are not certain exactly what it is they want. They probably have seen a stained glass window in a friend's home and liked it, or they may be intrigued by a stained glass lamp which they already possess. What they are not interested in is a "churchy" window (Fig. 12-23), and their one major fear usually is that's what they'll end up with. Not only do most individuals not have an idea of what they want, but they are often completely unaware of what stained glass windows cost. It would behoove you, therefore, when someone wishes to give you a commission for a window, first to find out how large an area is involved. Determine what the design is to be before quoting a price. Most professional studios charge by the square footage and by the design. The more complex the design, of course, the more labor is involved and the higher the price. Once the client understands this, you might show him various pictures of stained glass windows done either by you (preferably) or others, or sketch out a few quick designs for him so that at least you have something on paper that you both can look at and discuss. He may wish to have lines changed here or there, but without first showing him something he *can* change, no interplay of ideas is possible.

We have found it almost a matter of course that when husband and wife come into our studio to

Fig. 12-23. A decorative window from a church which is not "churchy" at all but quite charming. It is destined for a private home following an extension of its width and length to permit it to fit an existing opening.

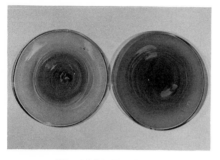

Fig. 12-24. Display of roundels.

Fig. 12-25. A display rack showing some different colors of opalescent glass.

Fig. 12-26. Acetates of windows for a restaurant.

purchase a stained glass window, the husband usually decides upon the design and the woman upon the colors. This is not a rule of thumb, but it happens often enough to almost make it one. Remember when choosing or showing colors, if you are using pastels to demonstrate with, to point out to the customer that the colors are not accurate for stained glass. In the long run it is best to use samples of stained glass to show the prospective clients what their window will look like (Figs. 12-24, 12-25). Be sure you have enough samples of color hues to show them and that you have enough choice of designs so that they might select either one in its entirety, or at least give you an idea of what they would like by pointing out a piece here and a piece there from which you can fabricate a total design for them. Most stained glass windows are chosen as abstract designs, though we have made a goodly number of pictorial windows for more specific instances. These, of course, allow a lot less leeway, being fairly well conceived in the mind of the clients. In some instances they may bring in photographs of animals or scenery they wish incorporated in the window. We recently made two such pictorial windows for a couple who own two horses and wanted them in stained glass exactly as they appeared in the photographs they left with us. Other examples of pictorial windows are "The Pirate" window and the "Garden Scene." These and other examples of abstract windows are seen in the color section of this book. Note here how color and linear quality go hand in hand. Abstracts are something else again, and the client may tend to lean more on the artist's suggestions here.

Once the client has decided on the design, you should get a deposit from him before doing any further work. After all, you now have to draw the design for him to scale and expend a good bit of time and labor for which you should be paid. You should spend no more than a week to two weeks on this, or the client will begin to become impatient and start calling you. Once you have the design drawn up, lay it out and have your clients in to examine it once more. They can then make any final changes they wish before you start cutting the glass. Specify that once glass is cut, no further changes may be made.

Another method of showing clients what their design will look like is to draw up "acetates" of how the finished window will appear (Figs. 12-26, 12-27). This involves painting with a special type of paint on clear plastic a small, exact replica of their window. It is a tedious and time-consuming project, and we do not advise doing it unless working on a very extensive project where a great deal of money is to be involved. The ordinary window for a private home does not necessitate the making of an acetate. Usually these are only produced for church work. If, however, your client insists on seeing a picture of his finished window, and he is willing to pay you for making the acetate, it is not all that difficult to do. Remember that it must be drawn to scale and colored in with the various color paints as best as can match the finished glass result you hope to obtain. Acetates, of course, can be used afterwards to show other clients what windows you have done in the past look like. They are much more impressive than pictures and will show more detail and more work to the client. They will also show him that you are a professional worker in every sense of the word, since acetates, to be effective at all, must be done well.

Color transparencies of your previous windows are also effective in helping sell yourself and your designs to a prospective client. We make it a point to take color transparencies of every window we do and a good many of our lamps and small hanging objects as well. Such transparencies can also be used in lecturing to groups about stained glass and in general educating the public, who are beginning to develop a great thirst for knowledge about this art.

2. *Pricing Your Work*

A constant question that we are asked, both in person and through the mail, by hobbyists and serious students of stained glass who want to begin to work at their craft and be remunerated for their efforts is, "How does one price a piece of stained glass?" The rule of thumb method, as we have stated for a window, is so much per square foot. This square footage is achieved by measuring the length and width and multiplying the two together in inches and then dividing by 144 inches to get the square footage. Most stained glass windows for private homes are usually measured in inches rather than in feet. Prices vary with the individual studio from $15 to $20 per square foot for simple designs such as diamonds, squares, or rectangles in a repeating pattern, to $50 to $60 a square foot for more complicated designs involving a great many more pieces of glass, and naturally, therefore, a great deal more cutting. We do not suggest that the beginner in the stained glass field charge his client according to the amount of time he feels the project will take him. He may find if he does this that he will have to

Fig. 12-27. More acetates—all drawn to scale.

Fig. 12-28. Beginning an acetate—the initial line drawing. This is a design for a transom and two side panels for a front door.

charge so much that he will simply lose the commission. Most individuals, during the first year or so they're working in stained glass, simply cannot work fast enough to justify charging by the hour. You will find as you progress that your time will cut down, but you will still be more realistic to charge according to the design and the size of the window. Many artists in the field charge according to what their ego tells them their artistry is worth. This is a completely subjective approach and you must herein let your conscience be your guide.

Many people have no idea how much labor is involved in even a simple piece of stained glass work. They may therefore be initially surprised at the price of any stained glass object. Yet these individuals are not too taken aback by the cost of oil or water color paintings or a piece of sculpture. It's a matter of education and exposure. The individual who will think $10 is too high for a hanging object in stained glass might not think $1,000 too high for an oil painting, yet a proportionate amount of artistic endeavor and effort may well have gone into both. Pricing is a real "no man's land," and in the long run, only you can tell what your objects are worth. You will soon find out whether they are under- or over-priced by either how busy or how lonely your workshop becomes.

3. The Work in Progress

Once your client has accepted the designs, it's a good idea to get a further down payment from him. You may or may not want to sign a contract. If you do, surely there will be a stipulation clause in it when the window is to be completed. Whether you sign contracts or not, it is always a good idea to finish the window as soon as you can without putting too much strain on yourself. Most people will want their window as soon as possible; if they press you for a date, don't be too specific. Try to establish a good working relationship with your client, one that assures *him* he is getting the best possible work for his money in the most reasonable amount of time, and that allows *you* to feel your creativity is not being suppressed by an inflexible due date and late penalties. If your client wishes to visit the workshop to see how his window is progressing, you may or may not agree, depending on his personality. We rarely have an objection to clients looking in on the work in progress. At the same time, they must be made to realize that any major changes at this point are not possible. However, you really don't have to worry about this; most clients are interested only in the finished product and are only too glad to leave you alone so you can complete the job as quickly as possible.

4. *Turning the Window*

Your 300-piece window is now leaded, soldered, and puttied, and lies on the worktable in all its glory. It now must be turned over so that the other side may be completed. Turning fairly large windows of so many pieces involves problems that don't exist in turning a small stained glass panel. To attempt to raise the window by two corners will simply fracture it right down the middle, as it will not be able to take its own weight without bending at the joints. As in so many other activities in stained glass, it is best to make haste slowly here. First, do not attempt to turn any good-sized window by yourself. Second, get a sturdy piece of plywood under the window between the window and the table, by raising one corner of the window slightly. Gently wriggle the plywood beneath it, while your partner, just as gently, pushes the window from below. Make sure the piece of plywood is somewhat larger than the window itself and thick enough to support the window without bending. Once the window is resting on the plywood, get another board and sandwich the window between them. You may then move the window almost any way you please. Raise the plywood and the window will come up with it. The weight of the window may then be transferred in standing position to the other piece of plywood, the first piece removed, and the window then laid back on the table with its unsoldered side uppermost and the first piece of plywood beneath it. Once this side is soldered and puttied, the window will acquire a greater amount of strength than it had previously. If it is over 3 feet by 3 feet, however, you may decide that the strength is still not sufficient to support it, and the window must then be barred.

5. *Barring the Window*

Below a certain size and with the majority of the pieces of the window being large ones, no barring is necessary. However, with windows consisting of innumerable small pieces of glass and in size above three feet by three feet, bars should be installed approximately every two feet. We no longer use the old steel bars wound with copper wire at the soldering areas. In barring windows we now use galvanized steel straps. Such straps have been coated with zinc, so that they are themselves solderable.

When you are making a window that you realize

will have to be barred, you should attempt to work the barring into the design wherever possible. Remember that these bars will run straight across the window, side to side, and may appear to show as an interference in the design. Oddly enough, the eye really does not see the bars after a while. The human eye is used to seeing things as a complete picture and not as individual bits and pieces. Therefore, although the bars may look rather interfering at first, the eye soon gets used to them and ignores their appearance. This is not to say that they should be simply thrown slap-dash here and there. Where they can be hidden behind lead lines, they should be. But where they cannot, the bar should not be left out simply for this reason. The window must have support where it is necessary, otherwise it will begin to buckle after a time, even in the sturdiest frame.

When you place your bars across the window, be sure to place them from border lead to border lead, even though molding will be supporting the border leads (Fig. 12-29). The molding can be sliced to allow the bar to fit into position. To bar a window simply across the mid-section and not carry the bars to the border leads is to lose at least 40 per cent of the strength of the barring. Cut your bars carefully, therefore, and solder them to each joint they pass over, making sure you press them as close to the joint as possible so as not to have a great gap of solder showing. Place the bars so that the flat side is vertical to the window. They will thus show less and yet exhibit more support. You will be astonished once they are in place how much firmer your window is.

Fig. 12-29. Barring a window. The zinc-coated rod runs the width of the window.

Whether you place the bars on the inside or the outside of the window is pretty much up to you. We prefer to place our bars on the outside of the window, as they show less. Inside or outside, be assured they will melt into the design—an invisible, but necessary, factor holding it together, like the putty and the solder. Enduringly visible is the artistic endeavor. This alone truly holds the window together or lets it fall apart.

6. *Installation*

It is entirely up to you whether you wish to install your commissioned stained glass window or not. This should be decided upon at the initial talks with the client. We generally do not install the windows we make. First of all, the process is time consuming and takes us away from the studio which is where we really want to be. Second, there is nothing really creative about installing a window. It's simply plain hard work. Third, the risks that you take involve possible cracking of pieces of glass which you are then responsible to replace at no extra charge. Very often, these cannot be replaced on the scene and the entire window must be removed back to the studio for the repair, which can take anywhere from one day to a week depending on which pieces have been fractured. Fourth, there is the matter of transporting the window to the site. Many windows won't fit even into the largest station wagon and a special truck must be hired for the occasion. And, fifth, many windows go in second or third floors and there is the problem of height to be considered if you happen to have a giddy head.

True, since it is your window, you may well want to see it through to its final phase and not trust the installation to a carpenter or glazier who may not know exactly how to handle *your* window. There is also the additional money to be made from the installation which can be considerable if the installation is a difficult one and if you have arranged to be paid by the hour. If, of course, you have arranged to be paid a flat fee for the installation (always a dangerous procedure) then you can lose quite a bit of money as well as time in setting the window. Many clients do prefer the artist-technician to be on the scene when the window is installed. They perhaps feel psychologically that it rounds out his interest in the matter—since he made the window he is the best one qualified to see it to its final resting place.

We advise the craftsman to consider strongly before agreeing to install any window. Very often the measurements given turn out to be inaccurate and you are then, rather unfairly, expected to fix them at the site. This involves anything from a little scraping of the frame to a general overhauling. Remember to try to allow for just this sort of contingency by using on the border of the window an H rather than a U lead. This additional channel may be just the amount of excess that can be shaved away and allow the window to fit properly.

There are, however, enough glaziers and carpenters around who certainly can set the window for you if you so desire. In many instances, when we are working on a new home or a home that is being renovated, the carpenter is more than likely on the premises when the window arrives and is quite able to put it into position.

The method we pursue is to have our clients call at the studio for their completed window which they are responsible for as soon as it leaves our building.

We attempt to crate it or give it enough wooden support so that it is mobile and will suffer no damage in transportation. This leaves us free to continue in the studio and create other windows rather than spend hours doing a job a carpenter might do more efficiently.

There are individuals who specialize in the installation of stained glass windows and if you are lucky enough to find them in your area, let them put the window in. They are experts in their field and they will end up pleasing both you and the owners of the window.

THE WORKING AREA

Any stained glass window reflects the studio from which it comes. It, therefore, behooves you to turn out more professional looking work by maintaining a neat and efficient studio with as many aids as possible. Studio "fixings" are not expensive; in fact you can make most of them yourself.

The Work Table

The work table can be made by laying a ¾-inch thick, four-by-eight-foot sheet of plywood on top of two saw horses and level it about thirty-six inches from the floor. This is about the right height for working while standing and will not necessitate your going on tip-toe or crouching over so that you get a backache. Such a wooden table top last for years, and when you do finally have enough nicks and chips out of it so it no longer forms a uniform surface, you can either flip it over to the other side, if it is finished on both sides, or just scrap it and get another. You will have more than gotten your money out of it by this time.

Instead of saw horses, you can make a frame out of two-by-fours. This will enable you to put shelves underneath your table for storage purposes. Be sure that your table is not wobbly; you will be doing a lot a nailing into it and using a lot of pressure against it both pulling and pushing to fit pieces of glass into the came. The more your table wobbles, the more compensating you will have to do. You can, if you wish, have a table smaller than four by eight, depending on the amount of space you have available. But, if you possibly can work it in, this size table will give you a joyous amount of room to spread out with one, two or even three projects going at once. Make certain that the top of your work table is level. You may place hooks along the sides on which to hang your tools, and as you continue to work in stained glass, you will begin to modify your work table to express your own working personality.

Fig. 12-30. Typical work table. Storage is provided below for boxes of six-foot lengths of came lead and sheets of pattern paper.

It's usually best if, when making the frame for the table, you allow a slight overhang for the table top. This makes for a sturdier working surface. Your table top need not be nailed down unless you have made your frame so wide that the top of the table barely fits it.

There is a constant struggle in most workshops for space. It's astonishing how rapidly space can be eaten up. Your work table, if planned properly, can give you a great many space saving areas which can be used to good advantage.

The Light Table

A good light table is a necessary adjunct to any stained glass workshop. It may be no more than a piece of glass propped on two bricks with a fluorescent bulb underneath it. The purpose of the light table of course, is to allow you to see the colors of glass. While the best way to look at stained glass is by natural light, this is not always practical, and a light table is the next best thing. It is especially useful when choosing colors for a stained glass window which will involve a great many pieces. You want to be certain that your colors will blend, not clash. To simply hold two pieces of glass up to the light is not satisfying enough, when what you really have to see is how five or six of the colors will mesh. Make yourself a good light table—it's not that difficult, and it will be well worth your labor by sharpening your color sense and allowing your final product to show itself in perfectly blended hues and tones.

The larger the light table, the better. This, of course, is limited by the amount of space you have at hand. It is important to leave as much space as possible for such a table. The best light tables are made of two-by-fours supporting a large piece (or several large pieces) of frosted glass. Use fluorescent bulbs at a reasonable distance below them (18 inches is about right for a good spread of light), of daylight quality if you can get them. This will furnish a truer type of light against which to see the glass (Fig. 12-32). Be sure you have enough bulbs to illuminate all the frosted glass that you have placed. Wire the bulbs together and attach a single switch. Don't have individual cords to each bulb which must then be pulled and plugged in a tiresome manner to get the table to light up. The light table should be a permanent feature of the workshop and not a fly-by-night type of affair which is constantly being taken down and re-assembled. Nothing is more wearing than repeating this process over and over as the tendency forms to avoid the whole thing and simply

Fig. 12-31. A light table with a portion of the glass top removed to show the bulbs.

Fig. 12-32. The light table, lit.

Fig. 12-33. Storage of glass in glass bins. Smaller bins sit atop the larger ones.

try to match one piece of glass against another by holding it against the overhead bulb. This will only lead to problems and mismatching of colors.

Glass Bins

The size sheet glass you are going to be working with is the size your initial bins should be made. Remember that stained glass is usable in almost all sizes for various objects and when you are finished cutting up a fairly large piece, you will be left with smaller pieces which still are valuable. It is necessary to allow for smaller bins to hold these different colors. Otherwise, they will scatter over the workshop and you will never be able to find them when you want them. Of course, these diminishing sizes can only be carried so far in bins. In our studio we have various size bins for various size pieces of glass and when the glass pieces eventually get too small to be practically placed within a bin, but yet are still too large to be disposed of, we use plastic shoe boxes, labeled as to the colors kept in them. It's a shame to get rid of glass scraps which you may shortly be looking for to use in small hanging animals or mobiles and, not being able to find them, have to cut up a large sheet to get these smaller pieces out of it. The key to the entire complexity is organization. If your workshop is well organized, you will be able to lay your hand on any color and size of glass as easily as you can find any one of your tools.

Tools

This brings us to the tools themselves and how to store them. There are two methods, either of which is acceptable and functional. One is to place pegboard along one wall of your workshop, or even along one portion of your work table. Then use pegboard hooks and hang your tools on them (Fig. 12-34). It depends on how many tools you have as to how much space you will need. You will find if you continue working in stained glass that your collection of tools will grow quite rapidly. Nothing is more frustrating than needing instantly a particular tool and not being able to find it—having to make do with something else and having your whole project go awry because of it. Usually the offending tool turns up just after the damage has been done. Save yourself a lot of aggravation and keep your tools neatly arrayed in the workshop.

If you do not have the room for pegboard, there are tool racks on rotating stands which are sold in most hardware stores (Fig. 12-35). One or two of

Fig. 12-34. Tools may be hung on pegboard . . .

these placed on your worktable with the tools in them should instantly satisfy any immediate request you might have for a particular working item. Glass cutters should be kept in a jar with steel wool soaked in turpentine at the bottom and they may be placed on a shelf or on the worktable within easy reach.

Whatever you do, keep your worktable clean. Nothing is more detrimental to good work than poor work habits. If your work table is filled with slivers of glass, tools scattered all over and pieces of pattern paper intermixed, you will have a high old time sweeping all of this debris aside just to clear a space for yourself to work. Each tool after it is used should be put back where it came from. Glass and glass splinters especially should be cleared from the working area, as they will interfere with future cutting and probably end up cutting you as well.

Fig. 12-35. . . . or kept in a rotating tool rack.

Lead Bins

Storage of lead can be a problem. If you only have a few pieces of came in six-foot lengths, you may find it feasible to drape them over a padded hook or hanger on the wall. If you are dealing with twenty-five strips or more, this is not a comfortable way to store them. You can build a box to hold your lead, either in three-foot or six-foot lengths, depending on the amount of space you have. Since lead comes in six-foot lengths, storing it as three-foot lengths would mean cutting it in half with the subsequent loss of a certain amount of material. However, space is the tyrant that holds sway over us all, and if this is its demand upon your workshop, you have no choice. If you are fortunate enough to be able to store your lead in six-foot lengths, you may find the best place to do it is directly under your work table on a sturdy shelf. Build a bin out of wood especially for the lead and put compartments in it for whatever different sizes you are using. Then, whenever you need a strip, you have only to stoop to the proper shelf on your work table and pull it forth. Be careful it doesn't tangle with the other leads. While a certain amount of labor may be directed toward building the shelf and the bin, you will find in the long run you'll be a lot happier storing lead this way. You will save a lot of time if everything is neatly arranged and in stained glass as in most other crafts, time is of the essence. The more you can cut your time down, the more objects you can turn out. Your workshop should be physically calculated to this end.

If you are unable to fit your lead bins underneath your worktable you might find a small area of the room where you can just rest them on the floor. In

Fig. 12-36. Window space always makes things look brighter.

this instance you will not need tops to the bins as you can simply lift the cames off the top as you need them.

Outlets

Try, if possible, to run extension cords from your existing outlets to the worktable itself. Many hardware stores carry outlet strips, which can be screwed directly to the work table and which will accept as many as three or four plugs at a time. While you may not need this many plugs in the beginning, you may find that later on they will come in very handy, as you may wish to light a lamp, plug in a soldering iron and perhaps a bench grinder simultaneously. It is awkward to have to keep stooping to baseboard sockets, in any event, and much more efficient to have a socket right where you are working. Be careful when extending the baseboard socket to the worktable that you do not place the extension cord where you will trip over it. Take enough time to run it along the baseboard to the table and perhaps up one of the table legs to the place where the socket strip will be placed. Then you won't have to worry about constantly stumbling over the wires in the middle of the room.

Soldering irons generally do not take so much current that you will find your circuit overloaded. If this should happen, of course, you must then plug in to some other circuit in the house.

Window Space

It's a sad fact but true that many beginning in the stained glass art end working in their basements. To most people this is the only room they have where such work can be done. Of course, one must work somewhere and a basement room is better than no room at all. Still, if possible, try to pick an area of the house that has some window space as you will need available daylight, preferably a north light, in order to fully appreciate any stained glass. While a light table is a fine working tool to get your colors to blend, the only real way to see a finished product is against true daylight.

Fig. 12-37. Kitchen triptych window done by the authors for Dr. and Mrs. Allen Lazar, Teaneck, New Jersey.

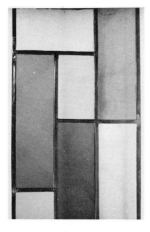

Fig. 12-38. Example of geometric rectangular window. Courtesy: Mr. and Mrs. Richard Fairfield.

CHAPTER 13

Making a Stained Glass Lampshade

The immense popularity of lampshades made of stained glass has led to an increasing amount of scurrying about in attics and basements for artifacts of this nature. Shades of every shape and form, even in poor condition, are selling today for prices no one would have dreamed of many years ago. Then they were being simply thrown away. This popularity has led to interest in producing new shades of this material. Since these items are of necessity hand made, making your own will cut store costs dramatically and will give you, as well, an idea of the basic principles involved in making such shades.

We intend to show in this chapter how a few different type shades are made, using both the lead came and the copper foil methods. You can, if you follow the instructions here given, provide yourself with a choice product and at the same time, have the fun of creating it (Figs. 13-1, 13-2, 13-3).

The multi-paneled lamp is of a pleasant and popular design and may be made in a number of different dimensions by varying the number of panels or making them individually smaller or larger in size. Multi-paneled lamps consist of long panels radiating from a central role and terminating in a skirt of some type. For purposes of illustration, we will use the simplest type of such lamp, which consists of a basic two-piece unit, single panel and single skirt. The craftsman must keep in mind that this design may be varied any number of ways. The panel may be broken up into a design of its own, or the skirt may be broken, or both. This is up to individual

Fig. 13-1. Examples of multi-paneled lamps. Left—the long panel, short skirt model which provides the basic form for almost all variations. To the right is seen one such variation, which may be produced by doing away with the skirt, shortening the panels and putting top and bottom halves together. A lovely hallway lamp.

THE MULTI-PANELED LAMP

Fig. 13-2. Another example of a multi-panel lamp. We see what can be done by breaking up both panel and skirt into a design. Panels are made as a unit and then folded together.

Fig. 13-3. A large paneled kitchen lamp with alternating panel strips. The bigger panels are broken into separate elements. Because of the somewhat squat appearance of this lamp a crown was added to give it more of a finished look.

Fig. 13-4. Hanging lamp, stained glass in combination with wood and metal.

taste and expertise, as familiarity with the medium develops. The basic principles laid down here, however, apply to any type of paneled lamp (Figs. 13-4, 13-5, 13-6, 13-7, 13-8, 13-9).

Supplies

We suggest that you outfit yourself with the following supplies: a large ¾-inch plywood board, approximately 4 feet square, a sharp knife, some leading nails, a good soldering iron, flux and solder, lead came of sizes ¼ inch "H" rounded and $\frac{3}{16}$ inch "U." You should have at least three six-foot lengths of the former and about four six-foot lengths of the latter. You should also have at least 5 square feet of your color choice of stained glass.

Preparing the Pattern

Our basic pattern is given (Fig. 13-10), and this must be directed into dimensions that will suit your own purposes. Our measurements for a lamp 16 inches in diameter, following the basic pattern shown, are as follows:

> *Panel A*—Eight inches tall, with a width at the top of 1⅜ inches and a bottom width of 4 inches.
>
> *Panel B*—(the skirt)—measures the same 4 inches at the top to meet the bottom of panel A, and measures 2¼ inches at its widest diameter from top to center of curved bottom. Panel B measures 1¾ inches at either end, from top to bottom. Twelve of these panels will, when put together, give you a lamp 11 inches high. Larger or smaller lamps must have the measurements changed accordingly. It is best when changing this basic pattern, to cut your panels out in cardboard first to make sure that you will be able to close your circle to the proper dimensions.

Be sure that your pattern is drawn exactly on graph paper before tracing it out on the heavier pattern paper. You will be cutting twelve exact pieces from this pattern, and it is imperative that the material stand up to it. If you are careless with your glass cutter and the pattern starts to fray, your pieces will begin to change shape and you will have problems later on. Better to cut another pattern if you are doubtful.

The panel B, or skirt, must match the bottom of panel A exactly, for the two pieces to fit later on. Even a $\frac{1}{16}$-inch difference here will multiply drastically as the pieces are being cut, and in the end you will have a lamp the top and bottom of which will

Fig. 13-5. Example of a small-pieced lamp shade, table variety, in the Tiffany style.

Fig. 13-6. Panels of a small three-pieced lamp laid out on the worktable to calculate the amount of bending that will be needed.

Fig. 13-7. The panels, now leaded, are being soldered together. Flux is being applied to a joint surface prior to soldering. Note the leading nails holding the panels in place.

Fig. 13-8. Bending the lamp. Each panel is bent a little at a time to take up the strain gradually.

Fig. 13-9. The finished product. Small jewels (navettes) have been leaded to the skirt folds to enhance the line of the lamp.

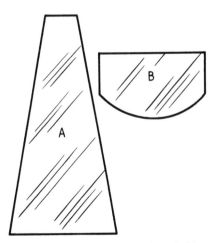

Fig. 13-10. Patterns for panels and skirt.

Fig. 13-11. Use of an L square to cut a long piece of glass to start a lamp. Note the position of the glass cutter. The lines within the glass will be running up and down.

Fig. 13-12. Use of the running pliers to "run" the score line. This is a useful instrument in this type of break.

Fig. 13-13. The pieces fractured with the running pliers. A clean break.

not fit together. So, take warning: cut your pattern correctly at the start and avoid a lot of grief later on. If you desire, you may even make your initial pattern out of a thin piece of sheet metal, but this material also has its drawbacks, as it must be cut *exactly* with tin snips. Be sure you get a thin enough piece if you're going to do this, to allow your glass cutter to ride freely along its rim.

Cutting the Glass

Having obtained a sheet of stained glass the color of your choice, cut from it twelve exact duplicates of panel A, and twelve duplicates of panel B (Fig. 13-10). It is best to cut a long strip from your piece of glass, measuring from top to bottom of the panel, with the lines running the way you want them (Fig. 13-11). Then lay your pattern on this long strip and cut your panels out, one at a time. Cutting on a bias this way, you may find your best tool to break out these score lines is a running pliers (Fig. 13-12, 13-13). You can cut panels very quickly with little wastage by simply laying your pattern first one way and then the other (Fig. 13-14). The edges of your glass should be as smooth as possible, and they will be if you use the running pliers technique. However, if you do have some very slight irregularities, don't worry about them, as they will be covered by the lead. Anything more than very slight irregularity, however, should be sanded away with abrasive paper (Fig. 13-17).

Next, cut your skirts out of the glass in the same fashion, by cutting one long strip and then laying your pattern along it and cutting out the pieces for the skirt (Fig. 13-18). Again, a running pliers will do very nicely to cut the straight edge, and glass pliers will pull away the curved edge with ease (Fig. 13-19). Remember, the pull of the glass pliers is "out" and "down," and use the edge of the table as your guide.

Once you have skirt and panels cut out of the glass to your satisfaction, sand them smooth and lay them aside. Many individuals prefer to alternate colors from one panel to another, or from one piece of skirt to another. We recommend the use of opalescent glass in all lamps. Such glass does not let the bulb show, and allows for an even diffusion of light throughout the surface of the lamp. Antique glass, or any clear glass, does not treat a bulb quite so courteously.

Preparing the Lead

Cut the ¼-inch "H" lead into twelve strips, each measuring 8 inches long, and twelve pieces of "H"

Fig. 13-14. Cutting the panels. Keep reversing your pattern. You may use running pliers for this or . . .

Fig. 13-15. . . . use the glass cutter fulcrum technique, or . . .

Fig. 13-16. . . . break by hand.

Fig. 13-17. Sanding a piece of glass on the wet-belt sander. This is a power driven unit feeding a circular belt. A fine spray of water sprinkles onto the belt from behind to keep the friction heat down. Small pieces of this belt are sold for manual sanding.

Fig. 13-18. Cutting the lamp skirts. As always the pattern is placed on top of the glass.

Fig. 13-19. The glass pliers will pull off the excess glass if used correctly. The pull is out and down.

lead, each measuring 1¼ inches long; the smaller pieces, of course, will be the ribs for the skirt. After you cut your leads, make sure the channels are not crimped at the edges due to the cutting. If they are, take your lead knife and pry them open so that the channel runs completely free along the entire length.

Measuring the Circle

Now lay all of your panels out side by side, not bothering to put any lead came in between them. You are simply trying to find out how much room they will take on the table, so that you will know exactly where to place your first panel as a starting point. You will notice, when laying them out, they form an almost complete circle.

Now take away all the panels, except the first one, which is your starting point. You will know now approximately where you will end up and how much room you will need for the entire circle. To the left of the panel that you have remaining, hammer in two nails. These will serve to support the side of the panel and keep it from moving. To the right of this panel, place one of the strips of your ¼ inch "H" lead. Make sure that it fits the side of the panel exactly, within the slot of the came. Push the lead firmly up against the panel to make sure there is no extra room for motion, and that the lead is indeed seated properly. Your lead came should not cover the entire length of glass, but a small strip of glass should be showing above and below. That is to say, your piece of lead will not be quite as long as the glass.

Now cut approximately 20 inches off one of the ³⁄₁₆ inch "U" leads and fit it over the top of the glass panel, making sure the glass fits into the slot of the "U" lead. Start the "U" lead almost at the end, but leave a little overlap to the left of the panel. Following this procedure, cut another strip of "U" lead of approximately 60 inches and drape it as best you can in a circle, so that none of this long length is hanging over the table. If any of it does hang over, it will be a constant drag on the portion you're working on and it will also tend to tangle and twist. Drape it around in a rough circle and keep it on the table in its entire length. Now fit the end portion of this "U" lead into the bottom straight edge of the first panel on which you're working. This also should fit exactly.

You now have in front of you the basic building block of your lamp. Each strip and each panel will follow successively from this one, and the same exact procedure will be employed (Fig. 13-20).

Fig. 13-20. Lamp panels are put together with lead ribs in between and strips of ³⁄₁₆" U coiling round top and bottom.

Building Your Lamp

Take your second panel and fit its left side into the right open slot of your first long "H" came. Continue the "U" lead on the top and bottom as you did previously, making sure to hold the top and bottom of the first panel as well as the second panel with leading nails. It is imperative that these panels be held securely so that they do not move and throw off your entire effort. Your third panel should be treated exactly as the second, and remember you are going to continue the top and bottom "U" leads concurrently.

By this time, you will see that the glass is starting to bend into the same circle that it took previously, and it is necessary to form the top and bottom "U" leads to fit into this circle. Do so. Make sure they are tightly pressed against the glass and that they are butting against the ribs formed by the "H" lead cames. They do not have to be butting exactly, since a small space between the two leads can be filled later with solder. If the "H" leads are a trifle too long, cut them down to fit. We do not want them to be overlapped by the top and bottom "U" leads, as this will leave an unsightly bulge at these points. Submit all your remaining panels to the same procedure, and when you are done, you will have an incomplete circle composed of twelve panels, ribbed with "H" lead came and circled top and bottom with "U" lead came, all pressed tightly against the glass and all held in place with leading nails.

Note, of course, that your last panel has on its right only an "H" lead, while your first panel has on its left no lead at all (Fig. 13-21). It is essential, during the next step, that you do not allow any solder to flow into the free channel of the "H" lead on the right. If you do, you will have quite a time melting it out or digging it out, and it would probably be better simply to substitute another piece of lead, should solder flow into the channel of this one. You may effectively prevent solder from flowing in, by taking a scrap piece of glass and placing it in the channel and holding it with a leading nail. This will make certain that no solder gets into the empty channel. A small piece of glass on top and bottom will do, since it's only the joints we are concerned with.

Soldering the Panel

Brush flux vigorously against all the joints and then run a small amount of solder over each joint, making certain that each is securely tacked. Be careful you do not burn a lead rib. If you do, you will

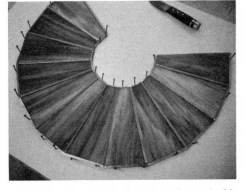

Fig. 13-21. The panels fanned on the worktable prior to soldering.

have to replace it, because it is impossible to repair it with solder and have it look right. If you do have to replace a lead, you must unattach all your leads to that point and remove the offending rib. It is a procedure best gotten over with once it happens. Don't pretend it didn't happen at all and just go on with the work. The further you progress, the more you will have to take apart later on. So, try not to burn the cames at all, but if you do, replace them then and there.

It is also imperative that you remember to solder only the side that is facing you. Do not turn over your panel and solder the other side. Once you have soldered the proper joints, trim the excess lead on the top and the bottom of the lamp and remove all the nails.

Bending Your Lamp into Shape

Care must be taken here, or your work to this point can be made useless in one easy step. With one hand, grasp the middle of the top circle of the lamp and bring it away from the board toward you. You should be standing, therefore, with the open circle facing away from you. Be careful while raising the lamp that the left hand panel, which has no outer lead rib, does not come away from the rest of the lamp. If it does, just push it into position again. It will slide easily into its groove. Very slowly, fold the lamp around away from you, a little at a time, being careful not to crack any of the panels. Try to give each panel a little bit of fold, rather than a whole lot on some and none on others. Each should take the same amount of strain. Should the lamp not fold smoothly, check the inside, that is, the non-soldered side, to see if the lead is crimping and preventing it from folding into shape. Remember, this is a critical stage where confidence, not exuberance, is required. Continue to fold your lamp until the free edge of the left hand panel inserts into the free flange of the "H" lead of the right hand panel (Fig. 13-22). Manipulate first the top and then the bottom into position (Fig. 13-23). Once you get the top in position so that it obviously has seated, solder it. Solder the top together while holding it tightly with one hand and then fit the bottom to meet and solder that. This way, you will only be dealing with one joint at a time instead of trying to fit both at once. If the top fits snugly and smoothly, be assured the bottom will too.

You now have the upper part of your lamp completed. Do not solder the inside, however. Place this much of the lamp on the board or work table

Fig. 13-22. Fitting the open glass edge of one panel into the leaded channel of the other end. They should go into place exactly.

Fig. 13-23. Soldering the bottom of the circle together. Hold the panels firmly with one hand.

and make sure that the bottom of each panel is resting on the table. This will automatically bring your lamp into proper shape. If you have a panel or two that is not resting on the work table, manipulate it gently by pressing around the surface of the lamp. It will automatically assume its position. If it still doesn't, check the inside, as a piece of lead is probably crimping and preventing the panels from moving smoothly into position.

Making the Skirt

Here you must use a piece of wood approximately four feet long and at least two inches wide. This must be fastened securely to the edge of your work table. You may either nail it down, or clamp it down with C-clamps if you don't want to have the additional trouble of prying it off the table later.

Now take one of your $\frac{3}{16}$-inch U leads, stretch it and open it with a lathkin, and lay it against the straight piece of wood with the channel facing away from you so that the flat end of the came lies directly against the wood. Take the first piece of skirt with the flat side toward you and insert it into the U lead, making sure it seats all the way into the channel. This is a deep channel and may fool you, so be sure that the piece of glass is well in place. Hold the left end of this first piece of skirt with a leading nail. Now take one of your twelve pieces of H lead which you have previously cut to a length of $1\frac{1}{4}$ inches and insert the right hand channel of this first piece of glass into a channel of this piece of lead. Follow this procedure with each piece of the skirt, so that when you are done, you will have a straight line of skirt pieces—the first one held at the left edge with a nail, and the last one having a lead rib on its right with an empty channel, also held by a nail or by another piece of glass into the channel (Fig. 13-24).

Next take another strip of $\frac{3}{16}$-inch U lead and starting at the left, press it firmly against the half moon edges of each piece of skirt, making sure it dips down far enough to meet each lead rib between the skirt pieces. This lead is quite malleable and can be pushed into shape with your fingers. You may also use a lathkin to get it into position. Don't be too concerned if there is a slight space between the lead rib and the U lead folding in towards it, as this space can be filled with solder. However, this doesn't mean you can leave a considerable gap here. If such a gap occurs, you probably have cut your lead rib too short and it must be recut. Work one piece of a skirt at a time and make sure that each one is held

Fig. 13-24. The skirt lined up and leaded.

securely with nails before going on with the next piece. When you are done, trim the lead margins on either end and solder all joints, making sure that you solder only those joints that are facing you. Do not solder the side facing the table.

Bending the Skirt

Remove all the nails and the strip of wood from your work table. Stand the skirt line on edge so that the straight edge is uppermost and the curved edge, of course, is resting on the table. Bend the line inward against the unsoldered side so that the free edge of the left side of the skirt inserts into the empty channel of the lead on the right (Fig. 13-25). Solder these two joints, again being careful not to let solder get inside the channel itself. You now have the two parts of this particular lamp completed.

Putting the Lamp Together

Place the top part on top of the skirt, making certain that the panel you are going to start soldering exactly meets the margins of the underlying skirt, because if this is off, all the other panels will be off. Do not worry if all the panels do not seem to meet the underlying skirt immediately. You will only be working on one at a time and if you are accurate on your first one, all the others must be accurate as well. If you are making a shade of alternating colors, you should decide at this time if you want the color of the skirt to match the color of the corresponding panel, or if you want it to match the alternating panel.

The Finishing Touch

Tack all the joints together with solder, working one panel at a time. Once you are satisfied that the skirt panels have met as accurately as possible, solder each joint firmly. Turn your lamp on its side, solder all the other joints and run solder in the area between the skirt and upper panel, both inside and out. For a smooth, finished look, flatten a piece of $\frac{3}{16}$-inch U lead and wrap it entirely around the lamp so that it covers the seam between the top and bottom parts of the lamp. This U lead, or belt, is soldered in place at the joints. Do the same with the inside seam (Fig. 13-27).

Your basic lamp is now completed and it is important that you clean it as soon as possible to prevent the glass from clouding and getting tacky from the flux. Vinegar and water is a good cleansing agent and can be used with a piece of steel wool to clean the entire lamp. We usually also use our cleaning

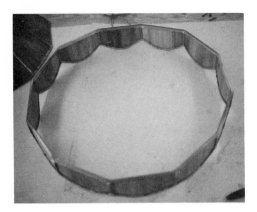

Fig. 13-25. . . . and bent into a circle.

Fig. 13-26. Putting the lamp together. Match up the first skirt and panel as perfectly as possible and the others will match up as well.

Fig. 13-27. The finished product on end showing the lead "belt" that covers the seam between panel and skirt inside and out.

and polishing powder to get off all the excess flux and residues. Follow this with any of the usual glass cleaners, such as Windex. The leads of your lamp will darken slowly with the passage of time, as will the soldered joints, although they will take somewhat longer. If you wish to give all the lead surfaces an aged or "antique" look, they must be "tinned"— that is, solder must be flowed over them and then antiquing patina applied with a stiff brush. This will provide a uniform, coppery finish that will do away with the rather shiny "new" appearance of your lamp.

Another way to make this same lamp is to lay the panels out in the same fashion as the skirt was laid out; that is, in a straight line along the table edge, using a long piece of wood as a guide. When the panels are laid out in this fashion, the strips of lead are placed between them with space between the lead and the top of the panels. The panels are then lifted in toto and wrapped around and folded down at the same time into the channels. It's a more difficult process and can involve a number of broken panels, if you are not careful.

When designing anything for foil, it is wise to keep a very thin margin between the pieces. If your design is going to be very precise, you may even cut the pattern without the use of pattern scissors, as the copper foil takes up very little room. Your glass cutting naturally must be absolutely precise. If it is not, it is best to use pattern scissors and allow for more play.

As a mold for this lamp, you may use a styrofoam ball or a plastic lamp shade, which may be acquired in many hobby shops, or a turned up wooden salad bowl. This makes a very pleasing shape for a lamp. On the surface of your mold, draw in your pattern, which you have previously worked out on a sheet of paper (Fig. 13-28). Most lamps of this nature have a repeating pattern of some sort. It is suggested that for your initial attempt, you do not get too ornate. Simple squares of glass will do to start with—perhaps an occasional diamond thrown in at measured intervals. You may even have a diamond pattern along the bottom of the lamp. We do not suggest that you make a pictorial type "Tiffany" shade at the very outset. When you feel yourself capable of proceeding to this extent, the principles you learn for the more simple lamp wil serve you in good stead.

Cover the entire surface of the mold with your design and make sure that the design is evenly spaced and is dimensionally exact. (If the design is a

THE MOLD METHOD FOR SMALL-PIECED LAMPS (FOIL TECHNIQUE)

Fig. 13-28. Initial sketch for repeating pattern. Small-pieced Tiffany type lamp shade.

Fig. 13-29. Laying out the pattern on the clear plastic mold.

Fig. 13-30. Form cut from glass to conform to basic pattern.

Fig. 13-31. Building up the glass pieces in sections on the mold. Other sections to follow are drawn in place on the mold.

Fig. 13-32. The lamp taking shape. More and more pieces of glass are being added, working around the top of the mold. Once this is complete, pieces will be added in concentric turns until the shade is completed.

simple one, you need not cover the entire surface of the mold with it, but simply one portion, so that you can then multiply this column around the mold.) Once this is done, retrace your pattern back onto pattern paper and cut it out. Then cut your glass to match the pattern. As each piece is cut, place it on the surface of your mold, starting at the top of the mold and holding it in place with either push pins, or in the case of plastic or wood that you don't want to mar, little pieces of plasticine clay (Fig. 13-31). The plasticine will serve to anchor the pieces of glass to the mold while still allowing you to remove them from time to time if you wish to look at them to check the colors. Work around the top of the mold, rather like knitting a cap for a head (Fig. 13-32). Do not work down a column at a time, as you will find your work, as it gets heavier, constantly slipping off the mold.

Once you have covered the top surface of the mold so that your work is beginning to flow downwards toward the base, you may remove this much, check it under the light, and if it is to your satisfaction, solder the pieces together. You may then remove the clay. The next line around the mold should be treated the same way. Thus, you will build up bit by bit along the surfaces of the mold. Remember, your pieces of glass must be small enough to conform to the bend of your mold without having corners sticking up in the air. Don't worry about soldering the pieces together firmly; just tacking them is enough initially. Remember to leave a hole in the top of your lamp for the socket and electrical wiring to come through. We have seen students get so carried away by the creative process that they foiled their lampshade directly over the top of the mold, thus making it more like a knitted cap in actuality, then a shade of stained glass.

Once the work is completed, you may lift it off the mold, solder all the joints together and bead it. It should also be soldered on the inside. You will be surprised how strong such a lamp can be when it is all soldered together.

More decorative effects may be brought into play after you have made a few of these simpler lamps. The effectiveness is all in the designing, which must first be done flat on a piece of paper, and then measured out to conform to the turn of the mold which you are using. If you want to make a swan, for instance, you must measure out the size of swan you want to use against the circumference of the mold at the place you want to use it. This will give you an idea how many swans you can fit into the space available. Half a swan is not better than no swan at all. Graph paper will help immeasurably here. Remember to leave space for the copper foil, which will be holding your pieces together.

We make absolutely certain of our dimensions by cutting our designs out of pattern paper and scotch taping them directly to the form to make sure that they will fit. This need not be done with all the figurations, but only with oddly shaped pieces that will form the crux of the design. A simpler way of doing this is to square off all such odd shaped pieces and take the measurement of this square around the form. The square then may be broken internally into any number of configurations. The possibilities of designing such lamps are endless, and the skill acquired with each will tend to make the next that much easier and vouchsafe courage for further experimenting in this form.

It is best to line the borders of your finished lamp with a piece of caming, such as a ³⁄₁₆-inch U. This gives a finished edge to the lamp. If you don't wish to do this, be sure you give an extra heavy coat of solder to the ends of the copper foil that form the lamp edges. Clean this lamp as before with cleaning and polishing powder and Windex as soon as possible after completing it, to make sure all the flux residues are gotten rid of.

A Few Things to Keep in Mind About Small-Pieced Lamps

(a) Originally these lamps were made by Tiffany from large molds, of either solid rock maple or aluminum. Such molds are difficult to obtain and are very expensive when they can be obtained. It behooves anyone making such lamps for sale to offer shapes which, at least in the beginning, can be obtained easily from materials at hand. As we have mentioned, salad bowls offer some of the most pleasing forms.

(b) Try not to draw directly on your mold, unless you can get the markings off easily. If you want to use your mold for more than one design, and you are using indelible ink to mark a design on the mold, you will shortly find yourself lost among a bewildering mixture of lines. Some individuals make a practice of drawing on their molds and then sanding away the inks. This is an extra and unnecessary procedure and one which simply adds more labor to a task already carrying enough labor of its own.

(c) Whatever you do, don't try to make one of these lamps freehand, that is, without any sort of mold, as in the flat table-top method described for the previous lamp. The copper foil does not bend well, and your small pieces will begin tearing through if you try to apply pressure to them to make some sort of bend to close your circle.

(d) Keep in mind you are initially applying solder to the small pieces, only to tack as few places as possible. Nothing is more frustrating than finding you have a piece that must come out, and having it so firmly secured it takes jack-hammer blows to loosen it from the rest of the design. Such force applied of necessity to get an unwanted piece away from your lamp will probably result in fracture or loosening of other pieces as well. If you only tack here and there, you can easily melt away the small bridgings of solder that hold the pieces together should you want to delete one of them from the overall design.

(e) Test each piece of glass that is going to make the curve of the mold at those areas where the curve is most acute. Don't make the mistake of placing your pattern paper against the mold, assuming the glass will fit simply because the paper does. The paper will bend; the glass will not, and simple as it may seem, many beginners overlook this fact.

(f) If you are using a styrofoam ball as your mold, you will probably only be able to use it once; however, these items are certainly cheap enough. They will not stand up to repeated exposures to the soldering iron. Use push pins to maintain the integrity of the pieces against the positionings in which you place them. If you intend to make a complete ball of stained glass, using a styrofoam ball as a mold, it would be best to make a half at a time, and then solder the two hemispheres together. If you are going to make a three-quarter globe using a styrofoam ball as a mold, then make the entire shade and dig the styrofoam out in pieces from below. This is the only way that you can do this and end up with a true form. The styrofoam is easily broken out with a knife. Such three-quarter globes provide difficulties in soldering inside joints, so be sure that the outside joints are very firmly soldered to sustain the shape and integrity of your lamp.

(g) You need not make an entire lamp out of small pieces. You may combine the small-pieced lamp with the paneled lamp described in the first section of this chapter, using small pieces as the skirt. If you do this, then you would be wise to make a form, either out of cardboard or heavy paper, and tack your small pieces around it, rather than laying them flat and trying to bend them around to form a circle.

(h) Most small-pieced lamps, due to their nature, end up looking very shiny and new because of the amount of tinning required. They are generally antiqued with antiquing patina to make them look old. This should be done as soon as possible after the lamp is finished, and before any great amount of oxidation has started to form on the soldered surfaces. The more oxidation that is formed, the more difficult the antiquing process will be. For quicker action it is best to heat the antiquing solution somewhat, and apply it when warm or hot.

(i) Small-pieced lamps are wired and hung exactly the same as any other type of lamp. They are quite stable and quite strong, and if you have soldered correctly, you should have no trouble with them coming away from themselves in mid-air.

(j) Don't be afraid to use plenty of solder, and make your copper foil edges as thin as possible. Don't worry about solder dripping onto the glass; the solder is not hot enough to crack the glass, and it can be easily scraped away afterwards. When you are beading, as a final step, it is wise to turn your lamp on its side, and not work on it straight up and down. It is difficult to solder in a straight up and down position, as the solder will keep dripping onto the table top. Put your lamp in a position best suited for you to work, and don't be afraid that it will collapse. If the joints are tacked sufficiently, your lamp will maintain its shape, even though it is not held in place any longer by the mold.

(k) Remember that chunks, and small jewels and three-dimensional effects may be worked into these small pieced lamps with telling effect. This is one of the most beautiful of all stained glass techniques and deserves to be done with delicacy and imagination. If you apply both of these to your labors, you will end up with a lamp that will be breathtaking in its final form.

One type of bent panel lamp, shown in Figs. 13-33 to 13-37, is actually made with flat panels, bent only at the joints. The other type contains bent panels, either in their entirety or as a topping to a small pieced skirt. Their fabrication requires the use of a kiln that is fairly deep and that will achieve a heat of at least 1500° F. They involve supplies not directly related to the stained glass art. We shall go into the making of such lamps in some detail:

BENT PANEL LAMPS

Fig. 13-33. Basic pattern for a bent panel lamp of one type. From top to bottom pieces are: crown, upper panel, lower panel, skirt.

Fig. 13-34. The pieces comprising the upper and lower panels are put together and joined as previously described for the skirt-panel lamp.

Fig. 13-35. The skirt is then added, having been put together flat and then bent to shape.

Fig. 13-36. The crown is first put together flat and then given a slight upward tilt.

Fig. 13-37. The completed lamp.

Fig. 13-38. A typical S-shaped bent panel for a lamp.

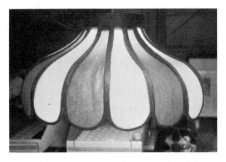

Fig. 13-39. A hanging lamp made of bent panels, each panel individually bent.

Calculating the Circle

The bent panel lamps can take either a single curve or a double, so-called "S" shaped curve (Fig. 13-38). The basic circle is dependent on the widest portion of each individual panel, regardless of the number of bends within it. You must, therefore, plan your circle from this measurement. If there is a certain diameter you wish to achieve, then you must divide it into the number of panels you wish to employ in your lamp. Bent panel lamps have an even number of panels, usually eight or more, of similar or alternating colors (Fig. 13-39). They may be held in place by either decorative brass stripping or white metal or lead came. The hobbyist would be wise to start with lead came, since the other metals are more difficult to work with, and must be factory shaped to specifications. The lead came the hobbyist can shape. In our studio, we work mainly with lead came and apply over it brass filigree, or decorative strips, as may be requested.

Once you have decided on the diameter of the lamp you wish to make, and you have calculated your circle, dividing this diameter among the number of panels, then you may go ahead and design the panel itself. Remember that your design must taper downwards from your widest point from which you have previously taken your circle measurement. Do not make the mistake of calculating your circle on a specific panel measurement, and then design a panel which grows to a wider measurement further along its length than you originally calculated.

Bending the Glass

Transfer your original panel design from graph paper via carbon paper to pattern paper. You may want to make a few different patterns to avoid the possibility of the single repeat pattern fraying due to the excessive cutting. You may, of course, cut a single pattern out of thin sheet metal, as we previously suggested for the multi-panel lamp. Then cut your glass exactly to the pattern, and lay your panels out flat, making sure that your measurements are exact (Fig. 13-40).

Making the Mold

Molds are of two varieties—they can be either drape molds or sagging molds. We generally use drape molds, as we find them basically more effective, but we have used sagging molds as well, especially for the more acute bends. Here the weight of the glass blank is used more effectively. (The glass pieces that you have cut in the flat are called blanks.)

Fig. 13-40. Two bent panels and their flat templates.

Your mold may be formed out of plaster of paris. Smooth it as best you can with a spatula as it is drying. You may make changes in this material fairly easily when it is wet, but once it is set it should be allowed to cure overnight undisturbed. The plaster of paris mold may itself be used in the kiln as a drape mold. We have had little success using plaster of paris as a sagging mold, however. Before using such a mold to bend glass, it must be heated in the kiln to approximately 1200 degrees and then cooled slowly for twenty-four hours. It is then ready for use. If after it has cooled, you find tiny cracks developing through its surface, don't be too concerned. However, if you find great chunks of the mold crumbling away, you must remake it and check the mixture of your plaster of paris more accurately. The mixture should have a rich, thick, creamy consistency and be as free of air pockets and individual chunks of plaster as it is possible to make it. Both air bubbles and such chunks will contribute to ruining the finish of your plaster of paris mold.

The other type of mold is made of terra cotta. This is a rough clay which can be molded into shape. It will harden as it is baked in the kiln and allowed to cure. Whether you are using terra cotta or plaster of paris, you must use a mold release substance coated over the mold so that the glass will not stick to the surface. We use Kay Kinney's mold release, which we have found works very well.

Once you have your molds all ready and your glass cut, you are ready for the final procedure. If you are using a drape mold, place the mold in the kiln with the hump uppermost, and balance your glass on top of it so that when it drapes over the mold it will exactly fall into place. If you are using a sag mold, then place your glass on top with the declavity away from you so that the glass will sag into the mold. With sag molds you must be very careful that no undercuts are present, or you will not be able to get your glass out of the mold. Each mold should be coated well with mold coat, and then the kiln should be gradually heated. Most glass bends somewhere between 1250° to 1300° F., depending on the color and the thickness. We bend all our glass by eye from a top loader kiln. We have found it too awkward to bend panels of glass using front loader kilns. Not all colors of stained glass bend at the same temperature, nor in fact, do all pieces of glass from the same sheet bend at the same temperature exactly. The cone firing method is, therefore, of no use here as each piece must be individually watched. Our molds generally last for five to eight bends before they begin to crumble from the constant use. Occasionally, molds will last for only one or two bends, so it would behoove the glass bender to make his molds as precise and as impurity-free as possible in order to get the most use out of them.

Fitting the Panels

Once you have all the panels bent to your specifications, you are ready to fit them together in the general shape of the lamp. If you are using lead came to hold them together, the best came to use is ¼-inch "U" round, which will follow bent glass more precisely and with less trouble than any of the other lead cames. Using such a lead, you would fit it directly against the edges of the bent panels, following such surfaces carefully and molding the lead against them with your fingers. Solder the ends where the lead meets and do each panel individually so that, when you are done, you will have all your panels rimmed with lead which has been soldered to meet at the top of the panel.

Bent panel lamps must be put together vertically, not horizontally, as it is difficult to form a circle once they have been laid out flat and tacked together. A small block of plasticine clay may be used as a stand to hold the panels upright at the correct angle at which they are to be joined (Fig. 13-41).

The panels must always be of an even number. Most bent panel lamps consist of eight or more panels, all evenly spaced. With the panels standing in the little blocks of clay, it is possible to move them around on the surface of the table and still not have them fall over. Use enough clay to keep them upright, but don't use so much that it gets in the way. Move the panels to the correct angles within their blocks of plasticine so that they meet at their juncture points, and tack them together with solder. You may have to maneuver them around here and there in order to get them to meet exactly. *Be certain* they are all at the same angle or your circle will not close, and if it does, it will appear deformed. With the panels tacked together and resting on the table, you may fill in with solder along the remainder of the lead lines where possible. The panels at the bottom may splay out from one another. Here they must hang free, supported by the juncture lines above. If they are fairly close up to a point before they tend to angle away from one another, you may use brass banding as decorative strips down the center. If your curved panels follow each other closely all the way down, you may extend your brass or copper decorative banding as far as you like. This banding should be soldered to the lead, from within the lamp so that

Fig. 13-41. Beginning to put together a bent panel lamp. The panels are put together vertically and are supported by plasticene. Once you have three of them tacked together they will usually support themselves, and additional panels may be added without the plasticene.

Fig. 13-42. The completed lamp. Filigree has been soldered over the lead borders of the panels and between the panels and the crown to give a more delicate effect. Many different styles may be designed.

no solder shows from the outside. When bending such strips to fit, it is wise to make a small styrofoam mold to use as a guide (Fig. 13-42).

When soldering, hold the band in the front with a protective mitten so that the heat does not burn your fingers, and solder it to the lamp from within. It takes only one or two areas to tack it well to the lamp. You may solder it right through existing areas of solder that are holding the panels together. They will puddle directly against the brass band from the heat of your soldering iron.

THE LANTERN

Compared to the three types of stained glass lampshades that we have been discussing, the lantern is quite simple. That does not mean, however, that it need be simple looking; nor that it must turn out less beautiful than the other lamps we have discussed. Most lanterns consist of four-sided panels, rectangular in shape, ornate or severe in design, with a long bulb within, which effectively lights up all the corners and angles. Each panel may be designed the same, or may be alternatively different (Fig. 13-43).

Start by designing a panel of your choice, remembering not to use too many small pieces, or you will detract from the overall effect. There is just not enough room here to overdo it with a Tiffany type procedure, although foil certainly may be used. The pieces need not be as small as in the Tiffany shade, since there is no angle or bend to climb. An old jewel or two or a few chunks may be used to advantage. The light coming through these faceted glass pieces will give a startlingly beautiful effect. Whether your lantern is a simple four-straight-paneled piece, or a more complex flaring design, or a top-bottom combination which must be fitted together (Fig. 13-44), it should be made as a mock-up in heavy cardboard before any glass is cut. The best cardboard comes from the sides of corrugated boxes.

Fig. 13-43. Lantern composed of four panels broken into a design in abstract. One panel shows the use of an old roundel.

You should treat the mock-up with the same respect and care that you intend to treat the final product in glass, for if the mock-up is incorrect or ungainly looking, your glass product will be the same. The carboard mock-up should show only the shape of each large panel, so that the proper angles between them may be achieved. Once these are cut, they should be taped together and made very sturdy. Keep this form in front of you while working on your lantern. The mock-up should be slightly smaller than your finished product to allow the glass edges to meet.

Once you have the mock-up to your satisfaction, cut your glass panels and place them against the form so they fall into the angles you have worked out. Tack them together with solder. Remove them from the mock-up when they are thus joined, and thoroughly solder them. You will find that by using the mock-up as a guide, there is much less chance of error in forming the angles between the panels. Ninety-degree angles are difficult to get exactly right and if you attempt to form them without the use of a mold, you will be thrown off on the entire lantern.

Don't worry if the 90° angles show with the solder not thoroughly filling in between them. Once you have your lantern well soldered together, take a strip of ³⁄₁₆-inch "U" lead, and flatten it into a belt, as was done with the first lamp we discussed in this chapter. This belt may then be run over the sides of your lantern and tacked top and bottom to form a seam covering.

The lantern is a non-circular type shade and its wiring poses problems which are slightly different from the wiring of the circular shades we have discussed. We will take this up in the next chapter.

Fig. 13-44. A more simplified lantern showing a small top and long skirt. The trick here is to get the angle right between them. Best use a mock-up for this one.

NON-CIRCULAR SHADES

There are types of stained glass shades that are neither square nor circular. We refer specifically to the star-shaped style lamp. This "star lamp" involves rectangles of glass built up along pre-determined panels to form a three-dimensional star effect. Although such a lamp looks complicated, as you take it apart panel by panel and see how it is put together, it devolves into nothing more than multiple rows of glass angled together to form the final shape. The mechanics follow closely the making of the lantern, except in an extended and more ornate form. Professional shops that turn out numbers of the same type of non-circular lamps make their molds out of wood or aluminum, so that they have a more lasting and more exact form than cardboard. Such molds are, of themselves, difficult and time consuming to make—in some instances, more difficult and more time consuming than the lamp itself.

In this category of non-circular shades, one may also include the triangular shaped, almost free-form shade, which itself is made up of small triangles, or variations of this basic geometric form. Again, this is first designed and then produced in a mold before any glass is cut.

Any shape lamp may be thus made out of stained glass—a most obliging material—providing a mold is first made as a guide. Your glass must then follow this guide in order to make the final product as precise and well thought out in appearance as it was in your imagination.

CHAPTER 14

Wiring the Lamp

Before getting on with the actual wiring of the lamp, it is necessary to discuss briefly the parts and pieces of equipment that you will be using to complete this activity. Starting from the top and working our way down, we have:

THE CANOPY

Fig. 14-1. Vase caps of different shapes and sizes.

Fig. 14-2. Two of a kind. A vase cap 9 inches in diameter next to a 2 inch brother. Lamp shades can vary this much in top diameter.

This is a decorative plate which fits directly to the ceiling and through which the electric wiring passes. Its purpose is twofold: to cover the hole in the ceiling made for the electric box, and to give purchase to the chain holding the lampshade. Canopies come in all styles, from very simple brass bowls to ornately carved, highly polished, or antiqued designs in metal. It is wise to pick a canopy that will not detract from your lamp. This doesn't necessarily mean the simpler the canopy the better. An extensively foiled Tiffany type shade should have a canopy of complimentary intrigue, not a bare metal cap. Conversely, don't overawe a lamp of plain geometric design with a baroque ceiling piece.

Canopies come with two types of center holes and with or without small side holes meant for screwing into the underlying electric box. In the latter instance, the center hole runs $\frac{7}{16}$ of an inch, and the two side holes are spaced $4\frac{1}{4}$ inch center to center. Our own preference is for the single large center hole, which is $1\frac{1}{16}$ inches, and which supports the lamp directly to the electric box by means of a decorative hangar unit. Some popular canopy finishes are brushed brass, black, bright brass, polished copper, weathered copper, chrome, and weathered antique brass.

If you are not going to place your lamp into a pre-existing fixture box, swagging it gives decorative and functional placement. A swag is nothing more than a loop of chain attached from one portion of the ceiling to another so as to walk your electrical wiring in a decorative form over to the nearest baseboard socket. Two swags will suffice for most lamps, but three can be accomplished for a large lamp, with equal or diminishing loops of chain. Both the lamp and the loops of chain are held by ceiling hooks, with "molly" screws. If you have any sort of heavy lamp, it would be best to place the ceiling hook directly into a beam. Be sure, when swagging, to run your chain all the way down the wall to the baseboard socket. Nothing looks more unfinished than running out of chain halfway down the wall, and continuing on with a bare wire.

You can either make up your own swag kit by purchasing the items separately, or if you aren't sure exactly what you'll need, you can purchase such a kit ready made with the correct amount of chain.

SWAG KITS

Fig. 14-3. Lamp hooks of different styles. Each is held to the underlying socket by a brass nipple.

DIE CAST LOOPS

This loop connects the chain to the lamp and also serves to hold together the two vase caps which stabilize the lamp. The wiring passes through its center hole. Loops are somewhat varied, and, like canopies, should match the lamp in style.

CHAIN

Chain is sold in three-foot lengths, and at least in the case of decorative chain, has each loop notched so that it may be readily opened with a pair of chain pliers. Anyone who has struggled to open decorative chain by gripping the loop on either side and pulling like mad with regular pliers will appreciate the ease of working with an instrument especially made for this purpose.

Chain is relatively cheap, and the use of the proper chain with your lamp will provide it with just that extra touch of appropriate decor. When passing the electric wire through the chain, it is not necessary to weave it through every loop. Every other one or every third one will do nicely, will give the same effect, and will require far less effort on your part.

Fig. 14-4. Chain pliers opening a link of chain.

CHAIN PLIERS

This specialized tool is calculated to open and close the links of decorative chain with ease. While the individual making only an occasional lamp may find that he can do without it, for anyone producing a number of stained glass lampshades which must be wired and set to be hung, it is a necessity.

SOCKETS

There are a number of kinds of sockets, some of which work for our purposes better than others. We find it best to use sockets with a set screw in the neck and which are keyless. We like the set screw, as it allows a definitive measurement to be made along the length of the nipple, and holds it firmly in place. Do not get a socket with either a chain or a push-pull switch; they are awkward to use, do not look well in the lamp, and will simply be in the way. Besides, you are going to be using a switch on the wall, or in the case of a swag lamp, on the cord. We do not use porcelain sockets, simply as a matter of choice. They are heavy, and we feel they add nothing to the fixture. Either a brass (brass or nickel coated), or bakelite socket is what we recommend. The bakelite has an advantage, in that it is a shorter socket than the brass, though it is a little more difficult to wire. Be sure to get one with a standard base. Such a base is held by a small screw in the socket, and it is best to take this off before you begin to wire the socket. The keyless brass socket also has a standard base, which is held in place by pressure locking to the cap. This, also, must come off before the wiring is done.

VASE CAPS

These are molded discs of brass, which rise tent-like from a flat plane to a shallow center peak where the nipple hole is located. One is placed inside the neck of the lamp and another ouside. When the two are then compressed by the outside lamp ring and the inside socket with a nipple acting as a lever between them, they neatly sandwich the neck of the glass and grip it securely all around. Such caps, of course, can only be used with lamps with round necks. They change size approximately every $\frac{1}{8}$" so it is better to first make your lamp and then fit your vase caps to the existing hole, rather than having a specifically determined center hole and trying to force your measurements to conform to it.

Fig. 14-5. A vase cap gives a finishing touch to the top of a lamp.

While vase caps come in unfinished brass, lacquered brass, and high polished brass, it is difficult to get them in any other color. The brass coloring may be changed chemically to an antique copper or a pewter, or you may paint the caps. If you do intend to paint your vase caps, be sure you are not applying the coat to a lacquered cap without first removing the lacquer with alcohol or acetone. For painting purposes it is always easier and cheaper to use an unfinished than a finished vase cap. Use a good grade of paint to avoid chipping later on.

There are those who argue that it is something of a waste to use two vase caps in a lamp. They feel the decorative cap should only be used on the out-side. For such individuals, check plates which are brass-spun round flat plates with an ⅛″ lip are available. We don't use them ourselves, since we believe a three dimensional object such as a lamp should be prepared to be viewed from all sides and should, therefore, look its best in every direction.

Furthermore, since a round lamp usually presents a cone shaped look inside and out, a vase cap which is cone shaped itself to a degree will fit much better than a check plate, which must of necessity leave an empty space above it to the top of the lamp.

Vase caps come as well in decorative form. Such devices have soft fencing in the form of an edge filigree, as well as an additional half-inch edge which tucks in the top portion of the lamp. This is particularly effective if you have a leading job you are interested in hiding. Remember when calculating vase caps to allow in your measurements for the top rim of lead covering your lamp, which should have the vase cap fitting neatly over it.

GLOBES

There are Duralite bulbs which can be used as globes. They are fat and sassy looking and give an air of importance to the inside of the lamp. However, if your lamp's inside dimensions are such that even this bulb will be lost in it, then you would do better with a globe.

Globes have their own problems. For one thing they require a different fitting operation. For another they require a hangar to support them. Hangars are essentially cast brass holders with three thumb screws that grip the lip of the globe. Make certain that these set screws turn easily. Remember they will have to be opened again to remove the globe in order to change the bulb. If you have to use pliers to turn them shut it will be very difficult to open them again without cracking your lamp. When you buy a hangar, check the set screws and make sure they fit. They usually are packaged separately.

NON-CIRCULAR LAMP FITTINGS

If you have made a lamp with a square or hexagonal top there is no reason why you cannot wire and hang it. Of course, you cannot use vase caps which come only in circular form. Two bars of galvanized steel should be measured across the top of the lamp at the strongest points, usually at two solder joints. Leave enough room between the bars for an ⅛″ nipple. This can then be caught from below by a brass check ring and led into the socket. Another check ring and nut will hold it from above and fix it to the bars. You can then apply the lamp ring and chain. If you don't want to be able to look up and see the ceiling through your lamp, cut a piece of thin sheet metal to fit the top. Drill a hole for the nipple and solder the sheet metal all around the top surfaces of your lamp. This will provide a holding plate and finishing plate at the same time. It is usually not necessary to solder the inside of the plate to the lamp. If your lamp is unusually heavy, you might want to consider placing a few galvanized steel supporting rods across the plate at requisite intervals and soldering them to the top surfaces of the lamp.

For lanterns, which are basically small squares as far as the tops are concerned, a flat plate leaves a somewhat unfinished look. Try your hand at bending your own decorative top for such pieces. A sheet of copper and an instrument called a "bending brake" will help you do the job. The bending brake provides a means of bending metal into requisite angles that leave only one seam to solder.

WIRING THE LAMP

Once you have decided on the measurement of the top hole, fit your vase caps top and bottom and measure the size nipple you will need. This nipple will run through the two holes of the vase caps from bottom to top. Enough should be protruding so that it can be caught by a lamp ring above, and below so that it can screw into the top of the socket. We usually start from below, screwing the nipple into the top of the socket and then tightening the socket set screw. We then place the nipple through the inner vase cap and upper vase cap. The top of the nipple is caught with the lamp ring and tightened so that the vase caps are held in place securely. Once this is done you can move your lamp in any direction without fear of the vase caps falling off. Measure the amount of lamp wire you will need. Lamp chain comes in three-foot lengths (which is the height from the ceiling that most lamps are hung). Measure your wire, therefore, slightly more than three feet. Pass the end of the wire from the top through the hole in the lamp rings, through the vase caps and through the top portion of the socket below. Split the wire; take the insulation off the split ends and wire the copper directly against the two screws in the socket. Once this is done tighten the screws, pull the socket up against the top, place the bottom of the socket holder in place and press it closed so that it snaps into the top of the socket.

With chain pliers open one of the links of chain, hook it to the lamp ring and close it. Now weave the lamp wire through the chain at every other or every third link. Be careful not to stretch the chain away from the lamp which is sitting on the table. The weight of chain can easily pull the lamp to the floor. This is especially true if you are using extra chain to make a swag. Unconsciously you may back farther and farther away from the table as you weave the wire through the chain. Your lamp can topple very rapidly.

Once you have the lamp wire through the chain, split the end of the wire as before, taking the insulation off and wire on a small lamp plug. Your wiring job is now complete.

CHAPTER 15

Free Form Objects

An object is considered free form if it is not to fit any predetermined borders. While this precludes its immediate use as a window, a panel of a door, fireplace screen or room divider, it allows the artist to concentrate solely on design unlimited by scale. Such pieces include shade pulls, animals, or plants which may hang in windows, mobiles, etc. We will concentrate in this chapter on the preparation of such free form objects of stained glass.

DESIGNING AND STYLIZING

There are a number of kits on the market containing everything from small animals made of pre-cut glass to objects composed of chunks or glass globs which can be put together by the use of lead came or just glued. However, it's more fun to design and style your own right from the beginning. Here's how it's done.

First, get your basic shape. If it's an elephant or a frog or a mouse with a mushroom, remember that the medium you are working in allows, indeed demands, imagination to show it off. Basic figurations for free form objects are plentiful. Pick up any magazine or Madison Avenue advertising and you will find ideas galore. The object is not to simply copy out these pictures and make them into stained glass. The idea is to *transpose* into stained glass and *adapt* for this medium a totally new creation, the idea for which may have simply been set in motion by a casual glance at a line drawing. You must style your designs so that they have some particular flavor —some whimsy or some dimensional quality which you, by adding to the basic theme, give a quality and

Fig. 15-1. Free form, free standing objects of stained glass include the Japanese dancing girl here shown (she's really a little night light).

162

taste to make it your own particular creation (Fig. 15-3, 15-4).

Free form hanging objects require a good bit of thought and design before they come to life in stained glass. If you cannot so treat a free form piece, then you had better discard it for the present and re-design for something else. It's really quite easy to just draw any stained glass hanging object and cut it and lead it. But if it has no particular point of interest other than its rather simple existence, its novelty will soon wear off. In our own designs we try to add a little extra something that will give the eye a replenished delight each time it looks at them. The little snail, for instance, has a roundel for its shell and two antennae made of copper wire with a little millefiore for an eye. The elephant has a three-dimensional trunk which seems to be reaching out at you, perhaps to ask for a stained glass peanut. The pop-eyed frog is exactly that—a small green animal whose eyes come directly out of his head, being glass doll's eyes, glued into place. Another frog who seems to be serenading his lady love has a guitar which is made as real as we can make it with actual copper wire strings and a three-dimensional arm holding it. All these are simple enough devices to add charm and intrigue to these small hanging objects, but they serve to attract attention, not only because the object is *made* of stained glass but because it is *designed* of stained glass. While each has some aspect of its character pointed up in its design, it is all the same important that this not be carried to extremes. An overemphasized "cuteness" can end up making real beasts of your glass animals.

The technique of making free form objects is somewhat different from the technique involved in making a window, panel or any other so-called "enclosed" object. What is used instead is the "wraparound" technique. This technique involves cutting out your pieces of glass to an exact pattern as has been described for a panel. However, once your pieces are cut and sized, each is wrapped around its border with a piece of copper foil or a piece of $1/16''$ U (back-to-back) lead. Care must be taken in the wrapping so that it is not sloppily done. The pattern should not involve too many complex angles and corners, as you will find these hard to wrap, especially with lead. Remember, that although small animals, mobiles and hanging "whatyoumaycallits" may boast of being "free form," even they, although not locked in the strict proportional confines of a window, bear

Fig. 15-2. A stained glass miniature piano designed for fun if not for sound. Small pieces of glass foiled together give the bend in the side. The piece measures about 6 by 5 inches.

Fig. 15-3. The "mini-lamp" here shown is more a decorative free-form object than a true lamp measuring approximately 9″ high and about 5″ wide. It makes a nice night light. (Courtesy: Heirloom Lamps.)

USE OF FOIL OR LEAD CAME

Fig. 15-4. The smallest stained glass window we've ever seen is contained in this bronze belonging to the Stained Glass Club. (Artist unknown.)

Fig. 15-5. An owl being bugged. No wonder the bird's vision is so clear: his eyes are washers. As for the bug, he is composed of small glass circles soldered together, with copper wire for feet and antennae.

Fig. 15-6. Leading up a snail. The single groove $\frac{1}{16}''$ flexible came can take sharp curves and angles with ease. The snail's body is a pressed roundel.

a proportional relationship in regard to their own innards. We advise that a pattern scissors still be used in cutting all inside lines of any fairly complicated design for the sake of a neat and compact entity.

$\frac{1}{16}''$ lead came should be stretched only minimally before use. If you pull too hard, you will narrow the channel to such an extent that your lead may be unusable and will, furthermore, become distressed— that is, thin surface break lines may begin to appear. If, however, you have a very thin piece of glass, you might stretch the lead more than once, allowing it a rest period between stretching of fifteen minutes to half an hour and then re-stretching it. You can thus lengthen the came about six to eight inches, a proportion subtracted somewhat from its width. Your very thin glass will now fit more securely into the wrap-around lead. Nothing is more annoying than glass which fits improperly into such a lead channel, flopping in and out against the extra width like a loose tooth.

Such jogging exercises of the glass may further be prevented by wrapping each piece of glass securely in the lead as tightly as possible, and even using glass pliers to press the came against points and angles, such as may be in the design. Please exercise a natural discretion when pressing with these pliers or you will end up with more pieces of glass than you originally allowed for. Unlike the regular "H" came, where each piece of glass is fitted into the whole like so many parts of a picture puzzle, back-to-back lead (or copper foil) is fitted around each piece of glass, pressed tightly against it and the ends then soldered. Each piece of glass, with its rim of lead or foil, is then placed back into position on the work drawing and securely held with leading nails. The glass cutting should be as accurate as possible so that the leads will lie true. The slightest bump or discrepancy in the cut surface of the glass will be magnified by the leading. Once all the pieces are thoroughly leaded up and each part back on the work drawing, solder can easily be flowed over the seams and the piece will be done with a dispatch that will surprise you. Back-to-back lead is recommended especially for beginners who are anxious for a finished product as quickly as possible.

We have found the easiest method of working with this lead is to lay a six foot came on the table, groove up. Starting at either end, we proceed to roll our piece of glass along it, using fingers to mold the lead against the glass in a temporary bind. We calculate in advance where our solder joint will be—that is, where our circuit of the glass will be completed—so that it will be hidden in a future seam. In other words, we want our lead to appear as an unbroken ring, so we solder it around each piece of glass only at juncture points with other pieces of glass. Thus, all individual seams are hidden. At this point, we cut our lead and with lathkin, pliers and fingers, introduce an urgent pressure of the metal against all surfaces until we are satisfied that a tight fit exists. Some workers like to use a glue in the channel to make sure their lead stays tight against the glass. While this is possible, it's an extra step and more time and should not be necessary if your piece is properly designed and if you have used a requisite amount of pressure to hold the lead against the glass. In the case of copper foil, the glue backing already exists on some of this metal when it is used for this sort of work.

Each piece of glass, after being soldered closed, is placed back on the pattern. It should fit the pattern exactly; any bump or crevice that did not appear in the original piece of cut glass and that has now suddenly arisen, should be suspect. Such discrepancies arise from inadequately wrapping the lead or from poor cutting of the glass. It is easier to fix it immediately, even if it means re-wrapping the piece of glass or even re-grozzing it, than to try to compensate for it in the piece of glass adjoining. This procedure of robbing Peter to pay Paul invariably winds up with the operator paying the piper.

Difficulty arises through careless use of the material. We have seen craftsmen, who ordinarily are the souls of discipline with copper foil and the general leading process, go completely mad when faced with the apparent freedom of back-to-back lead used in free form objects. Their glass cutting becomes careless and their pieces develop dissipated edges that stagger through the design in a sick imitation of the underlying work drawing. They seem to get the idea that since no strict outside limits exist and since solder will fill in all discrepancies, one might as well cut up a bit.

Unfortunately, solder used as filler does not substitute effectively for glass. It is also far more difficult to work with and does not tamely submit to being dumped into unwanted excavations in the design. In the long run, trying to fill in with solder will simply waste time and make your final piece look as though it were sandbagged against an air raid. So, if your pieces don't fit securely, it's a good idea to recut them. Just because the object is free form

Fig. 15-7. The completed project.

Fig. 15-8. Some hanging free-form objects. A seahorse.

POINTS TO KEEP IN MIND

Fig. 15-9. A couple of young ladies.

doesn't mean that it should be done with less care than any large window or panel.

In wrapping your lead, don't be afraid to use your pliers to get a tight fit. As we mentioned before, don't use them like a vise, but it is really not difficult to sense the breaking point of the glass and to apply pressure to that point. Do not use any pliers with deep or sharp grooves as they will certainly leave their imprint in the lead (Fig. 15-10). We have a pair of old glass pliers whose jaws we filed smooth, and they serve well for this purpose.

Fig. 15-10. Crimping a piece of 1/16″ came around a glass angle with pliers. Enough force is provided to produce a sharp angle in the lead without breaking the glass.

Both back-to-back lead and copper foil have one serious drawback. They cannot span, unassisted, long areas of glass. Where either is used over lengths of four inches or more without being strutted to another piece of lead, they develop in time a decided tendency to come away from the glass. This is true whether it be in the outermost rim or a long inner span. Separation will occur due the weight of the piece alone. It is most liable to happen either at the top or the bottom, but can occur anywhere the design allows a long span of lead.

Remember, therefore, when designing any free form object to allow for this tendency and not cut large pieces of glass which then can only be held by their border, one to another. Leads will come away.

Fig. 15-11. Stained glass elephant with three-dimensional trunk. This one happens to be pink.

This might also be kept in mind when placing loops for hanging on such objects. Since the best place to put loops is at the juncture of two or more leads, it would be well to involve such a crossroad in your original design and equally thoughtful to tie in other outside pieces as well. So you can see that even a free form item must have a solid basis in factual mechanics.

THREE-DIMENSIONAL EFFECTS AND DOUBLE GLAZING

Three-dimensional effects might be used to point up in your creation some feature of its character—as in the elephant, the three-dimensional trunk (Fig. 15-11) and the frog, the pop-eyes. The possibilities are endless. In making three-dimensional figurations, however, be sure not to overuse them. Only place them where they may be seen as pluses, not surpluses. Keep in mind that you're dealing with a small figure, usually 6 to 8 inches in diameter, and it should not become so busy that its charms leap at you rather than insinuating themselves so the onlooker has the fun of slowly discovering them. Most three-dimensional effects are best done with copper foil, rather than with the 1/16″ U came, no matter how thin you make it by stretching. The came simply does not have the mobility of the foil for this purpose. When considering a three-dimensional touch, it is wise to

Fig. 15-12. Some sample patterns.

hold the foiled piece that you are extending with a pair of small pliers as the heat from the soldering is easily transmitted to your fingers and you may end up dropping and breaking a piece of glass that may have taken you some time to cut. Try to avoid over-bracing such objects. The three-dimensional effect should appear a natural extension of the piece, rather than a tacked-on afterthought.

Double glazing is the art of using one piece of glass on top of another within the same area. Special leads are available for this with exceptionally wide channels. However, you may also use $\frac{1}{16}''$ U around each piece. Then solder them together one on top of the other. When properly used, double glazing will give an extra depth to the glass or a subtle change in color that neither piece has separately. Such procedure is especially effective in small shade pulls, where there is not much room expansion-wise to get any particularly individual effects, and so you must deal directly with the glass itself. We use antique streakies and double glaze either cathedral or antique glasses to get particularly beautiful effects in shade pulls. Since you're only using small amounts of glass, you may well find that the scraps that you have saved in your work bins will come in especially handy here. Be careful when employing double glazing that you do not put two pieces of glass together, the colors of which will clash with one another, or worse, totally block each other out. It's easy enough to experiment and see which colors go together well and which give the impression of depth before actually cutting them and soldering them together.

A good mobile is comparable to a three-dimensional graffiti. Whether it be impudent, profound, wise, witty or charming, it gives you a peak into the personality of its maker and a comment on his originality. Mobiles have a fascination for workers in the stained glass field. There is so much that can be done with them. We like to use long strips of glass interspersed with driftwood or pieces of bamboo for effect. Holes, of course, must be drilled in the glass which hangs completely unleaded from the supports. For this purpose, a glass drill is needed. The technique is described in Chapter 4. This again is another way of effectively using up glass scraps.

We present here—much scaled down—a few sample patterns of free form objects and mobiles that might be considered by the beginner. Naturally, these are simply designs and can be elaborated upon as the worker becomes more skilled in the craft.

Fig. 15-13. Rose with lead foil leaves and brass rod stem.

Fig. 15-14. A poodle.   Fig. 15-15. A cowardly lion.

Fig. 15-16. A locomotive. The flashlight is functional. The object is three dimensional.

MOBILES

Fig. 15-17. Three dimensional piano. A small music box may be placed inside.

SAMPLE PATTERNS

CHAPTER 16

Using the Glass Cements

There are areas of the stained glass craft not involved with the old medieval techniques or even the Tiffany techniques of the twenties. This comparatively new field has come about because of the revival of interest in the art and the consequent amount of material left over when major products are completed. Such material includes especially scrap glass and scrap chunks from dalles, as well as extra globs, scrap lead and bits of imagination which, like the extra crust of a pie, was trimmed away because it went beyond the confines of the immediate enterprise. Interesting endeavors can be composed by combining all these leftover elments, using the glass cements as a unifying thread. Here are a few of them:

Using Up Scrap Glass —
The Mosaic Window

On a piece of ordinary window glass draw a design of your choosing. This may first be sketched on kraft work paper and held beneath the clear glass as a guide, or you may draw it directly upon the window glass itself. Be sure the glass you are using is clean and free of grease. You may then fit your pieces of glass to the design cutting them to pattern, or you may prefer to simply use them as they are conforming your design to their accidental figurations which you may find especially pleasing for an abstract. The size of such pieces is your choice. Remember to leave spaces between them. When you have the pieces set to your satisfaction glue each one to the underlying window glass. We prefer to use for this either Bond #527, a good all purpose glass glue, or Bond G-r-rip,

Fig. 16-1. A "mosaic" window in process of construction. Stained glass is here glued to underlying window glass according to a pre-determined pattern marked on the glass itself. In this instance the stained glass pieces will not cover the entire surface but will stand out in bas-relief against the clear glass background.

168

which is another strong cement. Both of these dry clear without any "layering" effect, which is very important.

If you wish, you may cover the entire surface of the window glass with a foreground-background design, or just use a silhouette, that is, have only the foreground glued and standing out against the clear window glass beyond. Let your pieces stand for several hours until the glue sets. Don't worry about excess glue that may seep between the pieces.

Once the pieces of glass are firmly fixed in place by the hardening of the glue, take some black grout or liquid lead and fill in between the pieces of glass. The liquid lead we prefer is Met'l Bond, which comes in either black or gold color. Grout tends to give a much smoother, more even surface than liquid lead, which produces more of a rough, soldered appearance. Try to avoid getting liquid lead on the surface of the glass. In using liquid lead, which comes in a tube, be sure to squeeze the tube from the bottom. The material is thick and may break through the bottom if you are not careful. Some of this will of necessity seep into the glass, and when this occurs try to wipe it off immediately with acetone. If it should harden on the glass, you will be faced later with the task of scraping it off; otherwise it will give a sloppy effect to the finished piece.

This particular technique gives an interesting mosaic-like effect which can become quite ornate once you get the hang of it. It is similar to working with tile except that here you have: (1) a true stained glass modification of the window glass with control of the light penetrating the work and not just a bounce-back reflection as you get with tile; (2) an easier material to work with than tile, which requires a good bit of hand strength to continually operate the nippers; and (3) a material that provides an almost limitless range of hues and tones and therefore more span for the play of color sense. The project can be completed fairly rapidly—most such windows take only a few days—and the effect can be breathtaking. Stained glass may be used instead of window glass for the backing.

Drinking Glasses and Candle Holders

A method similar to the above is employed in placing glass scraps around drinking glasses. Here again, the glass is either cut to shape or the shapes selected, measured against the existing surface to a more or less precise extent, and then glued to the underlying drinking glass with the Bond #527 and grout or liquid lead applied between the surfaces. A

Fig. 16-2. An ordinary drinking glass being covered with small pieces of stained glass as decoration. Grout or liquid lead will be placed between the pieces.

most decorative object may be produced this way; there is a great demand for these in gift shops. Such a creation may be further extended by placing a lighted candle in the center. The flickering of this center flame as it passes over the stained glass embroidery chases the various colors like a moving neon sign.

Fish Tanks

One of the simplest methods of using glass chips is to employ them as colorful decor in the bottom of a fish tank. A fairly strong light at the top of the tank will set off the kaleidoscope of colors below. Fairly large pieces of scrap may be used here; arranged at random they will give the appearance of a multicolored grotto. You might prefer opalescents, which tend to reflect back the light more strongly then the antique and cathedral scraps though, placed properly, these will sparkle quite effectively, too. Nor will the glass hurt the fish, though you will be constantly asked the question.

Fusing

Access to a kiln considerably broadens the horizons of scrap use. Try this: Take a wall tile (preferably a white one to start) and place a few of your scrap glass chips on it (Fig. 16-3). Then fire to about 1450°F. and cool the oven very slowly, at least overnight. When you crack the kiln you will find the glass has melted into the tile in novel patterns. No two tiles will turn out alike. Each is a fresh creation. We must stress letting the oven cool slowly, for the coefficient of expansion of the glass and the tile are quite dissimilar, and if you open the oven too soon, hairline cracks will begin to appear in the tile's surface.

Of course you don't have to use tile as a base. You can take a small piece of cathedral glass cut to square or rectangular shape and use that. What comes out is an interesting carpet-like effect of free-form color which may even be hung as a small panel of itself.

Three-Dimensional Pieces

Three-dimensional objects—that is glass sculpture —can be created by gluing scrap glass together into interesting designs. You should have some basic form in mind initially, though this certainly may be modified as you go along by the character of the glass pieces themselves. The build-up may follow both horizontal and vertical dimensions. Such a sculpture may be as ornate as you care to have it become limited only by your sense of proportion and the amount of chips you have on hand. The end

Fig. 16-3. A wall tile which has pieces of stained glass fused to it.

result may be either astonishing or dismaying, but in either case such an exercise furnishes a discipline in spatial design which can be incorporated even into two-dimensional work.

Scrap Lead

Scrap lead needn't be separated as to size unless you particularly desire it. We only separate fairly large lengths—at least two feet or more—for studio re-use. Otherwise the smaller pieces just tangle the larger ones.

We favor using small pieces of scrap as the metal, rather than the came. A small hand torch will easily melt it down for re-use as weights in knife handles, bases for small standing lamps or stained glass chessmen. Impurities such as putty, flux, etc. will float to the surface of the molten metal and may be skimmed off with a ladle.

We make a great many stained glass chessmen for our stained glass chessboards using such "buttons" of lead as the heavy base for the piece, which will keep it upright and against which we may solder the intial buildup. Indeed, any free-standing form may use such a base to advantage with its easy solderability and rapid formation. As a mold for our chessmen base we use the bottom portion of a toy soldier mold.

Other types of molds for lead are available—anything from fishing sinkers to bullets. It's surprisingly easy to work with this metal (mold sets are sold as children's toys), and you'll be astonished how you can incorporate the results of these molds into use with your stained glass scraps.

Small pieces of lead came may find use as feet (you can cut their ends for claws) in small animals, as tails for same and as hooks for hanging panels. At the very least your scraps can be saved for sale to the junk man. He will be happy to give you the going rate per pound, providing you have ten pounds or more.

Fig. 16-4. You can melt your scrap lead on a ladle and pour it into such a mold, as shown, to make stands for standing free-form objects of stained glass.

PROJECTS FOR CHILDREN

Many children show an interest in working with stained glass. It's a good idea to keep them away from sharp pieces, however. There is a crushed glass which may be purchased which has no sharp edges and which may be used quite safely to produce the following:

Crushed Glass Designs

Acquire a few cookie cutters of various shapes and wrap ¹⁄₁₆″ U lead securely around them. Solder the joint and lift away the cookie cutter. Your lead now

Fig. 16-5. Two cookie-cutter patterns . . .

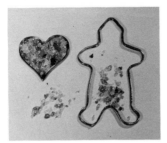

Fig. 16-6. . . . being filled with crushed glass.

Fig. 16-7. Following the spreading of the crushed glass evenly within the lead frame glue is flowed from above and allowed to percolate through the glass. Make sure you have wax paper underneath. When dry these medallions will glitter and sparkle in the sunlight.

should maintain the shape of the cookie cutter that it was pressed to. If not, compensate by hand to make it so. Place the lead on waxed paper and fill the bottom of it with a clear-drying cement such as Duco. Then pour crushed glass of whatever color you desire into the center of the lead, almost to the top. Add more cement until the mold is completely filled, gently tapping the sides in the meanwhile to make sure the glue circulates through the small pieces of glass. Several of these items may be made at one time. Put them aside to set for several hours and when the glue matures, you will have a true stained glass medallion. With the cement being colorless, there will be no blurring of the faceted effect you have created with your multi-leveled crushed glass chips. Simple? A child could do it.

Stained Glass Greeting Cards

A variation of the above technique may be done as follows: Cut a piece of window glass into a small square and acquire some stencil letters from your neighborhood stationery store. Try to get several sheets of the same type of lettering. Glue three or four such similar sheets together and cut the letters out into some sort of a simple word or two, such as "Greetings" or "Happy Birthday," etc. Arrange these words in the stencil format across the piece of glass you have cut. Apply scotch tape to hold them firmly to the surface of the glass and run scotch tape as well inside the letters themselves to form a surface that will not adhere to the cement. Next, pour a small amount of cement into the center of each letter, using a toothpick to make sure that you cover the surface of the glass within by spreading the cement evenly around. Next, pour a small amount of crushed glass chips into each letter, spread them with the toothpick, and follow this up with another thin coating of cement on top. When the cement has dried, you should be able to remove the stencil with little difficulty and you will have, in effect, a little stained glass greeting card which will furnish a good deal of delight to the child who receives it. This process may also be done by forming the letters with $\frac{1}{16}$" back-to-back lead and gluing the lead to the glass, though it is additionally complicated by adding this factor.

Stained Glass Jewelry Box

An ordinary cigar box will do for a starter. Paste over its top and sides some ordinary white paper to cover the writing and design. Draw a pattern of your own for the child to copy or let him create one him-

Fig. 16-8. Stained glass jewelry box. Step 1. Get a cigar box in good condition, cut a piece of pattern paper to the size of the top and draw a pattern. Children may just trace the shapes of some scrap glass pieces to fit the existing area.

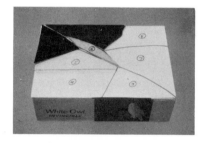

Fig. 16-9. Step 2. Glue the pattern to the top of the box and affix the glass pieces to it by means of a clear, quick-drying glass cement.

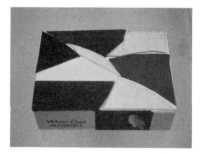

Fig. 16-10. Step 3. All the pieces are glued to the lid of the box. Move them as close to one another as you can while the glue is still workable, but remember to line them up with the borders of the box.

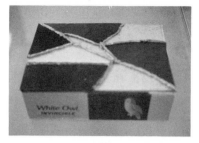

Fig. 16-11. Step 4. A plastic filler (liquid lead) is used to fill the cracks between the pieces of glass. Use enough to form a definite ridge between the glass patterns.

Fig. 16-12. Step 5. Cut a piece of glass to size (we have here used a green opalescent) and glue it to the front panel of the box. Repeat this process for all other panels.

Fig. 16-13. As a finishing touch you may place some glass globs or chunks in a free form or figurative design. We have added a small bird to the cover design which is made out of glass globs. His eye is a millifiori and his tail a piece of thin sheet brass cut into strips. Once your jewelry box has been let set long enough for the glue to dry, you may use a decorative contact paper to cover the inside. Cigars, anyone?

self directly onto the box using the glass globs as designing material. Once the design is decided upon, the globs may be glued into place, grout or liquid lead run between them and the sides may then be treated in the same fashion. Some colorful contact paper applied to the inside surfaces will complete the project with a neat and thorough disguise of the original material. You might like to try a more complicated version of this one yourself.

Sculpture

Glass globs or gems may be easily placed together in three-dimensional forms by children using either the #527 Bond Cement or the Met'l Bond liquid leads. In a freedom similar to finger painting, the children may here let their imaginations run rampant and many interesting creations can come from age groups nine years and even younger. Most children favor making small animals or tiny replicas of themselves with these globs and a good time is had by all. We suggest using globs, as here again there are no sharp edges to consider.

Lamp Shade

Take an ordinary glass globe, the kind that has a lip around the edge of the hole. You can affix over the surface of this pieces of stained glass as well as chunks and globs, held in place with one of the glass cements. Liquid lead, again, can be used between them. The child may draw his design directly onto the globe following the conformations of the pieces he has on hand. The pieces must be small enough to take the bend of the globe. An object of this type can then be hung on its own with a bulb inside it, and when lit will furnish the child with a Tiffany lamp of his own making.

A corollary to the above procedure is a far more advanced project, an actual stained glass shade of small dimension fabricated over a styrofoam ball. The styrofoam, of course, would have to be covered with wax paper so the glue would not adhere to it. This is not difficult as only half of this globe is made at a time. Naturally the pieces of scrap must be so arranged that they will glue to one another; a number of them must be cut to size and shape.

Fig. 16-14. Stained glass globs. Small globs and pieces of stained glass built up over an existing form will produce a beautiful display. Another good way of using up scrap glass.

Fig. 16-15. A couple of butterflies on a glass covered with glass chips and black grout.

CHAPTER 17

How to Paint On Glass

The art of glass painting is as old as the art of stained glass itself. The earliest fragments extant show painted detail. Such painted detail on a surface of glass must be done both with restraint and decision. The paint should never overpower the glass; it is present to embroider or modify it but to a specific artistic purpose. Some individuals feel that painting on glass adds a certain "impurity" to the stained glass art, which they would prefer not to see employed. Such people like their stained glass free of any surface modifications, preferring to enjoy the beauty of the colors in the glass itself. Be that as it may, there come occasions where, for the sake of detail in a pictorial window especially, painting on glass and shading of the basic tones of the glass are necessary and proper (Figs. 17-1, 17-2, 17-3, 17-4 and 17-5).

It was overpainting of glass toward the end of the Renaissance period that finally smothered the entire art. It is well, therefore, to keep in mind that when you paint on glass you are conspiring with it, not using it simply as a canvas which must be covered.

There are two major techniques, the fired and the unfired.

Here we find ceramic paint and glass paint per se. Ceramic, or china paint, fires at much higher temperatures than glass paint, between 1250° and 1350° F. Glass paint fires between 1050° and 1080° F. In addition, china paint is generally meant to be fired over a glazed surface. There is, therefore, a difference in the maturing temperatures between

Fig. 17-1. Small fired painted panel—a mouse under a mushroom. This quick sketch was done as an experiment in texturing fired paint. Only black trace paint was used.

THE FIRED TECHNIQUE

Fig. 17-2. Ten Commandments—non-fired paint.

Fig. 17-3. Owl. Example of fully stained and fired window glass. (Kay Kinney paints were used.)

Fig. 17-4. Bee ashtray (window glass). This piece was painted with Kay Kinney's Blackline and then sagged into a mold. (Courtesy: Edward Martin.)

the two paints and while a few china paints may be used on glass, what generally happens is either the glass melts before the china paint matures or the china paint simply does not get hot enough to melt into the glass and flakes off when the glass cools.

1. Glass Stainers' Paints

All fired paints used in the stained glass art are basically atmosphere proof. Glass stainer paints, especially, are calculated to withstand the sometimes dank atmosphere that accumulates in large buildings such as churches, which contain an immense amount of dead air throughout all types of weather. They will maintain their color indefinitely, even under such circumstances. Glass stainer paints are made mostly by the Hancock firm in England. They are water base paints and are quite difficult to use. For one thing, they are affected in their liquid state by weather. If it is too muggy they will not flow properly; if too cold they will tend to break up along the brush stroke. Their preparation also involves a certain tenacious amount of procedure. They have been used for hundreds of years and have proved superbly effective once the student learns how to apply them. To this end, a certain technique is definitive for good results, as well as the acquisition of certain supplies.

Supplies. Basic supplies necessary for use in any fired painting technique are: a glass pallet, a glass pestle, several different sizes of pallet knives and a supply of brushes (Fig. 17-7) of various types specific for use on stained glass. In addition to these brushes, you should have on hand whatever old paint brushes of small dimension you can locate. These will be used to give a stippling or other decorative effect to be worked into the paint depending on the character of the brush. You should also have a supply of toothpicks, quills, or sharp pointed bamboo sticks which will be used to pick away the paint for a design to show through. The glass pallet should be prepared by having sand rubbed into its center to provide an abrasive surface for grinding the paint.

Grinding. Before any glass stainers' water based paints are used, they must be ground. Scoop a few spoonfuls of paint out of the bag and place them on the center of your pallet. With your pestle catch them against the abrasive surface of the pallet and work the paint around the surface to make it as fine as possible. It may look pretty fine when it comes out of the bag, but it should still be ground so as to make it as amorphous a material as can be done. Only after it is ground should the other ingredients be added to it (Fig. 17-8).

Vinegar Trace Paint. This is a dark colored paint which is used for basic figure lines or specific design lines. It has no shadowing quality. It blocks the light out completely if it is used correctly. Mixed with water, vinegar and gum arabic, the paint is used rather thick with the gum arabic present as a sticking or setting medium. The amount of gum arabic to be added to the paint is always questionable and depends on the weather, on the amount of paint you have on your pallet and on your judgment. If the weather is hot and muggy, too much gum will tend to overstick to the glass and the paint will not flow smoothly. If the weather is cold, too much gum may break the paint line along a brush stroke leaving skips or spaces in the line. If not enough gum arabic is added, the paint can flow over the glass, but will not adhere well and will not fire correctly when it is placed in the kiln.

The method of mixing the paint is as follows:

Pile a small amount on the pallet in the center. Grind it thoroughly and then scrape it all together again into the center (Fig. 17-9). Make a little well or depression in the center and measure in some gum arabic and vinegar. Start mixing with a pallet knife (Fig. 17-10). If the mixture remains thick, add a little water or vinegar until it becomes pasty. A few drops more water at that point should do it. Try a few test brush strokes along the pallet to be sure.

Vinegar trace paint is painted on with a special long-haired brush called a tracer or tracing brush. The paint on the brush must always be worked "wet in wet," that is wet on the brush and wet on the glass, or it will "fry" when it is fired in the kiln. You cannot go over a dry painted line again with more paint or continue to add paint to a stroke which has dried. Such a paint line must be one complete stroke (Fig. 17-11). Assuming you have painted a stroke which has dried, if you are not satisfied with it, you must completely erase it from the glass surface and completely redo it. If you do not and you apply another coating of vinegar trace paint over or to it, the two areas will separate where they meet when they are heated and the overlying area will bubble up somewhat like an overcooked pie crust. This "frying" procedure can lead to a general flaking off of that layer of paint.

Vinegar is used as a medium for this paint. It furnishes a vehicle which burns out readily and

Fig. 17-5. Fired paint and sticklighting all through this panel. The bird's eye is etched. The scales on the snake are all painted.

Fig. 17-6. Basic supplies for fired painting—glass pallet, grinder and palette knives.

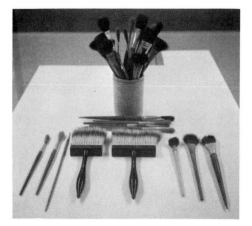

Fig. 17-7. A selection of brushes.

Fig. 17-8. Grinding the paint.

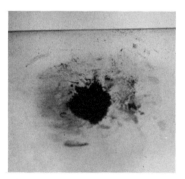

Fig. 17-9. The paint after its initial grinding.

Fig. 17-10. Further mixing of the materials with a palette knife. This allows for more control of the individual items going into the mix.

Fig. 17-11. Painting lines using a tracing brush and a stick—called a mahl—to steady the hand.

Fig. 17-12. Designing areas into the painted (but not fired) piece to modify and control the light coming through.

which allows the paint to flow quite nicely. A certain amount of water may be mixed in as well, but we have used vinegar alone with good results.

After the vinegar trace paint is dry and before it is fired, it can be scraped or modeled with a quill or a bamboo stick for design purposes (Fig. 17-12). It can be used as either a positive or negative surface; that is, put on an area and a design picked out of it or painted directly on an area as a design in its own right. This technique is more appropriately used with matt paint, but can be used with trace paint as well. Trace paint is fired by sight at about 1100° F., with the kiln turned off when the paint surfaces look to be somewhat shiny.

Painting with this material is a procedure that requires a good deal of practice. We suggest that you make yourself a "bridge" out of wood, in order to have something to rest your wrist on when using this paint. Such a bridge is easily produced by placing two small blocks of wood underneath a longer one and nailing them together. Before trying to paint any major project with trace paint, it is suggested that you practice on a piece of plate glass the various strokes that are necessary to acquire the requisite wrist motion. Using the long tracing brush is an experience in itself. For one thing, the brush must complete its stroke before the paint runs out of it. It is therefore wise to get the maximum possible consistency to your paint on the pallet and then "load" your tracing brush with it by putting the tracing brush into the paint sidewise and rotating it so that all the bristles are covered with paint. Of course, if you overdo this, you will have so much paint on your brush that when you tip it forward to get that neat thin stroke you want, a glob of paint will run off the brush and blot the entire area. It is necessary to learn just how much paint the brush will take before this happens. If you don't put enough paint on the brush, you will find that you may run out of paint in the middle of a stroke and since you cannot go back over the stroke or continue it without overlapping some of the dried paint, you have to erase the entire stroke and do it all over again with a brush containing more paint. Remember also that as you are working the paint on your pallet is drying out and the mixture must be constantly replenished with vinegar and possibly gum arabic if more paint is needed.

In order to keep the mixture as fluid as possible, it is a good idea to keep working your pallet knife over the pallet and keep mixing your paint between strokes so that you will have an idea just how fast it is drying out and how much water or vinegar is necessary to re-add to get it back to its proper consistency.

Gum arabic is generally purchased in powder form, but it dissolves well in water and it is as such that we generally store ours. Gum arabic will also dissolve well in alcohol, but to use it in this medium, of course, allows you far less time to work with the paint before it dries out.

It is also a good idea when working with vinegar trace paint to keep holding the glass up to the light to see how thick or how thin the paint is being applied. If you can see light coming through the paint, then of course, it is too thin a mixture and your basic reserve must be replenished with more paint. If the mixture on the glass is so thick that it is ridging, you will end up with a very uneven surface which may fry when it is fired.

Cleaning the Glass. None of the glass paints should be used on a piece of glass that has not been thoroughly cleaned prior to being painted on. The initial cleaning should be done with alcohol or acetone and the glass then allowed to dry. Both alcohol and acetone can form a thin film on the glass, which is very difficult to remove. Another way of cleaning the glass is simply to smear some of the vinegar trace paint on it (moist) and then wipe this off with a clean rag or gauze pad. Since the paint has tiny pieces of glass already in it—the basis of all fired painting on glass being a melting of small particles of glass into a larger piece of glass—the glass in the paint will have an abrasive quality of its own and will tend to clean the surface of the glass you are going to paint on better than any glass cleaner will do. Remember when cleaning the glass to clean as well the bottom surface, as any bits of paint sticking to this surface if placed in the oven will also become imbedded in the glass and you may get rather novel effects that you did not look for.

Technique. When you think you have the technique of the wrist motion pretty much under control and that the paint mixture is adequate for what you want to do, then you may practice tracing lines onto an actual piece of stained glass. This is always done on a light box or light table for individual pieces of glass. The technique of painting several glass pieces together will be discussed later on in this chapter. For your first attempt, it is best for you to try to paint one small piece of glass with a simple design and fire it to see how it comes out. In order to study the technique, you might paint several different types of lines—curved and straight, while resting your wrist on the bridge and swinging the brush in as guided a fashion as you can manage. Then fire these different strokes and see which technique and which mixture of paint works the best. Only in this fashion will you be able to guide yourself gradually into the art.

Place whatever lines you wish to employ in paint underneath the glass to be painted on between the glass and the light box. It will take practice to follow these lines at first, as your hand will tremble and globs of paint will probably roll from your overloaded tracing brush. But, if you persevere in this most difficult technique, you will be rewarded in the end by acquiring a "painting hand," which eventually will be able to apply the trace paint to even the most complicated outlines.

Matt Paint. Matt is a more transparent paint than the trace and can be put on the glass either thin or heavy, depending on the effect you wish to produce. It will always fire in a somewhat transparent fashion, however. Its medium is water and gum arabic or vinegar and gum arabic. It is put on with a soft paint brush and then "blended," that is, spread over the area to which it is to be applied with a special brush called a Badger Hair Blender. It's essential to have such a brush in order to accomplish the technique of matting.

A matt after it is blended out is usually stippled or worked with other brushes or with the fingers to get a uniquely embroidered texture. The amount of gum arabic included in the mixture will determine just what is possible to do with this paint. Matt paint is applied over the tracing paint after the tracing paint is fired. The use of matt, therefore, generally requires two firings, one for the tracing paint, then a cooling of the glass and then the application and firing of the matt. Occasionally, we try to apply the tracing paint and then the matt immediately to save ourselves a firing. This is often impossible to do as the spreading of the matt over the tracing paint will tend to blur the tracing paint outline. Of course, matt may be used alone. It is fired in the same manner as the tracing paint, but need not be fired quite as high. If matt is overfired, it will lose its color and end up looking quite pale. Both the matt and trace paints do fire out to some degree ordinarily.

Basically, matting is used for shadowing and filling in the background of a painted portion. It is

Fig. 17-13. The hair and beard have been painted with matt. Note the highlights and shadowing possible with this paint.

Fig. 17-14. More delicate matting shows on forearm and hand.

the charcoal of the glass painting world and may be applied thick or thin and in varied qualities and designs to give the effect of fullness required of any painting. Remember not to mix so much gum arabic into the matting that you cannot rub it off the glass easily and yet not so little that it just won't stick at all. Many odd visual effects can be achieved with the matt by adding alcohol to it, causing it to dry out quickly in interesting swirls, or dropping splashes of alcohol on it after it has dried. Our favorite method is the use of finger painting on the matt after it is laid down and dry. This gives interesting swirls and lines and is applicable especially to long flowing hair and beards. The pirate window (see color section) had matt applied to the entire surface of the building. A fine wire brush was then used to take out irregularly shaped thin lines throughout the surface of the matting to give the glass a grain that resembled wood.

2. Use of the Silver Stains

All glass stains such as orange, red, yellow, etc., are composed of silver nitrate in varied percentages. The terminology is somewhat misleading, since the color of a silver stain is not silver. Silver nitrate has corrosive properties which are not present in the paints we have been discussing so far. Do not use the same pallet for the stains as you do for the paints. When using stains, the pallet should be a coarser one as stains require much more grinding than do the paints. Grinding stains is a tedious procedure that may seem to be leading nowhere, as the material is continually moving out from under the pestle. Persist at it, however, for despite what you may think, you are accomplishing something. We prefer not to mix the stain with water before grinding, as we find that this gives us less control of the material and makes it harder to grind.

Stains do not work well from brush to glass. However, the same precision is not required as when you are painting. You are changing the glass color of an area with a stain. Needless to say, you should have a special brush for staining which should not be used for painting. Staining is usually done on the opposite surface of the glass from the painting and is always fired with the stained side down, that is to say, with the stained surface resting on the kiln wash. The stains fire at approximately 1000° F. Each time the piece is refired the color gets deeper. Silver stain (remember this is actually golden in color) does not keep well and is affected by light, so it is best to keep it in a dark bottle. It will not take well on all glass. Usually "white" or clear glass works the best. Quill type brushes are best to use as the silver stain will quickly corrode a metal ferrule brush, as it will a metal container. English glass takes oranges, reds and yellow stains best. German glass, in our experience, doesn't take stain well at all.

When grinding the silver stains, do not use a metal pallet knife. If possible, use one made of horn, as the silver will darken the metal considerably.

3. *Oil Base Paints*

Glass stainers' colors have a rather limited selection: in the paints mainly blacks, blues, browns and greens; and silver stains varying in hue from ruby to yellow. There are another set of glass paints based on oil, rather than water, called Drakenfield paints, which are equally as effective as the glass stainers' paints and yet are much easier to work with. The pallet of colors here includes every hue and tone that one could wish. Drakenfield paints are as permanent as glass stainers' paints and will not be affected by atmospheric conditions found in the home. Since these paints are not water based, they must be used with their own particular medium. This medium contains an oil–turpentine base. No vegetable oil can be used as a medium with the Drakenfield paints, as the carbon content in such oil is too great to burn out. Therefore, a non-vegetable oil plus a turpentine base is employed. It will take the Drakenfield oil base paint somewhat longer to dry on the glass than its water base cousin, but it will stick to the glass equally well and may be worked with much more ease than the water base material. No addition of gum arabic is necessary to oil base paint. The powder is ground initially on the pallet into a fine consistency, and the medium added until a thick paste is reached. A drop more medium is then added so that the paint flows readily from the brush.

Technique. Brush strokes may be gone over to a moderate degree with no consequent frying of the paint. These oil base paints may also be blended to show different tones of color, but experimentation must be used here to determine whether or not these colors will separate after heating.

While the oil base paints are much easier to use than the water base, there are still major problems of technique to be considered. Chief among them is the consistency of the paint mixed on the pallet. If this has been painted on too thick, you will find broken brush strokes where the material has bunched up when fired. Overfiring of this paint will also give you this problem, even if the consistency was correct at the time the painting was done. We have found the oil paints fire lower than the water base—1000° F. to 1050° F. Too much heat beyond this point begins to break up paint lines. Remember also that oil base paints, having a longer drying time than water base, will tend to smear if stick-lighting is attempted too soon after application. If this happens, you will do best to wipe the entire portion off and start anew, rather than try to clean up the smeared areas and just make more of a mess.

Stick-Lighting. Provided the oil base paint is allowed to dry, stick-lighting may be accomplished with relative ease. Because of the somewhat thicker consistency of oil base as compared to water base paints, you must be careful in working your sharp quill or stick when forming a design, so that you do not pull away more of the paint than is your purpose. Proceed very slowly, testing the consistency of the paint before you scratch away any long line of it. It may be a good idea first to take away a little from an outside edge to find just how tenaciously the paint is adhering to the glass. If you do happen to pull away more paint than you desire, one of the advantages of oil base paint is that you don't have to take the entire design back off the glass and re-apply it—you can simply touch up that single area.

Stick-lighting is used here as it is used with water base paint: to emphasize an existing paint line by placing a light line below it or to use the covering paint as a negative, scratching away those portions of it where you wish the color of the glass to show through. Remember that stick-lighting should never be an intrusive element in a design; it is a subtle emphasis, a logical shadowing of light along a painted surface which rather guides the eye than catches it. Fig. 17-5 shows an example of this technique.

Use of the Oil Colors. Probably the easiest color to use in the oil base paints is the black, whether it be *intense black* or *medium black*. The other colors have their own personal idiosyncrasies: difficulty in mixing, difficulty in getting them to flow to the glass from the pallet or brush or, as is most usual, difficulty in firing. Each color should be employed as a new challenge with new rules applying. The yellow color, for instance, tends in our experience to fire somewhat lower than does the black. We have fired both the black and yellow colors at the same temperature and found the yellow to break up along painted lines and bunch together, whereas the black remained quite solid and substantial. It is therefore cautioned that you do not fire different colors of oil base paint within the same batch, unless it is absolutely impossible not to. In that case, you must compromise against getting a perfect result with each color of paint against the necessity of time or expense in firing the kiln for single pieces.

Firing Technique. The firing technique for the oil base paint is exactly the same as for the glass stainers' water base paints. That is, each piece to be fired is arranged on either the kiln wash or the kiln shelf with the painted portion uppermost. If glass stain is to be fired, or if additional painting is to be fired on a reverse side of an already painted piece, then kiln wash must be used, as otherwise the painted surfaces which are turned down will adhere to the kiln shelf. If you do use kiln wash, be sure to make it as flat and as even a bed as possible so that the glass does not sag, even imperceptively, into small discrepancies in the surface.

Each piece should be so arranged that it is not touching its neighbor. Yet, you must try to use all room inside the kiln to the best advantage. Be certain prior to firing that the kiln shelf is clean and especially free of any small glass chips or paint from previous firings. Once the glass is in the kiln and placed properly, turn your kiln on to "medium" and lower the lid almost closed. Leave enough open so that the air within may be heated and driven out of the kiln. After approximately 15 minutes of this, close the kiln entirely and turn the heat up to maximum.

Watch the pyrometer on your oven carefully. It is only too easy to overfire a piece of glass painting and, once this happens, nothing can be done about salvaging it. The entire piece must be done over. We always fire by sight and check the kiln at approximately 1100° by opening the top and glancing within to see what the glass looks like. At about 1150° it is usually done with a nice shining appearance to the painted elements. We then turn the kiln off and close it once again, allowing the glass to cool very slowly over the period of the next twelve hours. It is possible to cool even fairly large pieces of glass more rapidly by cracking the kiln and leaving it open until the heat goes down to approximately 500°, then closing the oven again and letting it cool the rest of the way with the top closed. This is all right if you are going to be there watching the oven all the time. If you're not and the heat goes down too rapidly, you may end up cracking some of your pieces. It is better to simply let the oven cool by itself and then you don't have to be there watching it and worrying.

THE UNFIRED TECHNIQUE

For the amateur glass painter who doesn't have access to a kiln, there are available certain glass paints which do not have to be fired and which may yet achieve some sort of permanency on the surface of the glass. In no instance can such permanency be measured against the unqualified longevity of fired paint. At their worst, the unfired paints will come right off the glass just by your looking at them too roughly. At their best, they will form a very tough coating on the glass and will be almost impervious to any outside influence, except a soap pad and Brillo. Even with these, it may take a considerable amount of rubbing to remove the paint. While there are a number of different glass paints on the market, we have found the best of them to be Talens Vercolor. This material comes in half-ounce tins in a number of colors and may be applied with any cheap hardware store paint brush. The little cans should be mixed thoroughly before using and if the paint is too dark, a medium is provided which will lighten it. If too thick, it may be thinned with turpentine.

Talens paint comes as a liquid and no addition is necessary. It can be used as is right from the can. Be sure to cap the can firmly when you are done, or the paint will dry out. Colors available are yellow, orange, red, brown, violet, blue, olive green, medium green; opaque colors: white, grey and black. Talens colors are waterproof, reasonably light resistant, and they withstand rather high temperatures without fusing or melting. The colors dry to a high gloss and are non-toxic under normal use. They will adhere to any clean, smooth surface such as glass, china, ceramics, plastics and metals.

Uses of Non-Fired Paints

Non-fired paint is used most frequently for touching up a small decorative object, usually free form in nature. Very rarely is it used in even the small panel to add dimension to the glass. Remember that non-fired paint involves mainly trace lines; no real matting is possible. However, for use in painting faces on small animals or whiskers or eyes or even lettering in names, it comes in very handy. We employ it quite frequently in our smaller creations, such as the cornucopia, and we see it again in our cowardly lion with the twisted wire tail where the

Talens paint was used for face and whiskers. The most popular color is black, since this paint is used mainly for trace lines. But the other colors can be employed with equal effect with a little practice and style. There is nothing demeaning about using non-fired painting techniques.

Directions for Use

Rub the glass entirely dry and make sure that it is free from dust and dirt.

Stir the paint well and take away any overlying skins of paint from a previously used can. If you do not do this, you will be very liable to get small bits and pieces of the skin sticking to your paint brush and forming dollops of paint as you work.

You may dilute the paint, if you wish, with turpentine. The paint may also be diluted with medium, if you want to immerse an object in it to color it completely. The paint as is, without being so diluted, will prove too thick and will not cling well to the object to be immersed.

If you want to soften the brilliance of any of the colors, do so with the medium provided. If you wish to paint a design with these paints on a clear piece of glass, you may so employ them. To provide the greatest durability, such a window should be done with painted surface facing into the room, rather than outside, to best protect it. This durability can be strongly increased by muffling the paint if possible during one and one-half to two hours at 120° C.—for instance, in a furnace. The white color becomes a little yellow during this procedure. We see, therefore, that Vercolor may be fired if need be. However, we would suggest that this procedure be put over into the fired glass category and fired paints be used instead.

You may imitate a leaded glass effect with Vercolor:

(a) Put the sketch behind or between two sheets of clear glass. Then paint the diamonds or rectangles on both sides to cover the sketch in between. When the paint is dry, paint your black lines on the surfaces of both pieces of glass. Wait for that to dry, then turn the two pieces of glass to face each other and seal them together. This will give you a dimensional stained glass effect and will also protect the paint.

(b) Glue lead tape to make a design on the glass and then fill up the spaces between with Talens paint.

Do not apply colors in too thick coats and don't apply them too quickly one on top of the other, or you will end up having a wrinkling of the colors.

Although Talens paint is proof against fairly high temperatures, if you are painting on a lampshade, it is advisable that you do not put higher than a 40-watt bulb in it.

A striking effect is obtained by placing a sheet of tinfoil or silver paper behind the piece of glass painted with Talens paint and then place the whole in a frame. This effect can be further heightened if the tinfoil is first crumbled.

PAINTING PROCEDURE

When a stained glass window is ready for painted detail to be applied, that portion of it that is to be so treated, if it involves a number of pieces, is taken out of the window proper and "waxed up." If the entire window is to be painted, then all pieces are waxed up. This process involves placing the pieces on an easel made of plate glass. The pieces are placed exactly as they will appear in the final window with space left between them for leading. Each piece is then tacked to the underlying glass surface with hot beeswax at its corners. This material hardens almost immediately upon application, and it is also chipped away with equal ease when the painting process is completed and the pieces must come off the easel.

The easel is now set up, if possible, against a large window that has strong natural light—preferably a northern exposure. The painted lines are then applied with the vinegar trace paint and matting in the methods described above. First the vinegar trace lines that outline the basic features are placed. The glass painter copies exactly from the drawing that was originally designed for this window. When all the trace lines are in position, the pieces are taken off the easel and fired, following which they are re-waxed in position for the matting to be applied. If oil base paints are used for trace lines, we still use the water base matting for shadowing and fullness of line. When the pieces are brought from the oven a second time, they are examined for possible imperfections, and if they are satisfactory, they are then incorporated into the general leading procedure.

The design for leading the painted pieces had to be calculated for way back in the original cartoon. As we stated elsewhere, painted pieces must be so diagrammed that they will not have lead lines running through them at odd angles, interfering with the general flow of the painted elements. The face, for instance, should be painted all as one piece of glass, not splintered into three or four different pieces. The same holds true for hands and feet. Garments, of course, may be broken up gracefully with lead lines along the line of flow, as in most instances these pieces of glass would end up being too large to be fired.

For hobbyists painting on stained glass, it is simpler to wax up the pieces directly over a light table or a light box, since rarely do they have so many pieces to be painted that an easel is necessary. Remember that the pieces must be firmly held in place, especially when you are carrying the same paint line from one piece to another. Otherwise, when you come to lead up your glass, you will find that your painted lines do not match up and the pieces will not only have to be recut, but also repainted.

The only way of truly etching a piece of stained glass is to use hydrofloric acid on it. There are a number of pastes on the market and a number of power tools which can be employed to wear away the top surface of color of a piece of flashed glass. The grinding power tools are especially tedious. If you have made up your mind that you wish to etch a piece of stained glass, then you must be prepared to go into the use of this very interesting and somewhat dangerous chemical—hydrofloric acid.

ETCHING

Hydrofloric Acid

This chemical, which of necessity is stored in plastic bottles, though it is considered a weak acid chemically, is nonetheless a fairly dangerous one when it comes to human flesh. Be especially careful when working with it that you don't get it under your fingernails. If you do, you may experience a great deal of pain and discomfort before the acid stops burning.

Fortunately, most etchings on glass do not involve applying the acid to a very large surface. Single lines or small designs usually are the province of the etcher. However, should you wish to cover a fairly wide expanse of glass with acid, remember that the acid will fume up proportionally to the surface it has to work on and such fumes can be highly toxic. Therefore, do not work in an unventilated room, nor allow the acid bath to sit around where children may breathe the fumes.

Materials

(a) Materials needed are flashed glass, that is, glass where one color is laid on top of another.

(b) A plastic pan, shallow in depth, sufficient to hold the piece of glass to be etched.

(c) Plastic tongs.

(d) Beeswax, asphaltum or any "resist" medium which will protect those portions of the glass not to be attacked by acid.

(e) Hydrofloric acid in plastic container.

Procedure

The piece of glass to be etched is treated with hot beeswax or asphaltum smeared over all surfaces that are to be protected from the acid, that is, the back and the sides and those portions of the flashed surface that are not to be etched (Fig. 17-15). The design is drawn onto the area that is to be attacked with glass marking pencil. Either this area is initially covered with protect medium and then the protect medium cut away from it according to the space of the design (the easiest process), or the protect medium is flowed around the edges of the design if the design is rather simple, such as a diamond or a square.

Another method is to employ clear contact paper. This is thoroughly wrapped around the piece of glass so that all surfaces of glass are tightly encased within it. The plastic is then pressed against the glass surfaces to get rid of all possible air pockets and the design is stenciled and cut out of the contact paper on the applicable flashed surface. The principle is the same as using the beeswax or asphaltum, but it requires much less preparation and considerably simplifies the entire operation.

Once the piece is ready, it is then dipped into its bath of hydrofloric acid. Caution—do not put the piece into the plastic pan and then pour the acid on top of it as the acid may splash from it onto your skin or into your eyes. Place the piece of glass in its protective wrapping into an already present bath of acid, with the side to be etched either up or down, as you prefer. Depending on the amount of surface to be etched away, the process may take anywhere from ten minutes to half an hour. You will be able to tell how it is proceeding even if the surface to be etched is turned away from you, as you will be able to see directly through the glass to the new color that is appearing as the top layer of color is slowly eaten away by the acid. Use the small plastic tongs to move the glass around a bit, but do not overdo this jiggling, as you may tear loose some of the contact paper or other resist material and allow the acid to penetrate into other areas and effectively ruin the entire piece of glass.

Fig. 17-15. Contact paper is a good resist material for etching stained glass. The entire piece to be etched is enclosed in the plastic sheeting and the portion to be attacked by the acid has the contact paper above it cut away.

Fig. 17-16. Some problems with etching. Etching the wrong side of a flashed piece of glass.

Once the etching procedure has accomplished its purpose, remove the piece of glass from the acid bath and wash it thoroughly in running water, being careful not to allow the initial splashes to get on your skin. We generally submerse our pieces completely in a pail of water and then dump the water out and then let running water run over the piece of glass. The resist material is then taken off—if it's beeswax, it easily chips off; if it's contact paper, simply unwrap it—and your etching should stand out in bold relief against the background surface of the glass.

The Purpose of Etching

The basic purpose of etching is of course to save a lead line or two or three, especially in areas that may be so small that lead lines, or even foil, would look ridiculous. Etching places designs in the stained glass as a part of the larger window where the leading forms the metallic design. Etching can take out very very fine lines indeed in the glass and embroider the overall effect considerably. When used to advantage, etching can add a most unusual and beautiful effect. Like everything else in art, its overuse can lead to confusion and disharmony with the rest of the work.

Problems with Etching

The usual difficulty is that the worker mistakes the flashed side of the glass. If you do this, you can sit for several hours watching your acid bath and your glass never will change color, but when you lift it out you will find some fairly deep indentations in areas that according to your thinking should have changed color a long time ago. You have put the wrong side of the glass into the bath. Instead of using the flashed side, that is, the color that is on top of another color, you used the "white" side or the clear glass side that only shows color because of its opposite surface. It is very important that you are able to recognize which side of a piece of glass is the flashed side. Even if this requires grozzing a small corner in order to see where the color is, it is best to do this and be certain before wasting all your time setting up the material to be etched and finding out afterwards that you had the wrong side all along.

Another problem that frequently arises is the careless use of the resist material. Unless this material is thoroughly packed along all sides of the glass—and that includes the thin edges as well—the acid will get under it and attack and roughen whatever edges it can find (Fig. 17-18). The acid will also tend to seep

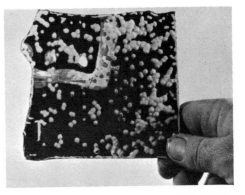

Fig. 17-17. One side of a piece of glass was left uncovered and placed in the acid. This is what happened to it.

Fig. 17-18. Careless use of the resist material. The acid has managed to seep under it and has begun to etch, inartistically, about midway along the bottom surface.

Fig. 17-19. The etched piece.

under edges of contact paper that are not thoroughly sealed down, especially around the design area where the stenciling has taken place.

In short, etching is a procedure that offers a great deal of power to the designer and can offer a great deal of frustration to the etcher if he is at all careless. If designer and etcher are the same person, it is not too difficult eventually to develop a split personality.

CHAPTER 18

Stained Glass Jewelry

In Shaw's play Caesar and Cleopatra, one of the characters speaks as follows: "Blue is the color worn by all Britains of good standing. In war we stain our bodies blue so that though our enemies may strip us of our clothes and our lives, they cannot strip us of our respectability."

From the ancient to the mod, things haven't changed much. While most of us may draw the line at actually drawing it on our bare skins, few among us, male or female, go totally unadorned. There is unquestionably present in the human spirit a wistful desire for plumage to make each of us a bird of a different feather. Originality and uniqueness are the two soldiers of a fortune raked in annually on this basis by top designers, some of whom will only make a limited amount of an item to keep its value up and its desirability secure. Here is your chance to design for yourself one of a kind novelties in the jewelry line made from stained glass, a material that is getting ever more attention in the fashionable boutiques.

Among these items are those strictly calculated for a short survival but an everlasting effect. Chief among them are the stained glass bras, which periodically reappear in the more sophisticated department stores in New York and other large cities over the country (Fig. 18-1). While they vary in detail, basically they are cups held together, either firmly by metal or loosely by chain, and supported over the wearer's neck, and or, shoulders. Each cup is made like a miniature Tiffany lamp, in small pieces, preferably in copper foil to keep the weight down and to

THE EYES HAVE IT

193

Fig. 18-1. One half of a stained glass bra. What happened to the other cup and the chain that connected them we don't know. Only this much was returned to us for duplication. We're convinced there's a story here somewhere but that would probably take another book.

Fig. 18-2. Stained glass belt buckle.

give a more diminutive effect. An actual brassiere may be used as the form. Needless to say, the endorser of this garb should be prepared for a certain amount of perceptual accuracy when going through revolving doors. We have seen some truly lovely designing brought into being in such items, but they are still pretty much for the woman who has everything. Modesty may be served by using opalescent glass. The less opalescent you become, the more risk you run of stimulating discussion, not so much of your work as your workmanship.

Stained glass vests also belong in this category of novelty items. They are not too difficult to produce. Essentially, you need only glass cut to size in rectangles, drilled with a hole in the top of each piece and a delicate thin chain to string them together. Unlike the bras, no soldering is necessary. You might sell a few of these to department stores as decor for their show window manikins. We have known individuals who did just this and so paved the way for curiosity about their stained glass work, which led to commissions in other more practical aspects of the art.

Less exotic, yet still a catching sight, is the stained glass belt buckle. Use only copper or brass as the basic metals here and if you use brass, make sure it isn't steel which is brass plated, as this will not solder. Having either made or purchased the basic buckle, any number of designs may be imposed upon it as the covering plate, or worked into the metal itself. Working with the metal presupposes the use of an enameling kiln and a knowledge of the enameling art. Imposing a stained glass decorative plate over the buckle is a much simpler process, which still gives a beautiful effect. With this, the best buckle to get is the type that fits a flange on one side into a groove on the other. Design your plate to completely cover these mechanics. Opalescent glass is best for this, with perhaps a jewel in the center; however, your imagination may well provide other effects.

Four or five breaks should be enough for the size involved, using copper foil as the holding agent. You can get as complicated as you like. A sense of completeness is added by running ¼-inch round lead around the outside of the buckle. This also adds weight. The entire face plate is then soldered to the underlying copper buckle and all lead lines can be then tinned and antiqued.

Remember that this is a performing art work and that stomachs occasionally peek over the belt line. Don't make your buckle so large as to have it nudging you, and remember, also, that it must be strong enough so it won't fall apart when pulled on. If you don't want to face-lift your buckle, you can work with it as is, using the sides and disregarding the steel tongue. Wrap adhesive backed copper foil around the sides and then tin it. What you have done is to provide a surface which is now amenable to soldering. From there, you can take it any way you wish to go, from foiling and soldering on small jewels or glass gems or chunks, to extending the buckle on over the belt. Just be careful that you don't interfere with the basic mechanism of the buckle. This technique can be applied also to the large plastic buckles on women's coats. The plastic won't melt from the soldering heat and with the increased size, more decoration can be added. Keep in mind that fundamentals of good taste should still be observed and the design should be planned and not just added slap-dash as the materials come to hand. Crushed glass, glued with the proper cement, will add luster to a plastic buckle, either by itself, or used sparingly as part of a larger design which also can be glued.

Stained glass belt buckles are among the most popular items produced in high school classes in introductory stained glass courses. The designs and imaginative endeavors going into the production of these items are truly amazing and seem to instill in this age group a determined effort to persevere in this decorative art.

The advent of the male sex into the garment industry's tides of fashion has splashed out a peacock urge that had lain dormant since the Restoration. As part and parcel of this change in clothing style there has come a demand for jewelry no longer limited to watch bands, tie clips, or money holders. A real swinger is the pendant.

As far as stained glass is concerned, this can be a circle, triangle, or square of glass with jewels poised over the surface, placed as part of the surface or simply a design within the glass itself (Figs. 18-2, 18-3, 18-4). A peace symbol is one of the first ideas that come to mind. Even so basically clear-cut a shape as that can be varied against its background, which may be circular or even heart-shaped to give a little additional impetus to the motivation.

Sometimes a jewel by itself, leaded or foiled, may be employed to good effect. If you are using jewels over a glass surface, they may be attached to the encircling rim of whatever basic shape you choose. Opalescent glass works very nicely for the background, but clear glass will also give a pleasing

PENDANTS

Fig. 18-3. Pendants—on the left a piece of costume jewelry foiled into the center of a leaded piece of stained glass; on the right the design set into the glass.

Fig. 18-4. Peace symbol—a pendant or, in larger form, a window hanging.

Fig. 18-5. Pendant—here's looking at you.

effect, since the swinging of the pendant will allow light to pass through it from all directions. If this is your desire, be sure to use colors in the overlay that will not cancel themselves out against the background. Jewels may also be glued to the basic shape, which should have foil or lead around it regardless.

We found a particularly effective pendant to be a square of glass with a glass doll's eye cemented to the middle of it (Fig. 18-5). We made these up for fun, and to our amazement found such interest in them that we sold numbers to gift shops and boutiques, which in turn passed them on, mostly to a youthful group of enthusiasts. It serves to illustrate how something so painstakingly simple can bring returns far and above its elementary fabrication.

A pendant, of course, consists of an emblem or design of some sort, supported by a chain. The chain we use is ordinary window sash, which gives more of an antique effect to the pieces. We had assumed initially that the more expensive looking the chain, the more appealing the finished product would be. In effect, what transpired was that the bright, new, and in some instances, ornate chain either took away from or clashed with the medallions. After much experimentation, we decided window sash was the best for our purpose, It not only was about the cheapest, but it looked best. The only process it had to be put through was a slight darkening in antiquing solution to get rid of its uncomfortably bright shine. The links can be separated with a screwdriver and pliers and rejoined once you have decided on the proper length. This chain is best cut with a good wire nippers. Unlike decorative lamp chain, you cannot use a chain pliers. A word of caution if you intend to use sash as a chain for pendants: It tends to shed its oxides onto skin and clothing. So don't use it in its raw state, but spray the chain with some sort of fixative. Those used to fix pastels or charcoal work well. Be sure to use something that will not harm the skin.

All told, pendants are among the most popular of the new jewelry for men; women, of course, have known of their charms for some time.

NECKLACES

A string of pearls is not the only decoration a neck may exhibit in the form of a complete circle of ornamental sparkle. Possession of a string of pearls also involves bank vaults, which is where such items rest most of the time. Between withdrawals, for parties where you really want to get out of your shell, you might try a string of ornamental glass designs—either nuggets of varying hues or foiled pieces of small abstracts. These can easily be hooked into a gold chain of plain design acquired at any jewelry store or soldered directly onto a copper chain. Gems (glass nuggets), we find, work about the best for this. They are without sharp edges, are durable and give enough weight so that you feel you have something on. Pieces of chunk glass with sharp edges filed smooth also give an interesting effect. We have seen such necklaces designed even tiara-like, with several tiers dropping off the main strand. It takes wit and imagination to design this sort of thing, but you may find it well worth your while. Such chunks or nuggets may be interspersed with small glass jewels. As with almost any stained glass jewelry, the use of adhesive backed copper foil is mandatory both for its incalculable ease of operation when working with such small pieces, as well as for the smaller weight, as opposed to lead, of the piece as a whole. Since the foil invariably has to be tinned, you would be well advised to take the brightness away with antiquing solution. Then the work should be spray-coated with fixative so the copper will not stain skin or clothing.

If you are thinking in terms of a tiara, you might like to try small figurines interspersed in the levels of chain with solder holding them to the different loops. Even three inches of width will suffice for the introduction of two or three of these devices, which might be animal, vegetable, or even abstracts of several glass jewels either fused or foiled together. The design is most important here; a very delicate touch is required.

A dummy torso of the type used for fitting blouses is very nice to have when doing this sort of work. It helps immeasurably both in the designing and actual fabrication of the piece to be able to see exactly how the various elements fall into place and how much bulk they produce. In fact, we feel so strongly about this that we urge you not to try necklaces unless you either buy or make some type of form which will give you the advantage of an onlooker. Without such perspective, you are liable to find the piece looks much better on the worktable than on you. Looking in the mirror helps somewhat, but it's an awful bother to keep taking the thing off and rebalancing it, and the tendency is to not try it on as much as necessary because of this.

PINS

Diamonds, say the blondes whom gentlemen supposedly prefer, are a girl's best friend. We have no intention of playing fast and loose with that proposition, but even best friends grow wearisome at times.

On those occasions, you might have Tiffany at breakfast by wearing a foiled stained glass pin on your lounging pajamas instead of your usual carat corsage. At least if you're a blonde, you might. The rest of us might well prefer diamonds; their accumulation is, however, an art and craft of its own and somewhat beyond our present scope. A finely wrought stained glass pin, all the same, is a jewel of its own to please the eye without pinching the pocketbook. We offer a few items of this genre:

The Bee

Two glass nuggets fused or foiled together compose the body on which a millefiore is melted for the eye. The wings can be cut from any scrap pieces of opalescent glass you may have flying around. Legs and antennae are copper wire. The tail is brown transparent glass on which black stripes are painted.

Fig. 18-6. The bee.

The Cat

A specially formed, fairly large glass nugget which, though only hinted at in the illustration, is two-toned, was used for chest and abdomen. We make such nuggets specifically for this type of jewelry. Our cat appears to be on the edge of a hiccough. The look of its eyes and the set of its tail, as well as its peculiar slouch, indicates a soothing prolongation of some stupefaction. Its eyes are actually glass fish eyes, which gives him the goofy look we wanted. His whiskers are copper and the tail is $\frac{1}{16}''$ U lead bent on itself. The head is a round nugget.

Fig. 18-7. The cat.

The Bird

He actually looks like he is giving the cat the raspberry, which may be another reason the cat doesn't look well. His pursed lips are small pieces of $\frac{1}{16}''$ U lead curled at the ends. We used a previously melted millefiore for the eye. Head and body are specially made streaky opalescent nuggets. The feet are two small glass globs fused together—though they may be foiled. He sits atop a branch made from a piece of brass rod and his tail is a thin sheet of brass cut into shape and sliced for feathers. (original design by Dorothy Harper).

Fig. 18-8. The bird.

The Owl

The owl is mostly eyes and body and is the most stylized piece shown. The eyes are nuggets carefully chosen for their effectiveness and foiled to $\frac{3}{16}''$ H lead which forms beak and head . . . sort of. The feet are $\frac{1}{16}''$ U lead or $\frac{3}{16}''$ divided and pulled slightly apart to form the toes. The tail is sheet brass.

The Tortoise

The trouble with a tortoise is that he's here today and here tomorrow; this one is no exception. Put him on the table, come back in an hour or two and you'll swear he's barely moved an inch. At least this one has an excuse; his feet are quite leaden. They support him, but that's about all. His body is a large, his head a small, round glass gem. There may be a smile on his face, but we can't tell from here.

All these small conceits are, indeed, pins and may be worn quite readily as stained glass costume jewelry. The pin is easily soldered to the back of the piece; make certain it is affixed firmly, as these items, once broken, are almost impossible to repair.

Here is another area of self-adornment where glass gems and nuggets may be used. Many novelty shops sell blanks for rings and earrings; it is easy to cement a particularly lovely or unusual glass gem into place and come up with one or more inexpensive yet unique pieces.

Whatever type of jewelry you decide on, remember that the workmanship should be as perfect as possible. The acid test of approval is to look at it carefully and wonder if you would buy it if you saw it displayed . . . and if not, why not?

Fig. 18-9. Owls.

RINGS AND EARRINGS

CHAPTER 19

The Crafts Show

The crafts show has become a popular, and for many exhibitors, a lucrative establishment. Over the past several years, corresponding to the tremendous explosion taking place in the crafts field generally, a great number of such displays have sprung up. Initially craft shows were taken in only as portions of larger art shows. Now, however, they fill up on their own with exhibitors invited from all craft operations to show their wares and demonstrate how they are made. Many such shows are still being produced by PTA's and church or other groups who are seeking money for a cause and who wish to benefit the crafts neighborhood in their community. A great opportunity is herein offered for beginners in stained glass, as they are sure to be noticed, being practically unique among all the other booths. Only recently has stained glass begun to be given a category of its own in craft shows. Initially it was buried under the general heading of "other multi-media," while Basket Weaving, Chair Caning and Egg Painting were listed alphabetically.

In many cases, stained glass is still not given its own specific category, but is listed rather limply under "Glass." This conglomerate title, which includes fused glass, blown glass, sea glass, old china and indeed in some instances, ancient eyeglasses has been enlarged, expanded and brought up to date by the discerning sponsors to include stained glass as well. Fortunately, the better craft shows recognize the fact that stained glass is an entity in its own right and treat it as such. We ourselves would hesitate to enter any crafts show that does otherwise.

The hobbyist interested in developing his craft

and interested as well in having people know what he is doing, might well take time out of his schedule to attend a crafts show or two to see what it is like. It is more than likely that he will be invited to participate, once enough people know of the work he is doing. More than likely, the invitation will come to him unasked. We receive notifications at our studio constantly of craft shows being put on in an area of four to five hundred miles or so around us and to which stained glass is a welcome entrant. After a number of years of attending such shows ourselves, we feel that the experience we gained might well be brought forth to help others.

The first thing you want to find out about your craft show is whether it's going to be held in a building or in the great outdoors. If it's outside, you must determine what the precincts are like. If it is in a building, you must be sure that there is a suitable nitch where you can show your stained glass to best advantage. Indecent exposure is not always a matter of legality. Often it is simply a question of taste. Craft shows can be held in some very peculiar sites and in very peculiar manners and it thereby behooves the exhibitor, no matter how desirous he may be for display of his items, to reconnoiter the area before participating in the show.

We arrived at one such indoor exposition to find all the windows covered with heavy drapes and no other available source of light by which to show our stained glass. Moreover, the drapes were not to be touched. This was not a crafts show per se, but we were invited as part of a larger art show and the other participants—oils, sculpture, water colors—were all accumulating the usual expressions of delight from the onlookers as they happily placed their various paintings on the walls and against their easels. We finally convinced the judges to allow us to pull the drapes back, but no amount of arguing would allow us to put any sort of hooks into the woodwork to hang our panels. We finally had to lean them against the windows, resting on the sills, and hope that they would not slip off.

We had arrived approximately 2:00 on the afternoon of a wintry, dull day. Setting up took about an hour and a half. A coffee break followed that, and, by the time the first guests arrived at 4:30, the light was already beginning to fail. By 5:00, when the show was in full swing, it was dark.

Stained glass does not have too much effect in the dark. We stood alongside our extinguished panels, while the audience passed us by completely. Almost

INDOORS OR OUTDOORS

completely. We did get an occasional individual who looked, shook his head, and said, "Isn't that awful." We assume to this day he was not talking about the quality of the workmanship.

Outside shows, however, also have their pitfalls. Many such shows occur in or around large shopping centers to get the traffic. Here, stained glass must also have its peculiar necessities catered to. One must insist on getting a booth not under the shopping center arcade where the light is poor, but on the edge of the arcade where at least some sunlight can stream through to illuminate the stained glass. Occasionally, sponsors of craft shows will take this into account and dispense booths to stained glass exhibitors where their material may best be seen. However, this is not usually the case and you had best double check.

Aside from this, such precincts have their own idiosyncrasies. One shopping center we exhibited at contained what seemed to be an inordinate proportion of children, all of whom wanted to touch everything. Stained glass is not overly responsive to touching, especially when the touching is actually more of a crumple. By the time we finished guarding our panels for the day, we were feeling somewhat stained and leaded ourselves.

A more conducive atmosphere for the outdoor show is the town or city park. Here at least the audience shows up because an art display is in progress, not because there happens to be a sale on refrigerators. Most parks have a lovely, green grassy area, which the mind's eye can see sparkling with sunlight and appreciative audiences. Reality, far more disconcerting, resolves the situation so that most exhibits are held somewhere in the woods while "keep off the grass" signs sparkle instead in the more aristocratic setting.

Here mosquitos, flies and occasional cicadas make up in enthusiasm for your presence whatever you may have lacked from other audiences, and since it has invariably rained the night before, you may find yourself knee deep in mud. Generally, the producers of the show scamper about enthusiastically pulling exhibitors out of the mire and scattering sawdust and gravel on the paths. A major difficulty, of course, is how to put one's panels so they might be displayed properly. Our lead pipe racks which we bring to outdoor shows for this purpose require a flat surface on which to stand. This meant literally digging one up. At our first outdoor show we made a mistake in not bringing chairs. Most of the other exhibitors had arrived with folding chairs at the ready. We had to snitch a quick use of their chairs here and there, when they went off to sell or enthuse over one of their canvases.

Remember that in many outdoor shows washrooms are non-existent and this generally involves a long walk back up to the Park Department area. There can also be no food unless you bring your own. At our first outdoor show we didn't bring our own and went hungry.

The only answer to resolving the uncomfortable situations inherent in the outdoor or indoor show is to know exactly what you're going into before you sign up. The general exhibitor information sheet which describes the show usually contains the size of each booth and the money that you will be charged for the space as well as conditions of sale and awards, etc. It may go into specifics, such as (1) teenagers available to watch your material if you want to wander around and see some of the show yourself, (2) where *exactly* the men's and ladies' rooms are, (3) where you may find places to eat in the area, and (4) where you may most conveniently park your car —to mention only a few. If it does, you're probably dealing with considerate sponsors with a good deal of experience. You can usually sign up without fear.

HOW TO DISPLAY

As we have indicated, displaying stained glass can present definite problems. We decided finally on racks, which we made as mobile as possible and which we never fail to bring with us whenever we agree to participate in any exhibitions.

These racks are made of ¾" pipe and screw together at elbow joints to form a very stable and well balanced affair from which may be hung several small panels and free form objects or just one or two large panels depending on their size. The racks form a rectangle rather like a clothes rack. The foot of each rack has a T connector from which two toes of pipe approximately a foot each spread out for balance. The racks stand approximately four feet high and measure four feet across.

The mobility of these racks is such that they may be put up and taken down easily and stored in the car. They go together rapidly, so that we may quickly put up for view whatever stained glass we have to show. Care must be taken in storing these pipes so that they do not rust, especially along the threads, or you will have difficulty putting them together securely. They must be threaded perfectly from the start or they won't go together. Once you have acquired a certain amount of efficiency working with these racks, you will find them enormously helpful in displaying stained glass at craft shows.

CHOOSE
YOUR SUNLIGHT

We touched on this previously in discussing the shopping center outdoor show. It's not enough to wait until you actually see the booth to complain; you must make it plain to the sponsors about the light at the time when you are considering joining the show. You must have a booth where the sun will best exhibit your stained glass. Occasional sponsors will agree to almost anything to get you to exhibit, but you are entitled to get this in writing and should insist on it so that when the day comes and you find yourself back in some dark corner, you will have someone other than yourself to blame. It's not that sponsors have anything against your media; they just do not realize how important it is that light be at your disposal. Every exhibitor is pretty much telling them the same thing because each wants to have the maximum amount of light at his booth. In no other craft form, however, is it a matter of such absolute necessity as it is in stained glass. Where possible, you should visit the area of the show beforehand so you can tell exactly where the best sunlight is to be found along the areas that are going to be used for booths.

BACK LIGHTING

Back lighting involves showing indoors and involves a totally different set of circumstances than the outdoor show. When you are showing indoors, unless you can somehow acquire a large window which admits plenty of light and against which you can place your panels, then you must rely on electric light to illuminate your work. Many art shows are held in private homes which have no space where stained glass can be readily exhibited. We bring along to such shows several powerful light bulbs with screw on type hangers, almost like Kleig lights. With these a wide luminesce is thrown over the glass, not just a pin point of light which the ordinary bulb will give—a bleary eye seen through a stained glass panel, illuminating nothing but its own irrelevance. Actually a fluorescent bulb would be best, but these are difficult to carry and even more difficult to hook up without actually making a light box out of each panel, which is impractical. Most people having such an exhibit in their home will be more than cooperative about letting you run extension cords from their outlets to supply your back-lighting. Try to keep the cords of reasonable length, and try not to make your back-lighting so intense that it blinds everyone going by from looking at the panels from the front—or indeed at anything else. At the same time you want to be certain that they are able to view your exhibit to its best advantage. You should be able to screw the grips of the bulb hangers to your pipe racks, aim the bulbs across the panel and toward the ceiling and switch on to exclamations of delight—which, of course, may be somewhat short lived if you happen to blow a circuit, so don't overload them.

Probably the best indoor method of showing stained glass is to acquire a sheet of "frosted" plastic, place that behind your glass objects and light it from behind. It may also be held from a pipe rack, from which it will diffuse the light evenly and make your stained glass stand out clearly. It depends on how much you want to carry and how much you want to put into the show.

WHAT TO DISPLAY

Of course you will bring your best works, not your worst for display. If you aren't sure which are which, you had better get some help from a disinterested party. Workers who feel all their efforts are of such poor quality as not to deserve showing, may be absolutely right. At the same time, many individuals have no judgment of their own work and must have an unprejudicial opinion to guide them. You should bring work that not only shows off your own capabilities, but that shows off the medium in which you are working. If you have several different types of items, such as lamps, panels, windows, and free form objects, you might try a sampling from each category. If you only have lamps or only panels, then that is what you must bring, but at least bring the best of them. A few very good pieces makes for a much more effective display than numerous shoddy ones.

THE DEMONSTRATION

Some craft shows have spots in the program where demonstrations of the particular skills required of various crafts are displayed. This is usually noted in the questionnaire accompanying your petition for space at such a show. We have found it always a good idea to demonstrate stained glass. Don't worry about feeling awkward and don't worry about not knowing enough. Keep in mind that you are not setting yourself up as an expert, but just trying to pass along information.

After you get over the initial strangeness of it, you will probably begin enjoying the demonstration and relaxing in the interest other people are taking in what you are doing. Remember you are under no obligation to give them a thorough course in stained glass technique; you're simply trying to acquaint them with the fact that such technique does exist.

So, don't make your lecture or demonstration too

complicated, or you will shortly begin to lose the interest of your audience. Make it brief. A good demonstration should take no more than twenty minutes. Make it succinct, so that within that time span you manage to demonstrate some of the techniques of glass cutting, tell them a little bit what stained glass is all about and show quickly how the pieces are put together and soldered.

PRICING YOUR WORK FOR SALE

There is no rule on how to do this. You must, however, keep in mind that no matter how long it may have taken you to make a free form hanging object, to most people it is only a small decorative piece and they are not prepared to pay you what you may think it is worth in terms of effort and time. In fact, if you are making one-of-a-kind items that are quite complicated and ornate, quite frankly you cannot afford to sell them. Your best bet is to make up five or six or ten of any one type of simple item, thereby splitting the labor among many rather than spending it all on one. In this way, you can price your pieces much more cheaply and still end up with a good return on your time. While it is somewhat difficult artistically to make any sort of mass produced handicraft, it is still better to vary the objects slightly to keep from being bored and yet be able to sell them. Of course, if you are going to make all your pieces extremely complex, you will still not be able to get the money out of them for the time that you have spent. Design them so that you can cut the pieces quickly and lead them quickly. There should be no provocative curves, no difficult leading points, etc. The person buying the work will not appreciate how much extra skill you put into it. He is looking at it as a colorful object that strikes his fancy.

Of course, if a piece is commissioned specifically, that is a different story and in that case you must carefully price it as a one-of-a-kind object, considering the amount of time, the material that you are going to spend plus the design. But, then, if a piece is commissioned, there is a definite interest in this specific object on the part of the buyer. He is not just picking it out of a shop window or from your booth at a show as a novelty. He will certainly appreciate the intricacies and the beauty of something that he is helping to create.

People tend to admire things vociferously until they discover the price. It is not a good idea to lower your price on an item because of this. If, however, this situation keeps repeating itself so that you feel perhaps the item is too high as it stands, you might redesign it, cutting down on the number of pieces of glass and the intricacies of the leading and then sell it at a lesser price at the next show or to the next gift shop. Of course, if you feel that the item is definitely worth the price that you have put on it, stick to your guns. You can, after all, always enjoy it yourself.

There is little you can do personally about advertising your presence in any particular art show other than by word of mouth. Most of these exhibitions have their own advertising which goes out to the local newspapers and, in some instances, if the show is an exceptionally large one, to national arts and crafts magazines. You should try to specify at the very beginning when you are sending in your application that the sponsors of the show be sure to include in their publicity that stained glass will be a part of the show. You might mention to your local newspaper that you're going to be in such a show. These newspapers are usually looking for items to print concerning local residents and will probably be happy to place this for you.

Once at the craft show you should have some sort of sign to advertise your presence and perhaps you might even make such a sign out of stained glass. This is simply done. Letters can be cut out of wood and glass of different colors placed behind it, or glass can be cut to shape and glued with glass cement to an underlying stained glass panel, in which case they will stand out in bold relief. If you want to get really fancy, you can design an actual leaded panel with your name or your studio name. Remember, a shoddy, simple sign is worse than none at all, so try to avoid advertising your presence as though your presence were unimportant. If you have any particular large piece of work that you have done, such as a fairly large window or large panel that you have produced for your own amusement, bring them and place them somewhere high above the booth so that people will be able to see over the heads of the milling that generally goes on at such exhibits, your unique calling card. If you have any little printed throwaway items which tell about yourself, your studio or your work, put them on the booth in front of you. You will be surprised how rapidly they will disappear. You may also be somewhat astonished at how few individuals afterwards will ever get in touch with you because of them. One or two may, and they may just be the right ones, but there is absolutely no relationship between the amount of literature that vanishes at these exhibits and the interest involved. People seem to

ADVERTISING YOUR PRESENCE

want to take whatever is free and in fact, in many instances, will try to grab some of the material that is not free. We have been to exhibitions where our demonstration items and books that were for sale had to actually be tied to the counter to avoid being swept away by the eager hands of the passing clientele.

Remember that the best advertisement of your presence in any show is yourself and you should be prepared to stay behind your booth and not disappear for hours during the day wandering around the exhibition hall. We have seen such exhibitors parading and it almost invariably occurs that when they vanish from their booth for a while is when the majority of people arrive and mill about with nobody to answer their questions and no one to sell them any of the items they might wish to buy. So bring a book and a chair and be prepared to spend the time as gracefully as possible. We have picked up a number of clients at such shows who later ordered stained glass windows for their homes. We also have been able to get a very good idea of what people expect in terms of prices for stained glass, as well as trying to educate some of the individuals as to what stained glass is all about. While many craft shows are not a worth while experience, there really is no way to tell which will be and which will not until you actually go through the time span.

Of course, if you find that the show is an absolute dud, there is nothing to stop you from packing your materials up and simply going home long before the show is over. We have done this too.

CHAPTER 20

The Gift Shop and Stained Glass

The gift shop is a great middleman between the working craftsman and the public. The crafts explosition has had its effect in the number of new and imaginative gift shops that have sprung up all over the country, specializing in hand-crafted objects. Others have both hand-crafted and machine-made material, providing the machine-made items have an appeal similar to the hand-crafted.

Unless you are a craftsman of long experience with an extremely good reputation, most gift shops will not buy your items directly from you. Instead they offer you what they call a consignment situation. This means they will show your items in their store for a certain length of time, and if the items are purchased, they will take a percentage of the purchase price and give you the remainder. Many individuals beginning to show their work around are a little disheartened by these terms. They feel that since they have done all the labor, the gift shop should buy the items directly. It's even worse, morale-wise, when, enough time having elapsed without the items being sold, the craftsman is presented with them once again.

At the same time, there are certain advantages to consignment from the standpoint of the craftsman. First is that his work is being displayed in an area where many people can see it. Second is the guidance that the beginning artist will get from many shops as to just what price to put on his work, what will sell and what will not. He can see quite readily whether the price is fair by how fast or how slow

CONSIGNMENT OR SALE

Fig. 20-1. One of the better gift shops of our acquaintance, everything in it is arranged with taste and all items are given a fair and equal showing. Craft shops such as "The Fat Cat" have begun to spring up all over the country.

the work moves out. He can then realistically arrive at some price that will still give him a good mark-up and allow the gift shop to get its percentage. Third, having his work in a gift shop allows the craftsman a certain status in the eyes of many individuals. It gives him a reference and a home base. Most people neither know nor care anything about consignment tactics. They are impressed by the fact that the work is being sold through a gift shop, and their estimation of the craftsman rises accordingly.

WHAT'S A FAIR PERCENTAGE?

Most gift shops consider 20% to be a fair price to take from your over-all price for each item of yours that they sell. We consider this quite a fair slice of the pie. There are shops, however, that will go as high as 25% or 33⅓%, and unless you are for some reason very fond of the people running such shops and wish to line their pockets, it would be much better for you to find a gift shop whose percentage is more reasonable. Remember, you must consider the consignment percentage when you decide on a price for your object, and if the consignment percentage is high, your over-all price will also be high, and your items probably will not sell. It's easy enough for the gift shop people to ask you to lower the price. If you do, however, you may be losing money, considering the amount of time and materials that you have to spend on the items under consideration. You should at least make 50% profit on small hanging objects—the gift shops' specialty. If you cannot make at least that, then it's not worth it, and you had either better find another gift shop or take that particular item off the market and redesign it so that it takes you much less time to fabricate it. We have seen many small objects in gift shops that were simply leaves or berries or apples or little pieces of fruit cut out of pieces of stained glass selling for between $3.00 and $4.00. Considering the gift shop mark-up to be 20% on a $3.00 item, the artist would be coming away with $2.40—certainly more than a 50% mark-up for such a piece of work. It is just these pieces that sell, whether of stained or crushed glass, and if you can move twenty or thirty of these a day, you are doing very nicely indeed, and so is the gift shop or shops which are accepting your work. It is (sadly) easier to sell twenty or so of these items than one fairly complex mobile that you may have labored over for some time. But persevere; the sale of enough of the small items will buy you the material and incentive to go on to bigger, and finally commissioned, works.

Fig. 20-2. Main display window seen from within. The stained glass objects are given individual room and not just hung helter skelter one in front of another.

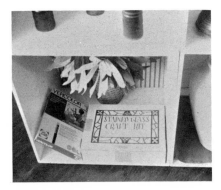

Fig. 20-3. Stained glass is featured in many craft shops. "The Fat Cat" goes in for some do-it-yourself items in this field . . .

Fig. 20-4. . . . as well as completed pieces such as lamps, mirrors . . .

Fig. 20-7. A different corner of the shop—rows of multicolored candles line the shelves.

Fig. 20-5. . . . and stained glass mobiles.

Fig. 20-8. Another corner—tastefully done.

Fig. 20-6. Different styles of stained glass lamps, while waiting to be sold, illuminate the precincts.

Fig. 20-9. Overall view of one section of the shop.

HOW LONG
SHOULD YOU LEAVE
ITEMS UNSOLD?

You had best consult with the owner of the gift shop on this. Only he will know how much interest has been expressed in your pieces. He may feel that after two months they should be changed, since they have not sold and people are getting used to them. Individuals who frequent gift shops and see the same stained glass hanging there month after month will tend to think the artist is not selling. This may be the truth, in which case it is wiser to put in a whole new display. Of course, if the items are continually moving, and you are continually replenishing them, you may not care about changing the display, unless you are tired of it yourself. Even a successful display should be changed at least four times a year and have new items added and the least successful ones removed.

SIGNING YOUR WORK

Fig. 20-10. There's even a stained glass window as part of the rear door.

All your work should be signed so that anyone buying it will know that it is a piece from your studio. Carbide scribers are available for this purpose. Even though people may not know your name or who you are, a signed piece of work always seems to appear psychologically more valuable than an unsigned one. If you can arrange to have an attractive little label printed which will describe your work with a short description of stained glass in general and how to care for it, you may find that this, hanging from your object, will attract attention and will become an additional incentive for purchase. People like to read about what they are buying; a label makes them feel that personal attention has been paid to their object, and the printing up of such small labels can be done with minimal cost. They may bring you great returns. We have such a label for our own work (Fig. 20-11).

EXCLUSIVELY YOURS—IF POSSIBLE

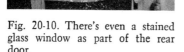

Stained Glass

STAINED GLASS CLUB
482 Tappan Rd.
Northvale, N.J.
07647

Created by:
ANITA DE

Fig. 20-11. Label for gift shop items.

It is our opinion that if you are placing your stained glass in a gift shop, it would be best if no other stained glass were present. To compete on a consignment basis is not practical. Many gift shops have stained glass from several different craftsmen in their shop and may even repeat the same general items. This certainly does not play fair with any of the contributing parties and can only serve to cheapen the articles in the public's eye. If you cannot get an exclusive with a gift shop for your work, we suggest that you take it to another gift shop. If a shop has been carrying your work and the owner feels that he would like to try somebody else as well, it is only common courtesy that he so inform you and that you then have a choice of removing all your work or leaving it with the competitive items. We feel very strongly that you should have an exclusive, at least for a reasonable length of time, so you may show your craft without having the effect diluted by the work of others in the same field.

There should also be a working arrangement with the shop, so that if someone comes in and wants a specific piece of stained glass fabricated, the gift shop refers them to you. This will still allow the shop to get their discount on the item and will allow you to get the commission. We do not think it particularly fair for a gift shop to refer a customer to another craftsman when they have your work hanging in their windows.

You may find your work getting so popular that an agent may contact you with a view toward displaying it at some of the gift shows that are held across the country. If this is the case, and if the work is good and price right, you will probably find yourself deluged with orders. These orders will come from gift shops all over the nation, wherever these shows are held. An instant business can suddenly develop. *Do not accept consignment terms.* Be sure to so inform your agent. Also be sure to check very carefully into the list of your prospective customers. Remember that your agent is simply taking the orders for a specific commission. You must pay this commission whether you get paid from the gift shops or not. It is your responsibility to make sure that you are dealing with reputable shops who will meet the terms of the agreement. You don't want to spend your time and effort turning out items which will neither be returned nor paid for. This is a very sad experience indeed.

Get a Credit Rating

Before even starting to function on any mail order, you should write to the firm placing the order and ask if they are rated in Dun and Bradstreet. If they are, you should consult these volumes at your local library and check their credit rating. If they are not listed, ask them to send credit references. If they don't do this, insist on payment in advance (pro forma). Some gift shops will refuse, and you will end up losing the order. It is worth it, for in the long run you would end up losing your labor as well. We make it a point never to deal with any shop that is not rated in Dun and Bradstreet, or that at least will not furnish several good credit ratings. Remember that even if you do get a good credit rating, most gift shops do not pay much before 90 days, and you will be sitting for quite some time before you get

MAIL ORDERS

Fig. 20-12. A unique gift shop item—a stained glass rose in a kiln-fired vase (formerly a beer bottle).

your money. Your agent, on the other hand, will want to get paid right away. The gift shop business can be very tricky. Sometimes your agent, for an additional percentage, will agree to do the billing for you and accept the loss of his commission on accounts that do not pay. This is something you might want to discuss with him.

Remember to Charge for Postage

When you are making up your invoice and the order is packaged and ready to go, be sure you add a charge for postage to the order. If you do not add it to the invoice, you will not be paid for it, and you will be losing that much more money from your total price. Reputable gift shops expect to be billed for postage and will simply add it to the check they send you. However, if it is not on the invoice, be assured that they will not figure it up themselves and send it to you. If you are sending items via UPS, be sure to add in the UPS charge on each package sent.

How Best to Send Glass

There really is no good way to send glass. We have tried sending items via UPS, Railway Express, Parcel Post, etc., and we suffer approximately a 50% breakage in the process. Naturally, if these items are of any great value, they should be insured, so that at least you will get your money back. However, to insure every item sent through the mail adds a great deal of time and expense to the overall procedure. In the long run, all you can do is insure very expensive items up to the hilt, try to let the cheaper ones go without any insurance, and hope for the best. Remember that you never really will know if the item got there in one piece, or if the gift shop at the other end simply dropped it. Unless you have a substantial operation going, you may find mail orders are more trouble than the whole thing is worth.

Billing Procedure

If your items are in the corner gift shop, you will not have to bill; the shop will send you a check each month for whatever they sold, plus an itemized list of what went out. However, if you are sending items to gift shops across the country, not on consignment terms, you must bill them religiously each month, or you will not get paid. No gift shop, in our experience, will send you your money unless they are so billed, and not once, but three or four times, in many instances. You should have a standard invoice printed up with your name and the name of your studio on it, and your invoice should include the date, the items sent, whom they were sent to, where the order was placed and with whom. A copy of this should also go to your agent. Then you must list the items that were ordered and when the order was shipped, how much the total came to plus postal charges, and then list the amount on the bottom. It is not necessary to go through this type of invoicing each time. You may send a balance due statement thereafter. Rest assured that you will probably have to do this type of follow-up, and don't be disappointed when it occurs. Of course, if you run into gift shops that are very slow payers, or that do not pay you at all, you must notify your agent not to accept any further orders from these individuals, unless they pay for the items in advance. Gift shops are notoriously loath to do this.

If you have worked up a fairly successful business making items for gift shops, you would best acquire a method of making them via mass production. You may require some help in this. In the long run it will be worth it. To do items on a mass production scale, you must cut out at least 30 or 40 of each single item. Do all the glass cutting first. When all the pieces are cut as smoothly as possible, place them together in piles and run back-to-back caming around them. The leading should be done on each similar glass piece of each item so that you go right down the line, leading and cutting while someone follows up with an iron, soldering the came closed. Pieces then are soldered as units, and then are all turned over on the other side and soldered. There are special glass cutting jigs available, machines which can be set to cut any number of one particular pattern, and investing in one of these can help considerably in getting your items turned out as rapidly and efficiently as possible.

Of course, this is not really what stained glass as an art form is all about. We see it, like any art, as producing one-of-a-kind items for specific sale or display. However, money is made by mass-produced items, and if this is your "cup of tea," you can certainly do well at it. Once you have made your contacts through the large gift shows via an agent, you will find that you probably won't have enough time to keep up with the orders. Be sure that your prices are reasonable—both reasonable to the gift shop, which usually adds a hundred percent mark-up, and reasonable to yourself.

Package your items as carefully as possible to avoid breakage. Straw or bubbled plastic is the best

MASS PRODUCING ITEMS FOR QUICK SALE

Fig. 20-13. Small stained glass kits—mass produced and ready to go. In order to make a profit on such items you have to sell a lot of them and be able to turn them out at a rapid rate.

PACKAGING

medium for protecting glass, as it seems to absorb shocks well. Crumpled newspaper is also good, but there is a great deal of time and effort spent crumpling the paper. You should not attempt to send any more than two or three items in a package, for if a particular package gets roughly handled, generally all the items in it will be broken. It's a good idea to have boxes made that will specifically fit the size items you are going to ship. Have enough space in them so the packaging material can be generously applied. Then you may pack these boxes in a carton and be fairly certain that they will get to where they are going safely. If items that manage to get through safely month after month suddenly start returning broken, you might want to check and see if some new postal employee or some new UPS driver might not be handling them a little too roughly.

PART V
Repair and Restoration

CHAPTER 21

Repairing Stained Glass Objects

Repairing stained glass involves totally different techniques from those required for building an object from the beginning. In many cases, it's a great deal easier to rebuild an item completely than to repair it, even partially. This holds especially true if the piece to be repaired is a panel with several portions broken out of the center, or a lamp with a broken bent panel or two which must be put back into the old brass holding material. Not only is the work involved tedious and difficult, but most of the objects brought in for repair are so dirty they must be cleaned before you can even see what color glass you're working with. The leads are generally so corroded that you can't get them to take solder at all, unless you scrub away like mad with a wire brush. That scrubbing may abruptly peel them right away from the glass, and then you must replace them anyway.

It's very difficult to tell an individual bringing an object in for repair that it would probably be much better to have the entire thing rebuilt. People feel you are trying to convince them because you can make more money that way. It is true that it costs more to rebuild, but if it's the end result that matters, the best end result for a thoroughly battered window or lamp is rebuilding—anything short of that is a compromise. Unfortunately, it is only on the fee that people want to compromise, not on your labor. They must be told emphatically that repairs on stained glass objects, like surgery, leave scars to a greater or lesser degree, and the piece, if subjected to careful scrutiny, will always look repaired.

It's a temptation for the beginner at this sort of thing to quote a low price to get the job. Unfortunately, he then finds that he cannot do it as it should be done. He tries taking shortcuts in order to match the fee, and is likely to come out with a product looking worse than it did when it was first brought in. It is always best to be absolutely honest with people and tell them that a repair job is not a restoration. Restoring something implies that it will be brought back to a state of pristine creation, while repair involves merely replacing a portion of the object so that it will once again be functional and decorative, but it will not necessarily be perfect. People may be willing to pay the price of repair, but they too often expect restoration for their money.

REPAIRING WINDOWS

The easiest windows to repair have pieces that are broken out near the borders. If the window is brought in with its frame, it must be taken out before any work at all can be done on it. You should not have to do this—no window should be accepted in its frame. Getting it out can be quite a time-wasting procedure, as well as involving the possibility of your cracking more glass, which you will then have to replace gratis.

You should get off whatever dirt you can with a rag or with Windex. As you are going to be getting your fingers pretty involved with the metal, it is wise to have it and the glass as clean as possible. Be careful when passing a rag over the surface of any old panel that you do not inadvertently stick yourself on a piece of turned-up lead or an old copper wire that was used to join a reinforcing rod. You can very easily cut a finger open by cleaning one of these pieces carelessly.

Once the window is clean and the leads are reasonably so, then cut away the border lead surrounding the broken piece. The broken glass should be pulled gently out of the surrounding came with glass pliers, and the point of a lead knife then passed through the channels to make sure that no small pieces of glass and putty remain inside. Place a piece of pattern paper beneath the opening, and with a sharp pointed pencil, follow the design exactly, passing it on to the pattern paper. Do this exactly to the point where the border lead has been cut away and use a ruler to join the two ends of the design to take the place of the border lead. Then enlarge your design very slightly to allow for the leads covering the two neighboring pieces of glass. Cut the design out of pattern paper and check the pattern in the space. Then cut a piece of glass to shape. Your glass should fit exactly into the empty space, snapping into the empty channels of the lead with the least bit of tapping from a leading knife handle. You may then replace the missing portion of border lead and solder it to the lead on either side.

In many cases, you will find old putty within the empty leads surrounding the broken glass. This should be thoroughly cleaned out with your leading knife blade, and once the new glass is back in place, new putty should be applied. Never skip this step. It is one of the most important guidelines in repair that all replacement pieces of glass be puttied. This very often holds true in lamps as well. The putty helps fill in areas that are not exactly to dimension, and also helps strengthen the repaired area.

For windows or panels that have pieces broken out in their centers, the repair is considerably more complicated. Several methods may be applied here.

The Tinker-Toy Approach

This, quite simply, involves taking the entire window apart to the point of the missing piece, or pieces. You must cut away the border lead and work your way through all the sound pieces of glass between the border and the area you must fix. In complicated windows, this can involve a great number of pieces of glass and a great number of pieces of lead, for, needless to say, all the lead must be cut away as the glass is removed. There is the additional risk of breaking a number of these glass pieces, thereby having to replace quite a few more than you originally figured on. There is also a lot of putty scraping involved, since before any of the pieces of glass can be removed, you must pass the point of your lead knife under all surrounding caming to break away the extremely hard putty. This must be done on both the front and the back of the panel, and the more pieces you get out of it, the more difficult it is to turn back and forth because the unsteadier it gets. It's a cumbersome method, but once you get to the area of the break, you can fit the new glass exactly. You then back out the way you came in, replacing leads, glass, and putty as you go. The finished product will certainly be well-repaired and the process gets easier, of course, as it goes along. In fact, it's a lot easier putting the window together than it is taking it apart. As with most repair jobs, the most difficult portion is preparing the object for repair, not the actual repair operation itself.

The tinker-toy approach involves a great deal of time, a great deal of effort, and you should be getting paid a great deal of money, depending on the complexity of the work at hand. It actually is a restoration. Most people with a broken window, however, are not willing to pay the price that this type of repair would have to cost. In most instances, the worker will apply this technique only to windows that he has picked up in an antique shop and is repairing for his own use. In such cases, the labor and the time are his own, but so is the finished product. Old windows, some of surpassing beauty, can occasionally be found in antique shops with portions broken away. Because of these fractures, the windows can be had rather inexpensively. They can be restored by the method described above.

The tinker-toy approach requires a good craftsman with a steady head. If the window under consideration is of a fairly complicated design, it is best before taking it apart to make a pattern so you will know how the pieces go together again. Designs tend to appear logical and inexorable when the pieces are together; when the pieces are scattered all about your worktable, the possible combinations are staggering. An easy way to make such a pattern is by taking a piece of brown kraft paper, holding it over the panel, and pressing your fingers along the lead lines. This will indent the paper, and when you lift it, you will have a rubbing of these lines which will not only give you the design but the exact spacings of the glass as well. You can then darken these lines with a magic marker. This method serves far more purpose than a quick sketch drawn on a piece of scrap paper to be deciphered with difficulty later on. A rubbing is really the only way; it can be a great time saver and will furnish a great measure of security, which you may need as you progress.

Be gentle removing the sound glass. If you break a piece you may not be able to match it. Keep scraping your knife into the leading, sinking it progressively deeper to get the putty out so the piece can be wiggled free. Be careful that the old glass doesn't suddenly snap and your hand flies back against a neighboring piece of glass. This is one of those all too frequent accidents that accompany repair work. Another is having your leading knife slip into a carelessly placed bracing hand.

The Lead Flap Approach

This method is also used in repairing central portions of broken panels. It may be summarized as follows: Flap up the edges of the surrounding lead came as best you can so that the top flanges are at right angles to the surface and fit the glass as closely as possible, approximating it to the space left for it.

This procedure works best for diamonds or squares or rectangles, and it works worst with free form pieces, and especially pieces with sharp points or acute inner or outer curves. The specific technique is as follows:

1. With the point of your leading knife, thoroughly explore all channels of the surrounding came that still exist in reasonable form. If any of the channels are torn, or if the leads are in poor condition, they must be cut loose from the glass and replaced with new leads. This must be done before any glass is cut. When cutting old leads away, be careful not to crack any of the glass they adhere to. Very gently, with your lead knife, first cut one surface to the glass and then turn the panel over and cut the other; then pushing the came from behind with your knife blade, you should be able to pry the old lead loose. With your lead knife scrape the piece of glass now uncovered to remove all putty from its surface, and replace the lead with a new piece, soldering it to its neighbors. Once you are satisfied that the leads are firm and that the channels are completely empty, you are ready for the next step.

2. With your glass pliers, bend the flanges of the leads upright so that they end up as close to a right angle to the surface as possible. Cut all soldered joints. It is only necessary to do this on one side of the panel. The came on the other side should be left alone to form a shelf for the glass to rest on. You have then a hole surrounded by came which has, sticking out below, a small flange in horizontal position, with the flange above in vertical position. This should allow you enough room to wiggle the glass back into the space provided for it.

3. Place a piece of pattern paper underneath the opening and with a sharp pointed pencil, as before, make a pattern of the existing space. You must enlarge this pattern to compensate for the horizontal shelf of lead below so your glass will be about $\frac{1}{16}''$ larger than the pattern.

4. Cut your glass to shape after enlarging the pattern and smooth all edges with abrasive paper. If you have cut your pattern correctly, you should be able with the help of your lead knife to wiggle and pry this new piece

of glass into the opening. It should sit firmly on the bottom flanges of lead. Naturally, it should match as closely as possible the color of the piece you removed.

5. Check with your lead knife to make sure that the glass is sitting properly, and then, using the blade of your lead knife or a putty knife, smooth down the raised flanges of lead so they now cover the upper edges of the glass. Where the leads meet, the area should be soldered. Once this is done, your piece should be seated quite firmly back in the leads. Try to use a very smooth glass pliers when bending the flange; otherwise the grozzing teeth will leave their marks in the lead, and these are impossible to get out.

The difficulties with this procedure are manifold. For one thing, the glass cutting must be absolutely precise, and no matter how precise your glass cutting is, if your initial pattern is not correct, you will still have trouble with the glass. Many times we have cut patterns, using the stiff pattern paper, which fit the space quite readily, but the glass consequently cut from such a pattern would not go in at all. This may easily happen, for the paper pattern can take subtle forcings and small bends to make it fit, which the glass will not put up with. Thus, while the paper pattern may seem to be sitting properly, this is only an illusion because of its very small thickness, as opposed to the thickness of the piece of glass that is to follow it. So don't be discouraged if you've cut your glass precisely to pattern and it still doesn't fit. You will have to back and fill, placing marks on the glass with a glass pencil at the areas of contact and grozzing these away until your glass finally does go into the space provided.

You must fight the tendency to over-grozz. The grozzing must be done a tiny bit at a time. If you do too much grozzing in any one space, be assured that when the glass sits in, you will have a hole between the glass and the lead at that point, and the whole piece will have to be re-done. Grozz and fit, grozz and fit, and eventually the glass will go into the space. However, this may still not be the end of your troubles, for the lead rim which has been dislocated upwards may not want to come down again without looking something like a crumpled sheet. Lead so treated tends to get a somewhat ragged look when placed back over the glass, and to the extent that it does your repair will be noticeable. You can avoid a good bit of this ragged appearance in the lead by bringing it both up and down very gently and a little at a time. Patience is what is really required here. Some workers try to rush through repair jobs because the very nature of "repair" seems to indicate that it is a non-creative piece of work. It may well be so, but that does not mean that it should be sloppy.

All the same, you may find no matter how much patience you exercise, that you're left with a piece of lead that looks rather tattered and worn and which stands out like a sore thumb. This is one of the difficulties of this technique, and you can only try to ameliorate it by smoothing the surface with lead knife or putty knife blade over and over. Watch the pressure you apply. When you bend the lead up, it will help if you take a lead knife and cut it at the corners where the tension is at its worst, rather than letting the lead tear away at these areas. This not only will allow for a neater solder joint at the site when you are done, but it takes a lot of the strain off the central portion of the flange, so that the whole flap can move as a unit. Above all, do not use any other than a glass pliers to bend the lead upwards. We purposely use glass pliers because they are the widest-jaw pliers we have. To attempt to use electrician's pliers or grozzing pliers is simply to make the lead look even more torn and tattered than it would otherwise.

The Half-a-Lead Replacement Method

A third technique of replacing these difficult central portions of glass starts by taking your lead knife and cutting away all the leads surrounding the space to be replenished. That means all the neighbor leads are cut completely away leaving the empty space surrounded only by borders of glass. Pattern paper, as before, is placed beneath the space to be filled and a sharp pencil used to promote the pattern upon it. However, here the pattern need not be enlarged for there is no lead to compensate for. Once the pattern is cut, it should be fitted into the space to see how closely it matches. If it does not match well, mark where it is off and cut a new pattern. Once you have a pattern that fits accurately, cut your piece of glass to match, and, holding the glass from beneath, push it up into the space and see how it sizes up. It should fit as closely as possible to the bordering surfaces of glass, leaving only the space for the lead between.

Once you are satisfied that this is the case, take some plasticene clay and make a bed underneath the glass space to support the surrounding pieces. It should be a very thin bed so that it does not lift the panel away from the table surface, but it should be there to hold all pieces of glass from moving. Press your new piece of glass into the space and onto the bed of plasticene clay so that it is firmly held there. Remove with a toothpick any plasticene that oozes up between the glass. Next, measure the size leads you will need, always remembering to match them to the type of lead used throughout the rest of the panel. Cut your leads to size. Then cut them in half, right through the heart of the lead, cutting them as close to the center of the lead heart as you can. Do not mix up these matching halves, or you will end up with a very poor fit in your panel. Take a half of each piece of lead and run a small amount of glass glue down its side. Then place each piece on the panel covering the empty edges of glass. Press each piece down firmly and allow a few moments for the glue to begin to take to the surfaces of the glass which, incidentally, must be thoroughly cleaned. The ends of the lead should then be soldered together and any glue seeping out from beneath the channels should be immediately wiped away.

Allow several hours for the glue to set and then turn the panel upside down and remove the thin plasticene bed. Clean off the sides of the glass and now, being careful to place each remaining half lead on top of its brother piece in the same direction as it was cut, repeat the process of the leads as before. When you are done, you will have a neat appearing surface that to all intents has a single H lead holding two pieces of glass together. This type of repair is probably the best appearing for the least amount of work and will give a very fine looking surface if it is done correctly. As the glue dries, the leads will cling quite firmly to the glass and there should be no chance whatsoever of the repair coming apart.

A slight difficulty with this procedure is encountered when shaving away the old lead from the surrounding surfaces of glass. Always use your lead knife here and make sure that it is sharp. Lead will come away usually by nicking it at a corner and running your knife blade through the heart right along the surface of the glass. The major cause of concern is mixing up the two halves of your new leads, so that when you go to put them together, they don't match, leaving one side standing out from the glass. Mark these halves very carefully and make sure you mark exactly how the cut runs so that when you go to match the top surface with the bottom, you won't have them backwards. If you keep your lead separated and remember not to put the head of one at the foot of the other, you will find that they go together with great ease.

Another source of difficulty is encountered with the glass itself. If the cutting is so close that one surface of glass is actually touching another, you will not be able to force your leads between them to allow the cut surfaces to go together properly. This will also lead to standing away of the lead. Conversely, if your glass edges are too far apart, you may find that the lead came is not sufficient to cover them completely, and you will be left with a space. You have no choice here but to recut your glass. It is best to find this out before the leading process begins. That is why you must size your cut piece of glass up against the space provided.

These three methods are the major ways in which a stained glass window or panel may be repaired. There are conjoinings and modifications of these techniques which may apply to special situations, but in general, using the methods described above, you should be able to repair, and repair quite well, any window or panel that comes your way.

REPAIR OF BUCKLED WINDOWS

You may find in an antique shop, or a friend may show you, a window that has no broken pieces, but a lot of bent ones—at least so it may appear at first glance. What has happened is that the bracing of the window has given way, and the leads have allowed the glass to buckle forward. Simply leaning on the buckled portion in an attempt to push it back into shape is neither sufficient nor healthy. If you're ever asked to repair one of these windows, don't be misled, as the individual owning the window may be, by the fact that because there are no broken pieces to replace, the job is an easy one. The chances are that it's far more difficult than simply replacing a broken piece or two. It's an insidious type of window illness that shows on the surface as being much less of a disease than exists within. You may judge the extent of the problem by realizing that if the window were to continue to buckle, eventually the pieces of glass would commence falling out of it. In point of fact, windows that are badly buckled must be taken completely apart and completely releaded. There is no other way to fix them. If the buckling is just beginning and is only in one small portion, you might get by with a new reinforcing rod and pulling the old lead cames back into place against it. The chances are that you won't even succeed with this unless you put a lot of labor into it, to say nothing of the fact that once the window begins to buckle in one area, it will probably begin to buckle in another shortly thereafter.

Remember that releading any old window involves a certain amount of initial unleading, and this is really a job that will form the majority of the work in progress. Therefore, if you are calculating a price be sure you don't neglect the preparations prior to the restoration. We fell into such a trap some years ago and paid heavily for it. For while it was true that the windows we were dealing with were simple enough to lead up, getting them to that stage alone was more than worth the cost of the entire procedure. So, consider how much work you will have to go through before you can actually begin to start the work that the customer feels he is paying you to do.

REPAIRING FREE FORM OBJECTS

Some gift shops are notoriously hard on objects they have up for sale and you may end up unhappily repairing a great many of your own. However, on the off chance that someone wants you to do such a repair job on one of theirs, don't shirk it. Repairs on mobiles or small animals are usually quite simple. For one thing, the back-to-back lead allows for a good deal of mobility in moving pieces around. It's simple enough to cut the outside lead and all struts to the broken part, bend them aside, slide the broken pieces out, and replace them. The object is then bent back into shape, and the bordering leads soldered together. Of course, if the piece is smashed in several areas, it would not be worth repairing, since the cost of such an operation would probably be more than the entire piece is worth. Its owner should be notified that it would be cheaper for him to buy another one.

REPAIRING LAMPS

Two types of lamps are to be considered, the straight panel and the bent panel. The difference in repairing these two objects is considerable. We will discuss the straight paneled lamps first.

Straight Paneled Lamps

Repairs may be necessary either for long pieces of skirt or paneling, or for some of the small pieces within the skirt. Such small pieces must be totally removed and replaced, necessitating removal and replacement of the pieces around them. Since most of these pieces are foiled, there is no way but to take the area apart and rebuild it. Happily, this will not be too extensive a procedure, because such skirts can only be so deep, and usually there is only one, or at the most, three pieces of sound glass between you and the fractured area.

Repair of lamp panels can be accomplished best by the technique of stripping away the top surface of the two adjoining H lead cames. This allows you to remove the offending panel or pieces of same, cut a new panel to the shape of the remaining space and replace it on the half leads remaining below. Since you are cutting away only half of the remaining came you cannot match it perfectly with the new half that you must cut. It is best therefore to cut away as much of the heart of the new half leads as possible, cutting each half with metal shears right to the flat surface of the lead itself. This will allow you to put the half lead on top of your new piece of glass with no bits and pieces of heart remaining to form obstructions between it and the half lead below, which has most of its lead heart still remaining as a projection upward between the new panel and the neighboring panel. Be sure before replacing your new half lead that you stretch it so that it will be as firm and as straight as possible, and don't forget to run some glass cement under it so it will cling firmly to the underlying glass. Such a repair usually is accomplished quite readily. If there is a top flange of lead holding the panel, this can easily be bent upwards to release the old panel and then down again on top of the new panel. Allow the glue to dry for several hours and your lamp is as good as new. You needn't fear that the heat of the bulb will disturb the glue in any manner, as glass cement takes very high temperatures before it begins to run.

Repair of Bent Panel Lamps

These are probably the most difficult repairs to accomplish. Their problems increase both with the number of curves involved in the bent panel (that is whether it is a simple U-curve or an S-shaped curve) and whether the piece of glass is held to the frame by clips of metal or by an actual channel built into the frame itself.

The clip-in type panels are the easiest to work with. You just make your new panel (see Chapter 13), using one of the existing panels as a guide and fit it into the frame using clips to hold it in place. It should fit quite accurately if your mold was made correctly. Even S-shaped panels will fit pretty well into a clip-in type frame. However, the S-shaped panels that are held in a metal groove which is itself soldered to a frame are very difficult to work with, and all such repairs should only be taken with the understanding that the end result may not be perfect. In addition, if any soldering is to be done on the old brass, this will show no matter how you try to disguise it chemically.

If you have to deal with a bent panel lamp whose panels are attached in this manner to the frame, try to make your molds and your pattern as accurate as possible. You may have to cast four or five panels before you get one that will even come close to fitting into the space left for it. Even at that you will probably have to grozz the panel here and there to get it to fit. Grozzing a bent panel, especially a newly fired one, is a risky procedure, for the strains now present in the glass make it a very uncertain entity to work with. Very often you may decide to grozz off the smallest amount from one edge and suddenly find the panel has broken in half. Nonetheless, without grozzing you probably will not get the panel to fit into the lamp correctly. One of the reasons bent panel replacement is so expensive is because of this very fragility of the panels. When the lamp was first made, these panels were all bent on steel molds and were all pretty much alike. Any variations could be made up easily in the metal. Such can no longer be done, for you are left only with a tyrannous space which you must fill in every nook and cranny. There is no way you can move the metal around to allow for modifications in the glass. In any event, the chances are that your glass will not fit perfectly within the brass groove. If this is the case, copper foil your panel after making sure all the edges are smooth and widen the brass space sufficiently to take the copper foiled edge. Then, with a very stiff brush, go over the old metal until it is shiny. If you do not do this, it will not accept the solder. Flux the metal and the copper and run a bead of solder between them so that the panel is securely locked in place.

The shiny surface must be aged somewhat to match the rest of the surface. This can be done either with antiquing solution or a mixture of hydrochloric acid and sulphur, a very noxious smelling substance which should not be used in an unventilated area. This will instantly darken the newly laid solder and get it as close as possible to the color of the rest of the lamp. Do not change the color of the solder until you are finished soldering, as once the color has been changed, you will not be able to solder along this surface any longer. With S shaped panels fitting into a predetermined groove, the best you can hope for is a panel that will not stand out too severely from its neighbors and that will be firmly held in place both by the pressure of the lamp frame itself and by the soldering technique that must invariably be used to lock it into position.

Almost all stained glass repairing, if done on a minor scale, is not remuneratively successful and should be reserved for fixing your own stained glass objects or doing favors for friends. If you're doing it on a large scale and can thus work on several jobs at a time, it can be financially rewarding. However, you must learn to split the time involved among several projects, so that you may be molding a panel in the oven while rebuilding one window and dismantling a third. Each single procedure involves certain waiting periods—for instance waiting for the glass cement to dry when using the half-lead method —and these waiting periods may be best employed on another repair job. Only in this way will you be able to make such jobs pay, so that you may supply your more creative endeavors.

A Final Word

This far we've come together, but hopefully this is not as far as you, the reader will choose to go. The paths are open; if we've pointed a direction or incited an involvement we've accomplished our purpose.

Above all else, backlighting the information, is the pleasure that working with stained glass can give. Amid the instructions, cautions and guidelines moves the spirit of the craft—the fun and intrigue that brought you to it—which cannot be captured in a book concentrating on technique. If some of our own enthusiasm shows through, so much the better. Without such enthusiasm not a line could have been written.

From its inception, stained glass has been somewhat less than a spendthrift of its secrets. We are reminded that early workers on the island of Murano were kept under strict surveillance. If a glass worker managed to leave and did not obey an order to return, his nearest relatives were put in prison. If he still remained obdurate, an assassin was sent to kill him. This rigorous deterrent to tourism and communication persisted in spirit if not in letter over the centuries. No general sharing of knowledge in the craft was considered until roughly the turn of the century, and most of those books are now out of print.

Much still remains to be written; many of our chapters could well be books in their own right. Perhaps one day one of our readers will accomplish such a task.

We'd like to read it.

Bibliography

Amaya, Mario. *Tiffany Glass*. New York: Walker & Co., 1967.

Anderson, Harriet. *Kiln-Fired Glass*. Philadelphia: Chilton Book Co., 1970.

Beyer, Victor. *Stained Glass Windows*. London: Oliver & Boyd, 1964.

Bowers, R. S. *Drawing & Design for Craftsmen*. London: Cassell & Company, Ltd., 1916.

Burton, John. *Glass: Handblown, Sculptured, Colored*. Phila.: Chilton Book Co., 1967.

Chagall, Marc. *The Jerusalem Windows*. New York: George Braziller, Inc., 1967.

Davidson, Marshall B., ed. *American Heritage History of Antiques from the Civil War to World War I*. New York: American Heritage Bk. Div., 1969.

Davis, Frank. *The Country Life Book of Glass*. Glasgow: University Press, 1968.

Delamotte, F. G. *Medieval Alphabets and Initials for Illuminators*. London: E. and F. N. Spon, 1911.

Dierick, Alfons. *The Stained Glass at Chartres*. Berne: Hallwag, N.D.

Drake, Maurice. *A History of English Glass Painting*. London: T. Wernew Laurie, Ltd., 1912.

Gandy, Walter. *The Romance of Glass Making*. London: 1898.

Hancock, E. Campbell. *The Amateur Pottery and Glass Painter*. London: Chapman and Hall, N.D.

Harrison, F. *The Painted Glass of York*. New York: Macmillan, 1927.

Harvard University. *Glass Flowers from the Ware Collection in the Botanical Museum of*. New York: Harcourt, Brace and Co., 1940.

Johnson, James Rosser. *The Radiance of Chartres*. Studies in the Early Stained Glass of the Cathedral. Phaidon Press, Columbia University Studies in Art History and Archaeology No. 4. London: 1964.

Kinney, Kay. *Glass Craft: Designing, Forming, Decorating*. Philadelphia: Chilton Book Co., 1962.

Knowles, John A. *Essays in the History of The York School of Glass Painting*. New York: Macmillan, 1936.

Koch, Robert. *Rebel in Glass: Louis C. Tiffany*. New York: Crown Publishers, 1964.

Lee, Lawrence. *Stained Glass*; Oxford Paperbacks Handbooks for Artists. Oxford University Press, N.D.

Lethaby, W. R. *Leadwork: Old and Ornamental*. London and New York: Macmillan, 1893.

Lubke, Dr. Wilhelm. *Ecclesiastical Art in Germany During the Middle Ages*. Edinburgh: Thomas C. Jack, 1870.

Marchini, G. *Italian Stained Glass Windows*. New York: Harry N. Abrams, Inc., 1956.

Mayer, Ralph. *The Artist's Handbook of Materials and Techniques*. New York: Viking Press, Inc., 1940.

Metropolitan Museum of Art. *Medieval Art from Private Collections*. New York, 1968.

Metropolitan Museum of Art. *The Year 1200*. New York: Edited by Konrad Hoffman. 2 vols., 1970.

National Geographic Society: The Age of Chivalry. 1969.

Osgood, Adelaide H. *How to Apply Royal Worcester, Matt, Bronze, La Croix and Dresden Colors to China* (also serves for glass). New York: Osgood Art School Pub., 1891.

Pilkington, James. *The Artist's Guide and Mechanic's Own Book*. New York: Blake, 1844.

Piper, John. *Stained Glass: Art or Anti-Art*. New York: Reinhold, 1968.

Plowman, George. *Etching and Other Graphic Arts*. New York: Dodd, Mead & Co., 1929.

Reyntines, Patrick R. *The Technique of Stained Glass*. New York: Watson-Guptil Publications, 1967.

Rorimer, James J. *The Cloisters: The Building and the Collection of Medieval Art in Fort Tryon Park*. New York: Metropolitan Museum of Art, 1963.

Saint, L. & Arnold, H. *Stained Glass of the Middle Ages in England and France*. London: Black, 1913.

Sauzay, A. *Marvels of Glass Making in All Ages*. London: Sampson, Low, Son and Marston, 1870.

Schmutzler, Robert. *Art Nouveau*. New York: Harry N. Abrams, Inc., 1962.

Schuler, Frederick W. & Lilli. *Glass Forming: Glass Making for the Craftsmen*. Philadelphia: Chilton Book Co., 1970.

Sherrell, C. H. *Stained Glass Tours in France*. New York: John Lane, 1922.

————. *Stained Glass Tours in England*. New York: John Lane, 1910.

————. *Stained Glass Tours in Germany, Austria & the Rhinelands*. New York: John Lane, 1927.

————. *Stained Glass Tours in Spain & Flanders*. New York: Dodd, Mead & Company, N.D.

Snell, Henry James. *Practical Instructions in Enamel Painting on Glass*. London: Brodie and Middleton, N.D.

Stained Glass Club. *The Glass Workshop Bimonthly Magazine*. Edited by Anita Isenberg.

Sturgis, Russell. *A Study of the Artist's Way of Working in the Various Handicrafts and Arts of Design*. 2 vols. New York: Dodd, Mead & Co., 1905.

Twining, E. W. *Art and Craft of Stained Glass*. London: Sir Isaac Pitman & Sons Ltd., 1928.

Van Tassel, Valentine. *American Glass*. New York: Gramercy, N.D.

Werck, Alfred. *Stained Glass: A Handbook on The Art*. New York: Adelphi, 1926.

Wethered, Newton. *Medieval Craftsmanship and the Modern Amateur*. New York: Longman's Green and Co., 1923.

Whall, C. W. *Stained Glass Work*. London: John Hogg, 1905.

Winston, C. *Ancient Glass Paintings*. 2 vols. England: John Henry Parker, 1927.

Woodforde, Christopher. *The Norwich School of Glass-Painting in the 15th Century*. London: Oxford University Press, 1950.

Materials Listing

All supplies mentioned in the text are available from The Stained Glass Club, 482 Tappan Road, Northvale, N.J. 07647. A catalog is available listing materials and their prices. The club itself is open for membership for both beginning and advanced workers in the craft as well as professional studios. Members are entitled to discounts on selected items, special sales on bulk items, a full year's subscription (6 issues) of the club magazine "The Glass Workshop" and they have the advantage of using the club as a source of information. In addition, new members receive an instruction book of their choice from among a selection in our catalog.

Index

About the
Authors

Anita Isenberg was born in New York City and attended high school in Tucson, Arizona, and then went on to the University of Tempe in that state. She did graduate work in art and design at the University of Paris and at that time her interest in stained glass came to the fore.

She was an apprentice at William O'Connor's Castle Hill Studio from 1963 to 1966 and after that time she opened her own studio, the Stained Glass Club, to promote the craft of stained glass among hobbyists as well as a commercial art venture.

She has executed commissions for windows, room dividers, lamps and shutters in New York and New Jersey and she repairs antique stained glass for such people as Beatrice Weiss, the noted Tiffany collector, among others. Mrs. Isenberg, under the name "Anita De," is also editor of her own journal of stained glass and the allied arts, *The Glass Workshop*, which enjoys a large circulation in this country and goes to subscribers in such places as Manila, Curaçao, Puerto Rico, France, Mexico and Canada.

Seymour Isenberg is a graduate of Horace Mann School in New York City, Syracuse University, and Kansas City College of Osteopathy and Surgery. Although a practicing physician, he is an active stained glass craftsman and works closely with Anita Isenberg in the Stained Glass Club. He is the author of another book, *How to Multiply Your Real Estate Sales*, and is a contributor to medical, crafts and wildlife journals.

Dr. and Mrs. Isenberg live in Northvale, New Jersey, with their son Arthur.